U.S. IMMIGRATION

A Reference Handbook

Other Titles in ABC-CLIO's
**CONTEMPORARY
WORLD ISSUES**
Series

Books in the Contemporary World Issues series address vital issues in today's society such as genetic engineering, pollution, and biodiversity. Written by professional writers, scholars, and nonacademic experts, these books are authoritative, clearly written, up-to-date, and objective. They provide a good starting point for research by high school and college students, scholars, and general readers as well as by legislators, businesspeople, activists, and others.

Each book, carefully organized and easy to use, contains an overview of the subject, a detailed chronology, biographical sketches, facts and data and/or documents and other primary-source material, a directory of organizations and agencies, annotated lists of print and nonprint resources, and an index.

Readers of books in the Contemporary World Issues series will find the information they need in order to have a better understanding of the social, political, environmental, and economic issues facing the world today.

U.S. IMMIGRATION

A Reference Handbook

Michael C. LeMay

A B C ⬤ C L I O

Santa Barbara, California • Denver, Colorado • Oxford, England

Library of Congress Cataloging-in-Publication Data

LeMay, Michael C., 1941–
U.S. immigration : a reference handbook / Michael C. LeMay.
    p.   cm. — (ABC-CLIO's contemporary world issues series)
Includes bibliographical references and index.
    ISBN 1-85109-543-8 (alk. paper) 1-85109-548-9 (e-book)
    1. United States—Emigration and immigration—Government policy.
2. Emigration and immigration law—United States.   I. Title: US
Immigration.   II. Title.   III. Series: CLIO's Contemporary world issues.
JV6483.L46   2003
325.73—dc22
                                                    2003021522

08 07 06 05 04   10 9 8 7 6 5 4 3 2 1

This book is also available on the World Wide Web as an e-book. Visit www.abc-clio.com for details.

ABC-CLIO, Inc.
130 Cremona Drive, P.O. Box 1911
Santa Barbara, California 93116-1911

This book is printed on acid-free paper ∞.
Manufactured in the United States of America

This book is dedicated, in loving memory,
to my maternal grandmother,
Bertha Decker Lenger,
who at age nineteen immigrated from
Germany to the United States in 1887.
Her courage and experience instilled in me,
at age seventeen, a life-long interest in immigration.

Contents

Preface

U.S. Immigration: A Reference Handbook examines immigration policy in the United States since 1965. It focuses on the forces that shaped immigration policy as the nation and Congress reacted to changes in the flow of immigration, in part the result of the Immigration and Naturalization Act of 1965. As the flow of immigrants altered in volume and as immigrants' nations of origin, reasons for immigrating, and legal status changed, policymakers struggled with revising national immigration policy within the context of increasing globalization.

For several decades, immigration policy remained on the national agenda as a topic both substantive in its importance and timely in its impact. The United States stands alone among nation-states in the degree to which it has absorbed immigrants. It is now home to residents born in 170 other nations of the world. An amazing two-thirds of all persons permanently immigrating throughout the world are individuals, and often groups of refugees, seeking to enter the United States. The tens of millions of immigrants who have entered the United States since 1965 have profoundly influenced the culture, economy, and politics of this nation of nations.

How the vastly various groups of newcomers have mixed and mingled here provides a story of compelling human interest. Immigration policy intended to control the flow of newcomers is itself an interesting blend of four main elements: (1) the impact immigration has on the nation's economy, (2) how immigration affects the very nature of the mix of race and ethnicity that makes up the American people, (3) how that flow affects nationalism, the composite sense of "peoplehood," and (4) considerations affecting national perceptions of foreign policy needs. Sometimes these four elements seem to work more or less in harmony with one another, essentially reinforcing each other and characterizing an "era" of immigration policy. At other times, they work against each other, and the contending forces that seek to influence immigration policy will each emphasize different elements. In all

xiii

cases and periods of time, however, these four elements are key to an understanding of U.S. immigration policy.

Immigration policy is an important topic to examine in that it affords an opportunity to gain insight into the complexity of the policymaking process itself. That process is best understood according to an approach popularized by Professor James Anderson in his book *Public Policymaking*. In it, he rather succinctly defines public policy as "a purposive course of action followed by an actor or set of actors in dealing with a problem or matter of concern" (Anderson 1979, 3; see also Ingraham 1987, 610–628). There are some important aspects to keep in mind when examining immigration policy in particular. Immigration policy is regulatory in nature, involving the imposition of restrictions or limits on the behavior of both individuals and groups and dramatically affecting the economic, political, and social environment (Anderson 1979, 126–128). It is an *intermestic* policy area—that is, one that involves an inherent weaving of both international and domestic policymaking considerations. Immigration law performs an essential *gatekeeping function,* determining at any given time who will or will not be allowed entry (LeMay and Barkan 1999, xxvii). To better understand immigration, one has to examine the laws concerning it. The magnitude of the problems associated with the process of permanent immigration has led to many and varied laws since 1965, the most important of which are summarized in this volume.

What is here characterized as the *revolving-door era* of immigration policy reflects the time since 1965, which is also seen as an era of globalization. Enactment of the Immigration and Naturalization Act of 1965 marked an ending to an open-door policy for immigrants coming from Western Hemisphere nations. Cessation of the Bracero Program in 1964 and the closing of the door to open immigration from Western Hemisphere nations led to an increasing backlog of applicants from Latin America and renewed problems of coping with illegal aliens entering, for the most part, from those nations. In 1968, continuing difficulties in dealing with large refugee flows led President Lyndon B. Johnson to issue a proclamation by which the United States agreed to adhere to the United Nation's Protocol on the Status of Refugees.

In 1976, the continuing struggle to deal with the difficult issue of seemingly ever-increasing numbers of illegal aliens prompted Congress to amend the Immigration and Naturalization Act of 1965. This amendment was the first of several attempts to cope with the problem of illegal immigration. Mass refugee movements linked to foreign policy concerns led to the enactment and implementation of several "parole" programs to handle Chinese, Cuban, Vietnamese, and Soviet refugees; these programs culminated in the Refugee Act of 1980.

The 1970s have been described as a decade of *stagflation,* an unprecedented mixture of double-digit unemployment and inflation rates. These economic conditions and the shift in the national origins of both legal and illegal immigrants—from northwestern Europe to Latin America and Asia—led to calls for sweeping changes in immigration law. Among the more dramatic was the enactment of a new approach to discourage illegal immigration—employer sanctions—embodied in the Immigration Reform and Control Act (IRCA) of 1986.

Heightened fears that illegal immigrants placed an undue burden on state welfare systems resulted in laws withholding various welfare, medical, and even educational benefits from illegal aliens and even from legal resident aliens, as exemplified by California's Proposition 187 (1994), the Personal Responsibility and Work Opportunity Act of 1996, and the Illegal Immigration Reform and Immigrant Responsibility Act of 1996.

Since 1965, changing global conditions and resulting legislative reforms contributed to a major shift in the sources of immigration to the United States. The more than 20 million legal immigrants who entered the United States during this era came from dramatically different places than had those entering previously. Nearly half of the total wave came from Western Hemisphere nations (South and Central America), and about 35 percent came from Asian nations; those coming from European nations made up the rest, approximately 15 percent of the total.

A recession and continuing softness in the U.S. economy, adjustments in the economy to its increased globalization, and, especially, foreign and national security concerns resulting from the events of the September 11, 2001, attack on the New York World Trade Center Twin Towers and on the Pentagon led to serious proposals for a major overhaul of U.S. immigration policy. The new reforms enacted include a massive restructuring of the Immigration and Naturalization Service (INS), moving its various functions to the new cabinet-level Department of Homeland Security. As this is being written, there are also proposals before

Congress to reconsider a temporary-worker visa policy and to revise asylum and naturalization processes. Concern over the human rights of international migrants raised proposals about how
best to deal with such issues as human trafficking and with the
dual nationality aspects of a new world order, with its increasing
multiple allegiances. These developments suggest that perhaps
the United States is entering yet another era of immigration policy, one perhaps characterized as the "storm-door era." Policy
blocks the revolving nature of the immigration flow and attempts
to implement an immigration policy reflecting "Fortress America," just as many of the European immigration-receiving nations
seem committed to maintaining a "Fortress Europe" immigration
policy. Still other proposals grapple with state-building and humanitarian intervention and how they affect refugee status and
protection. Concerns centered on the issues arising from the
shared borders with Mexico and Canada are among the more
prominent of new immigration reform topics.

This volume reviews U.S. immigration policy since 1965 and
reveals an ongoing struggle for control of the substantial immigration process. The laws and court cases discussed herein tell a
story of periodic attempts to achieve a politically acceptable consensus about *procedural justice* in how the nation regulates the influx of newcomers into its area of sovereignty. This book focuses
on a *group theory* model for studying public policy (Truman 1951,
15–17), which assumes that the interaction among relevant interest groups is a central fact of politics. The group serves as the essential link between the individual and government. Group theory views politics itself as the struggle among groups to influence
government policymaking. It portrays the central roles of the political system as managing group conflict by setting the rules of
the game in which the conflict is played out, arranging compromises and balancing interests, enacting such compromises into
some form of public policy, and enforcing these compromises
through the enactment and implementation of law. It demonstrates that a key to a better grasp of immigration policy is the *dis-
parities in political power among competing interest groups.*

As with other volumes in the Contemporary World Issues series, this book aims to provide a starting point for research on the
topic by high school and college students, scholars, and general
readers as well as by legislators, business people, immigration activists, and others. It provides an overview of the topic of how immigration policy has changed since 1965; provides a detailed

chronology of U.S. immigration policy as articulated in laws and important court decisions; offers biographical sketches of many actors involved in the immigration policy arena; summarizes facts and data and offers selected primary documentary source material; provides a directory of relevant organizations and agencies, an annotated list of print and nonprint resources, and a glossary of key terms; and closes with a thorough index. I hope it will give the reader the information needed to better grasp the complex economic, environmental, political, and social aspects of the vital issue of immigration facing both the United States and the international community of today's new world order.

Michael C. LeMay

Acknowledgments

I wish to acknowledge librarians everywhere, and especially the reference librarians at California State University–San Bernardino. Without their quiet dedication and tireless and too often unsung work, books like this could not be written by authors like me for readers like you.

References

Anderson, James. 1979. *Public Policymaking.* New York: Holt, Rinehart and Winston.

Ingraham, Patricia. 1987. "Towards a More Systematic Consideration of Policy Design." *Policy Studies Journal* 15 (4): 610–628.

LeMay, Michael, and Elliot R. Barkan. 1999. *U.S. Immigration and Naturalization Laws and Issues: A Documentary History.* Westport, CT: Greenwood Press.

Truman, David. 1951. *The Governmental Process.* New York: Knopf.

1

U.S. Immigration Policy since 1965

Reflecting its essential gatekeeping function, U.S. immigration policy has been divided into several distinct eras, each characterized by a "door" image (LeMay 1987). From the nation's founding until about 1880, U.S. immigration policy could be viewed as being in its "open-door era." During this phase, "old wave" immigrants came mostly from northwestern Europe. From 1820, when the country first began keeping count, until 1880, approximately 10 million immigrants arrived, mostly in two great surges. In the first, between 1845 and 1854, Irish and Germans dominated the flow. In the second, from 1865 to 1875, British and Scandinavians contributed significantly, and the influx of Irish and Germans continued to be substantial. Immigration policy during the open-door era not only allowed relatively easy entrance, it often actively recruited immigrants.

A nativist political reaction to this wave of immigration set in, led by such groups as the Know-Nothing movement and the Ku Klux Klan and promoted later by the budding organized labor movement. These groups advocated a restrictionist approach. The era of immigration policy from 1880 to 1920 has been called the "door-ajar era." During this period, immigration to the United States shifted from people from northwestern Europe to people from south, central, and eastern European nations. Nearly 25 million immigrants made up this wave of so-called new immigrants. Policy was aimed at managing the flood of newcomers and focused on restricting individuals on the basis of certain characteristics, such as literacy, medical conditions, moral turpitude, and an assessment of their likelihood of becoming public charges.

During this era, however, Congress enacted the first avowedly restrictionist legislation targeting a specific racial and national-origin group. The Immigration Act of 1882, commonly known as the Chinese Exclusion Act, passed in May 1882. It stopped virtually all immigration by Chinese laborers for ten years. Its impact was dramatic. In 1881, nearly 12,000 Chinese immigrants entered, and nearly 40,000 arrived in 1882 before the law took effect. Their numbers fell to 8,031 in 1883 and to a mere 23 by 1885. The law also prohibited the naturalization of Chinese immigrants (Bennett 1963, 17).

Organized labor and nationalist groups advocated and Congress enacted in 1885 the Alien Contract Labor Law, known as the Foran Act. The Knights of Labor, the Order of American Mechanics, and various patriotic, veterans', and fraternal associations began a strident anti-immigration campaign (Divine 1957, 3). Groups such as the American Protective Association, a large and politically powerful Protestant secret anti-Catholic society, held restrictionist positions questioning the economic value of and the need for immigration. They assumed that different groups were more or less able to assimilate into U.S. society and considered this ability to be the criterion for assessing the desirability of immigrants (LeMay 1987, 55; Jones 1960, 257–258). Their positions presaged the blatantly racist restrictionist arguments of the early 1900s. In 1888, Congress amended the Chinese Exclusion Act of 1882. The amendment, called the Scott Act, extended the act another ten years and banned the return to the United States of any Chinese laborer who had gone back to China.

A depression in 1891 spurred renewed efforts to reduce overall immigration even more effectively. Concerns over Japanese immigration to the mainland, beginning mostly in the 1880s and peaking by 1920, led to increased political strength for the restrictionist advocate groups. The American Protective Association, the Knights of Labor, the Asian Exclusion League, and the Immigration Restriction League, for example, strongly advocated a literacy test as a device to limit immigration (Pitkin 1975, 36).

From 1907 to 1911, a special immigration commission—the Dillingham Commission—met and studied immigration policy. Its massive forty-two-volume report, issued in 1911, advocated openly restrictionist policy, including a literacy test. The commission clearly accepted the racist theories of the Immigration Restriction League (LeMay 1987, 69).

Congress overrode President Woodrow Wilson's second veto of an immigration bill in 1917, signaling that the tide in favor of restrictionist immigration policy was at an irresistible level. The Red Scare in the summer of 1919, reflecting a xenophobic fear of Bolshevik radicalism, set the stage for a new era of immigration policy, which I have elsewhere called the "pet-door era" (LeMay 1987, 73–102).

The pet-door era of U.S. immigration policy, from 1920 to 1965, overturned a century-old policy of an open door to immigration. The xenophobic efforts to adopt and enforce effective restrictionism essentially closed the door to all but a favored few. During the 1920s, pro-restrictionist forces convinced Congress to pass a series of laws (in 1921, 1924, and 1929) basing immigration on quotas of national origin. These laws stemmed the flood of immigration (from about 25 million during the forty years of the door-ajar era) to a comparative trickle (just over 6 million during the forty-five years of the pet-door era). As the law intended, the source of immigrants coming to the United States during the pet-door era shifted from mostly south, central, and eastern European nations back to those coming overwhelmingly from northwestern European nations.

The Immigration and Naturalization Act of 1965

Just as the quota approach to immigration reflected the racial ideas and fears of the pet-door era, the new era ushered in with enactment of the Immigration and Naturalization Act of 1965 reflected concerns of the civil rights movement. President John F. Kennedy's election in 1960 opened the way to a frontal attack on the quota system itself. While serving as U.S. senator from Massachusetts, Kennedy wrote *A Nation of Immigrants* (1958). In his book, Kennedy made obvious his favorable attitude toward more immigration. Adding to the momentum for change, the civil rights movement pushed the nation and its leadership to seriously question and reevaluate the racial bias of many of the nation's laws. Immigration law was no exception. The post–World War II decades chipped away at the quota system. Special acts, nonquota immigration policies, and refugee/escapee laws ameliorated a quota system that was simply too inflexible and too racially biased to be continued. The healthy economy of the early and middle 1960s enabled even organized labor to favor a more liberal immigration policy. By 1965, the traditional supporters of the national-origin system were unorganized and mostly inactive. Sen. Edward Kennedy (D.–Mass.), the youngest brother of the president, led the Senate forces seeking fundamental change in immigration law.

Senator Kennedy met with leaders from the American Coalition, the American Legion, the Daughters of the American Revolution, and the National Association of Evangelicals. They registered no significant opposition to eliminating the quota system (Chiswick 1982, 33; LeMay 1987, 110). Senator Kennedy argued persuasively for a bill that President Kennedy's administration had submitted to Congress in 1963, which did not pass. President Lyndon B. Johnson resubmitted that proposal on January 13, 1965. It was introduced into the House by Rep. Emmanuel Celler (D.–N.Y.), then chair of the House Judiciary Committee. In the Senate, it was introduced by Sen. Philip Hart (D.–Mich.). Among the thirty-two official cosponsors were both Sen. Robert Kennedy (D.–N.Y.) and Sen. Edward Kennedy (D.–Mass.). The Kennedy immigration bill sought to balance five goals: (1) to preserve the family unit and to reunite separated families; (2) to meet the need for highly skilled workers; (3) to help ease population problems created by emergencies, such as political upheavals, Communist aggression, and natural disasters; (4) to better the understanding of people cross-nationally through exchange programs; and (5) to bar from the United States aliens who were likely to represent adjustment problems due to their physical or mental health, criminal history, or dependency or for national security reasons. The act replaced the national-origin quota system with a preference system that allocated immigrant visas within each foreign state as follows:

1. First preference: unmarried sons and daughters of U.S. citizens
2. Second preference: spouses and unmarried sons and daughters of permanent resident aliens
3. Third preference: members of the professions and scientists and artists of exceptional ability
4. Fourth preference: married sons and daughters of U.S. citizens
5. Fifth preference: brothers and sisters of U.S. citizens
6. Sixth preference: skilled and unskilled workers in short supply
7. Seventh preference: refugees

President Johnson signed the bill into law on October 3, 1965, in front of the Statue of Liberty in New York Harbor. Some significant changes in the immigration flow resulted. In the decade after the bill's passage, total immigration increased by nearly 60 percent. The number of immigrants from some countries increased markedly: Greek immigration rose by 162 percent; Portuguese immigration rose by 382 percent; overall Asian immigration rose by 663 percent. Asian nations exemplified some of the most remarkable changes: Immigration from India rose by more than 3,000 percent; from Korea, by 1,328 percent; from Pakistan, by 1,600 percent; from the Philippines, by nearly 1,200 percent; from Thailand, by more than 1,700 percent; and from Vietnam, by more than 1,900 percent. Immigration from European countries declined overall by 38 percent. Those registering the largest negative percentage changes were Austria, whose immigration declined by more than 76 percent; Ireland, by more than 77 percent; Norway, by more than 85 percent; and the United Kingdom, by nearly 120 percent (LeMay 1987, 113–114).

The act's third preference category, a provision for professionals, was especially important to opening up immigration from Asia. Korean and Philippine health professionals entered in exceptionally large numbers. They, in turn, could then use the family preference category to bring in their family members (second or even later the fifth preference categories). By the late 1970s, more than 70,000 medical doctors alone had immigrated, so that by 1980, there were more Filipino physicians in the United States than native-born black doctors. Nurses and other medical technicians from Asia also used this provision to come in large numbers.

The 1965 act, however, was almost immediately outmoded in its provisions for refugees. The act set the annual preference limit for refugees at 10,200, which at the time seemed generous. Events in Cuba, Vietnam, and Haiti soon outstripped that limit's ability to cope with the demand for entrance by refugees.

Refugee Acts

In 1966, Congress passed a law that adjusted the status of refugees from Cuba, from whence alone came more than 800,000 refugees between 1960 and 1980. The 1965 law defined refugees as those fleeing communism or trying to leave the Middle East. It did not consider to be refugees those fleeing right-wing dictatorships in the Western Hemisphere (such as the government of François "Papa Doc" Duvalier in Haiti). The collapse of the South Vietnamese government in 1975 precipitated another large pool of refugees fleeing communism. Between 1975 and 1979, more than 200,000 Vietnamese came to the United States. At first, President Johnson responded to the refugee flow by issuing a proclamation in 1968 reaffirming the U.S. adherence to the UN Protocol on the Status of Refugees. With the fall of South Vietnam, Cambodia, and Laos to Communist forces, hundreds of thousands of refugees sought to come to the United States. In 1976, Congress amended the Immigration and Nationality Act after establishing an Indochinese Refugee Resettlement Program in 1975. By the end of the decade, these refugee pressures and the growing anxiety over an estimated 1 million illegal aliens entering annually prompted Congress to establish a Select Commission on Immigration and Refugee Policy (SCIRP) in 1978. Congress further addressed the issue in a major revision of prior law concerning refugees by passage of the Refugee Act of 1980. In addition to making the regulation of refugees more systematic as well as increasing the number of such persons who could be admitted, the act recognized the new category of "asylum seekers." The 1980 law redefined "refugee" to include people from anywhere in the world, not just Communist countries or Middle Eastern nations. It expanded the annual limit for refugees to 50,000 and raised total immigration from 290,000 to 320,000.

The 1980 act created the Office of the United States Coordinator, which was charged with monitoring, coordinating, and implementing overall refugee policy variously administered within the Immigration and Naturalization Service (INS), the Department of Justice, the Bureau of Refugee Programs at the Department of State, and the Office of Refugee Resettlement in the Department of Health and Human Services. The act's change in the definition of "refugee" increased the number of potentially eligible people from 3 million to 15 million. The question of refugee status is a complex one involving political, social, economic, and legal ramifications. Trends in political turmoil throughout the world led to what has been called the global refugee crisis, and since the 1980s, more than 15 million persons have become refugees. Such international movements of people are greater than in any other period of recorded human history (Ferris 1985, 105).

During the 1980s, the populations of the industrialized world became almost inured to the waves of refugees coming mostly from Third World nations. But since 1989, the movement of refugees has reached levels not seen since the end of World War II, when hundreds of thousands of Europeans began migrating from eastern Europe to the West: 100,000 people left the former Soviet Union, and 250,000 East Germans, 300,000 Bulgarian Turks, 230,000 Poles, and more than 20,000 Romanians emigrated.

This shift in the nation of origin of massive refugee movements with the sudden outpouring from eastern Europe heading to the West partially explains why the reduction in tensions between the East and West did not significantly alleviate the world's refugee problems. The current trend also involves a change in the world's image of the refugee, from the picture of an emaciated Ethiopian child with a bloated stomach seeking relief from famine in a dusty desert camp or someone fleeing war, civil unrest, or natural disaster, to today's image of a person seeking better economic opportunity or political liberty.

In its various provisions, the Refugee Act of 1980 allowed for as many as 70,000 people annually to enter the United States because they have a well-founded fear of persecution on account of race, religion, nationality, membership in a social group, or political opinion. In 1984, for example, 61,750 such refugees were admitted (LeMay 1987, 123). Such refugees tended to arrive in large numbers from given countries at given times—that is, they arrived in mass asylum movements. From 1960 to 1985, for example, nearly 800,000 refugees fleeing persecution came from Cuba, as did about 340,000 from Vietnam, 110,000 from Laos, nearly 70,000 from the then U.S.S.R. and about the same number from Kampuchea (Cambodia), 30,000 from the then Yugoslavia, about 25,000 from mainland China and Taiwan, nearly 20,000 each from Romania and Poland, and about 10,000 each from Czechoslovakia, Spain, and Hungary (LeMay 1987, 123). Despite changes in the refugee flows, most of the world's refugees flee their native lands driven simply by the attempt to stay alive—like the 4 million refugees in Africa and the 5 million Afghans encamped in Pakistan and Iran.

Receiving nations tend to accept refugees from countries with whom they have had some historic ties. Between 1975 and 1980, for example, the United States took in 677,000 refugees who were then mostly Soviet Jews (two-thirds of all Soviet émigrés came to the United States), Indochinese from countries with whom the United States had military alliance (that is, from South East Asia Treaty Organization [SEATO] member states), and people from South or Central America and the Caribbean. That total exceeded by three times that of any other receiving country and was almost as many as the other major receiving nations combined. England

and Canada were major receiving nations for refugees from former Commonwealth colonial states, and Germany has traditionally taken refugees from the Middle East (*World Refugee Survey*, cited in Papademetriou and Miller 1984, 264).

As William Brubaker, a noted immigration scholar, put it, "Massive postwar migrations have posed a fundamental challenge to the nation-states of Europe and North America. They compelled countries to reinterpret their traditions, reshape their institutions, rethink the meaning of citizenship—in short, to reinvent themselves as nation-states" (Brubaker 1989, 1).

The world's increasing economic and political interdependence, coupled with an easing of transportation and communication difficulties, made receiving nations of the industrialized world more accessible than ever. The worldwide population explosion, rising poverty and unemployment in developing nations, the accompanying political and social turmoil, the resurgence of ethnic and religious tensions, and periodic natural disasters act as powerful push factors driving international migration and refugee waves to an unprecedented scale.

The plight and problems caused by the influx of Haitians, who came as "economic refugees" and who, not incidentally, were black, raised other perplexing issues for U.S. policymakers. The Vietnamese and other Indochinese refugees were largely political allies whom the members of Congress felt some moral obligation to assist and to whom the population was generally willing to extend help; the black Haitian poor were another matter. The Vietnamese were mostly well-educated, middle-class persons. Two-thirds of them had held white-collar occupations in Vietnam, and 24 percent were from professional, technical, and managerial occupations. Less than 5 percent were farmers and fisherman (Montero 1979, 23). The Vietnamese tended to acculturate more rapidly than had any previous group of immigrants from Asia. Haitians, by contrast, were treated as illegal immigrants fleeing dire economic conditions, not political repression. They were not allowed in under the refugee status. Arriving in ever-increasing numbers starting in 1972, their legal status was clouded for years as the Department of State and the country grappled with what to do with them. As economic refugees, they were accorded neither aid nor public support such as that given Cubans, Vietnamese, Hungarians, or Soviet Jews. They were held in detention camps for years, and upon their release, they were not aided in finding jobs or housing or otherwise acculturating to life in the United States, as were the political refugees.

Haitian refugees were mostly illiterate, had low job skills, and had language problems that made them easily exploitable. They often lived in conditions of near-slavery as migrant workers. Public opinion saw them as a special threat to the labor market. Their influx focused attention on the increasing problem of illegal aliens, estimated at between 3 million and 6 million during the 1970s and 1980s. That issue has largely dominated debate over immigration policy since the early 1980s.

The Flood of Undocumented Aliens

Throughout the 1970s, problems associated with "economic refugees," such as the Haitians, drew increasing public attention and concern among policymakers. In 1970, the INS apprehended about a quarter-million undocumented aliens attempting to cross the nation's borders, mostly along the 2,000 miles of porous border with Mexico. By 1986, the number of apprehensions had risen to nearly 2 million. In 1978, SCIRP estimated the total illegal immigrant population in the United States at between 3.5 million and 6 million. Hispanics comprised the vast majority of such undocumented aliens, in contrast with illegals who entered "with papers," such as student or tourist visas, and then simply overstayed and became illegal aliens. About two-thirds of undocumented aliens were Mexicans driven north by poverty and unemployment at home. Many had come themselves or were relatives of those who came as temporary workers during the Bracero Program years (1941–1964).

The volume of *legal* immigration rose dramatically in the 1970s as well, to nearly 4.5 million for the decade. That level was the highest since the years 1910–1919. Net immigration for the 1970s, estimated at 5.4 million, was among the highest if not the highest of any decade in this century. These "fourth-wave" immigrants were typically young, with about 60 percent being in their prime working age years of sixteen to forty-four. That age cohort made up about two-thirds of those coming illegally, whereas less than half the total population fell into that age range. New immigrants were overwhelmingly Asian and Latino: 34 percent came from Asia; 34 percent from Central and South America; and 10 percent from the Caribbean. Only 16 percent were from Europe, and the remaining 6 percent were from Canada, other continents, or "unspecified" nations. Fourth-wave immigrants were better educated, on the whole, than those who had come during earlier eras. A high percentage had college degrees. They were more highly urbanized than prior generations of immigrants, and nearly 90 percent of them settled in ten metropolitan areas within the United States. They were highly concentrated in six states: California, Florida, Texas, Illinois, New York, and Arizona (LeMay 1989, 8).

Fourth-wave immigrants were more diverse than those arriving earlier, with sharp cultural and social differences among them. Central and South American immigrants included middle-class refugees escaping political conflict as well as rural residents fleeing turmoil and seeking economic relief. Professionals from Argentina had little in common with laborers from Colombia. Refugees from the Caribbean basin included Spanish-speaking Cubans, English-speaking Jamaicans, and residents of French-speaking islands (for example, Haitians). The tens of thousands of Indochinese refugees ranged from the primitive Hmong mountain people of Laos to sophisticated urban dwellers from Saigon. Sikhs from India or Buddhists from Korea mingled with entrepreneurs from Hong Kong (Muller and Espenshade 1985, 15).

Mexican immigrants, who made up roughly 63 percent of Hispanic immigrants, especially undocumented ones, tended to come from rural and small-town areas, fleeing dire poverty. They often exhibited a "sojourner" mentality: Since in their new country they resided geographically close to their native areas, they often returned to their place of origin, thereby keeping family, social, and other cultural ties strong. They came from near-feudal societies. Although earlier waves of immigrants had been eager to become U.S. citizens, having come here expecting to remain permanently and often having cut formal ties to their sending countries, Mexicans—especially the undocumented—considered the border a nuisance rather than a barrier. They often moved back and forth, retaining strong Mexican ties and slowing their rate of naturalization.

Although both push and pull factors are and always have been involved in the immigration process, push factors seem to have become more important since 1980. Worldwide population growth has certainly contributed as a dominant push factor. As noted in SCIRP's *Final Report,*

> One of the greatest pressures for international migration is and will be world population growth. Projections of this growth show more than a 50 percent increase

from 1975 to the year 2000, from 4 billion to 6.35 billion. . . . 92 percent of this growth will take place in
countries whose resources are least able to accommodate the needs of new population. . . . World economic
and political instability would be threatened by the
sudden, large-scale population moves which could result from widespread political or economic chaos in developing nations. (SCIRP 1981, 19–20)

The Crisis of Border Control

A growing sense of crisis arose from the conditions characterizing
the 1970s. Widespread dissatisfaction with the nation's ability to
control its borders registered in the mass media, general public
opinion polls, and within the government. During the Iranian
hostage crisis, which lasted for about two years during the administration of President Jimmy Carter, the nation was shocked
when it was revealed that the INS did not even know how many
Iranian students were living here, let alone how many were doing so illegally. Many Iranians whom the INS was able to identify
as being subject to deportation simply failed to attend deportation hearings or to leave when told to do so. Several hundreds of
thousands were estimated to overstay their visas annually (SCIRP
1981, 8–9).

Enactment of the Refugee Act of 1980 clearly indicated that
Congress was ready, willing, and able to reexamine immigration
policy. Failures by the INS to enforce policy and control the borders, coupled with the rising numbers of both legal and illegal
immigrants, led to broad support for a new policy and a bipartisan effort to enact one. The special bipartisan commission
SCIRP had been established to study immigration policy. Its recommendations became the foundation for most of the immigration reform acts of the mid-1980s to mid-1990s. Its recommendations were reflected in the move to impose employer
sanctions (the Immigration Reform and Control Act [IRCA] of
1986), to increase restrictions on legal immigrants, and to with-
hold various welfare, medical, and educational benefits from illegal aliens and even from legal resident aliens (Immigration
Act [IMMACT] of 1990; Proposition 187 in California; the Personal Responsibility and Work Opportunity Act of 1996, and the
Illegal Immigration Reform and Immigrant Responsibility Act
of 1996).

Illegal Immigration, IRCA, and the Employer-Sanctions Approach

Organized labor moved to deal with the threat from illegal aliens during the 1970s, which saw increasing unemployment and recession, hitting the lower-wage jobs especially hard. They convinced Rep. Peter Rodino (D.–N.J.) that undocumented aliens were taking jobs that rightfully belonged to U.S. citizens. Led by the AFL-CIO and the International Ladies Garment Workers Union and assisted by the National Association for the Advancement of Colored People (NAACP), which saw illegal immigration as threatening to the status and jobs of poor urban blacks, organized labor moved Rodino to propose an employer-sanctions amendment to the Immigration and Naturalization Act of 1965, essentially eliminating the "Texas Proviso" (Perotti 1989, 83–84). The Texas Proviso had favored growers and other employers of illegal aliens by exempting them from criminal action for hiring undocumented workers, although it was still illegal for workers to immigrate without documents.

Sen. Edward Kennedy, Representative Rodino, and Rep. Joshua Eilberg (D.–Pa.) linked employer sanctions with limited legalization (amnesty) and antidiscrimination provisions. Sen. James Eastland (D.–Miss.), a friend of the growers who opposed the employer-sanctions approach (led by the National Council of Agricultural Employers and the American Farm Bureau Federation), insisted that any reform of immigration policy that did not have a foreign-worker program, making it acceptable to growers by replacing illegal workers with an expanded H-2 temporary-worker program, was unacceptable to him. At that time, Senator Eastland chaired both the Senate Judiciary Committee and its Subcommittee on Immigration and Naturalization. He effectively killed immigration reform bills in committee.

In 1977, the incoming Carter administration became involved. President Carter's new secretary of labor, F. Ray Marshall, was a University of Texas economist who had long been interested in the issue. The Carter administration, however, was split on the issue. Secretary Marshall and Attorney General Griffin B. Bell favored a limited amnesty and a tamper-proof work-eligibility card. The commissioner of the INS, Leonel J. Castillo, and White House aides led a campaign for a generous amnesty program and deplored the civil liberties implications of a work-eligibility card.

Representative Rodino, long frustrated because even though

cabinet-level commissions, including one in both the Ford and Carter administrations had recommended approaches similar to his (including employer sanctions, legalization, and stronger enforcement measures), despaired that nothing could pass the Senate because of Senator Eastland's intransigence. It was at this point that President Carter and Congress, prompted by Senator Kennedy and Representative Eilberg, established the SCIRP. Although Representative Eilberg had little trouble getting the SCIRP blueprint approved in the House, Senator Kennedy had to use a parliamentary trick to avoid its being killed again by Senator Eastland, then about to retire. Senator Kennedy, as incoming judiciary chair, viewed SCIRP as a way to carve out for himself a pivotal role in any legislation on immigration reform or employer sanctions. SCIRP met, studied the issue thoroughly, and issued its final report in 1981. The report ran to more than 450 pages and was supplemented by a staff report in excess of 900 pages. Its recommendations covered the full spectrum of issues involved in the immigration debates.

SCIRP recommended closing the back door to undocumented immigration while slightly opening the front door to accommodate more legal immigration. It emphasized a need to define immigration goals more sharply and to provide a more effective structure to implement those goals by setting forth procedures to ensure fair and efficient adjudication and administration of U.S. immigration laws. SCIRP maintained that immigration unquestionably served humanitarian needs and that continued immigration was in the U.S. national interest. Although noting that immigration entailed many benefits to U.S. society, it also recognized the nation's limited ability to absorb large numbers effectively. Acknowledging that its first priority was bringing illegal immigration under control, SCIRP advocated setting up a rational system of legal immigration and recommended a modest increase sufficient to expedite the clearance of backlogs in order to reunite families, recommending that numerically restricted immigration be increased from 270,000 to 350,000 (SCIRP 1981). SCIRP emphasized the enforcement of existing laws via the imposition of employer sanctions, an increase in law enforcement, an amnesty program, and a restructuring of legal immigration. Although each of these ideas had been formulated before, SCIRP linked all these proposals together. It *legitimized the duality* of the employer-sanctions/legalization approach, saying, in essence, that one could not work without the other. Legalization would allow the INS to concentrate its efforts on border apprehension, while employer sanctions would "demagnetize" the pull of the economy drawing the continued influx of undocumented workers to the United States. The SCIRP's *Final Report* set the agenda for all subsequent discussions of and proposals to reform immigration law—including some of those still being advocated. Its prestige gave weight to proposals and ideas that heretofore had been stymied in congressional committees.

SCIRP's emphasis on the problem of undocumented immigration as "the most pressing problem" associated with immigration shaped and limited the focus of debate over immigration policy reform for the next two decades. Its *Final Report* issued a clear message: "Most U.S. citizens believe that the half-open door of undocumented/illegal migration should be closed" (SCRIP 1981, 104).

The administration of the incoming president, Ronald Reagan, responded to the findings of SCIRP by establishing its own Task Force on Immigration and Refugee Policy in March 1981. Chaired by Attorney General William French Smith, the task force presented recommendations to the president in July 1981. Those recommendations are summarized here:

1. *Amnesty*. Aliens living in the United States illegally since January 1, 1980, would be permitted to remain, would be made eligible for resident-alien status after having been here for ten years, and would then be free to seek U.S. citizenship (estimated number, 5 million).
2. *Guest workers*. A program allowing 50,000 Mexicans to enter the United States annually to work temporarily would, over several years, gradually increase the number of such workers up to hundreds of thousands annually.
3. *Employer sanctions*. Employers with more than four employees who "knowingly hire" illegal aliens would be subject to fines up to $1,000 per violation.
4. *Boat people*. Boats carrying Haitians would be intercepted. Detention camps holding as many as 6,000 people would be set up pending their deportation hearings.
5. *Enforcement*. A 50 percent increase in the INS budget and the addition of 1,500 new officers to the Border Patrol was recommended to enhance enforcement of immigration and labor law.
6. *Immigration limits*. Annually, 610,000 new immigrants to

the United States would be allowed, with a special preference being given to persons from Canada and Mexico (LeMay 1989, 37).

By fall of 1981, the House and Senate Judiciary Subcommittees on Immigration, chaired respectively by Rep. Romano Mazzoli (D.–Ky.) and Sen. Alan Simpson (R.–Wyo.), had translated the SCIRP and task force recommendations into legislative proposals that they considered essential as incentives to cooperation among the groups competing over the issue. The Simpson and Mazzoli bills were introduced into their respective chambers in March 1982. Committee hearings in both chambers were held, and the bills reported out by mid-May. The Senate bill passed that body by a vote of 81 to 19 on August 17, 1982. The House bill, saddled with several critical amendments, required the introduction of a clean version, sponsored by Representative Mazzoli and Rep. Hamilton Fish Jr. (R.–N.Y.), after passage of the Senate version, and the full Judiciary Committee finally approved the Mazzoli-Fish version of the bill in mid-September.

The Senate and House versions differed, however, and overlapping jurisdiction led Speaker of the House Tip O'Neill (D.–Mass.) to refer the House bill sequentially to four committees: Education and Labor, Agriculture, Ways and Means, and Energy and Commerce. Each considered the bill, and it finally reached the Rules Committee in December during the lame duck session of the Ninety-Seventh Congress. By the time the bill reached the House floor, more than 300 amendments had been filed, showing strong opposition. It died on the floor.

In 1983, with the Ninety-Eighth Congress, Simpson and Mazzoli renewed their efforts by reintroducing versions of their bills identical to those passed in 1982. Agricultural interests, headed by the Farm Labor Alliance and advocated by Representative Fish, developed a proposal for a guest-worker program. Rep. Edward Roybal (D.–Calif.), a leader of the congressional Hispanic Caucus, proposed an alternative bill that focused on tougher enforcement of existing labor laws and minimum-wage laws to clamp down on the hiring aspects of illegal immigration as a substitute to the employer-sanctions approach.

The bills moved through their respective chambers once again. The Senate again moved more readily to passage, with Senators Simpson and Kennedy working out compromises on employer sanctions, amnesty, and asylum-adjudication provisions. In the House, the Mazzoli bill again moved sequentially through the four committee referrals. Representatives Mazzoli and Rodino, with the backing of the Reagan administration and the House Republican leadership, pressed for quick floor action. The pending 1984 elections, however, once again led to obstructive amendments, and passage of the bill was delayed until June 20, 1984, when it finally passed by a slim margin of 216 to 211. With passage in different versions in the two chambers, the bills were sent to a House-Senate conference committee, where it failed to achieve an acceptable compromise and died.

In May 1985, Senator Simpson introduced a new version of his bill, without the cosponsorship of Representative Mazzoli. In the House, Representative Rodino introduced a bill similar to the version that had died in conference committee in 1984. Again, the two chambers eventually passed different versions of the proposed reform law. The White House strongly backed the Senate version, and the Senate Judiciary Committee rejected all attempts by the Senate Democrats to make the Senate version more like the House version. After the conference committee again seemed unable to reach a compromise, the issue seemed to be a corpse going to the morgue. A small group of legislators long committed to passage of immigration reform, however, refused to let it die. In October 1986, they fashioned a series of key compromises enabling passage in October 1986. Rep. Charles Schumer (D.–N.Y.) met with Representatives Rodino and Fish, Rep. Howard Berman (D.–Calif.), Rep. Leon Panetta (D.–Calif.), and Rep. Dan Lungren (R.–Calif.). Their fine-tuning of the bill's provisions led House members to agree on the package of provisions, including numerous points designed to protect the rights of temporary workers. They secured Senator Simpson's approval of the compromises as well. After a decade of dealing with proposals to reform immigration policy, Congress was finally in a mood and in position (with elections over) to act. Further deterioration of the Mexican economy led to 1.8 million INS border apprehensions, a record high. That fact, and the growing conservative mood of the country, seemed to convince opponents of the bill that continued resistance would probably lead to even more restrictive legislation in 1987. The Hispanic Caucus split on the bill, with five of its members supporting and six opposing it. The split of the Hispanic Caucus enabled the congressional Black Caucus to split on the bill as well: ten for and eight opposed.

The House passed the compromise conference bill measure by 238 to 173 on October 15, 1986. The Senate approved it 63 to 24 on October 17, 1986. The president signed it into law on November 6, 1986, as the Immigration Reform and Control Act of 1986 (IRCA).

The Impact of IRCA

The long and rocky road to enactment of IRCA was followed by an equally bumpy effort to implement the complex and often contradictory law. The compromises enabling its passage sowed the seeds for difficulties in implementation. Employer sanctions did not seem to work well in demagnetizing the draw of the U.S. economy. A number of documents were accepted as valid demonstrations of a person's eligibility to work. These provisions simply fueled a phony-documents industry enabling illegal aliens to continue coming to the United States and employers to continue hiring them without fear of legal penalty for "knowingly hiring" undocumented workers. Because of enforcement problems faced by the INS, the number of undocumented aliens successfully crossing the border declined for only a very brief period. Within a year, illegal immigration was at pre-IRCA levels.

Equally difficult was the implementation of the amnesty, or legalization, program. The program did result in the legalization of more than 3 million applicants. But the INS had no prior experience in dealing with such a program, which involved a 180-degree change in what had been the prevailing philosophy and tradition of the agency. Illegal aliens who met the criteria for legalization distrusted the agency, and only after extensive involvement by nongovernmental organizations (called qualified designated entities, or QDEs), some of which became legal advocates against the INS's implementation of IRCA's legalization program, did the INS come to amend its procedural rules allowing extensive approval of applicants. The record of approval of applicants varied across the country and by type of category of applicant. There were essentially three legalization programs: the regular program referred to as Legalizing Authorized Workers (LAWs), a Seasonal Agricultural Workers program (SAWs), and a Cuban/Haitian Adjustment program (LeMay 1994, 88–96).

IRCA authorized a 50 percent increase in Border Patrol staff, but actual staff increases fell short of that due to difficulties in recruiting and expanding training staff and facilities. As the Border Patrol increased in size, so did its duties. After 1986, the interdiction of drug traffic across the borders became a prime focus (due to the 1986 Omnibus Anti-Drug Law). Border Patrol agents shifted their emphasis from alien apprehension and smuggling to work with the Drug Enforcement Agency on Operation Alliance. The agency also expanded the number of staff being used to guard refugee camps and to identify, prosecute, and deport alien criminals (Bean, Vernez, and Keely 1989, 44).

Another concern about IRCA was whether or not its employer-sanctions provisions would result in increased discrimination against foreign-looking and -sounding individuals, particularly those of Latino heritage. Several attempts to study whether IRCA increased job discrimination were conducted. The Department of Labor (DOL) did an exhaustive review of the research evidence on the impact of immigrants. DOL concluded that the market forces that characterize dynamic labor markets seem to effectively absorb and integrate immigrants, both legal and illegal, in a manner that makes their effects indistinguishable from those of other workers at the aggregate level. DOL found few instances of outright displacement of native workers.

The most important studies on the impact of discrimination were a series of three annual post-IRCA ones conducted by the General Accounting Office (GAO). The GAO's third report found that there was, indeed, widespread discrimination that was the direct result of IRCA (GAO 1990, 3). The report indicated that the law resulted in citizenship discrimination, estimating, based on employer responses, that because of the law, an additional 430,000 employers (9 percent) began hiring only persons born in the United States and not hiring persons with temporary work-eligibility documents. In all, the GAO estimated that 891,000 (19 percent) of the 4.6 million employers surveyed nationwide began one or more discriminatory practices as a result of IRCA (GAO 1990, 7).

Further evidence of such discrimination came from charges filed with the Office of Special Counsel (OSC) in the Department of Justice. A report by the Mexican American Legal Defense Fund (MALDEF) and the American Civil Liberties Union (ACLU) released in November 1989 found IRCA to be a source of increased discrimination against foreign-looking or -sounding people, as did a New York State Assembly Task Force on New Americans study released in November 1988 (LeMay 1994, 122).

The Immigration Act of 1990 (IMMACT)

IRCA heavily emphasized the issue of illegal immigration. The law was enacted only after protracted struggle and only by incorporating several key compromises, which resulted in unintended outcomes when the law was implemented. Congress soon took up proposals for immigration reform that were not addressed by IRCA or that were intended to refine its approach when its implementation ills became obvious.

On March 15, 1988, the Senate passed another Kennedy-Simpson bill by a vote of 88 to 4. This measure addressed a number of aspects of legal immigration not dealt with by IRCA and also had a few provisions to address what were seen as problems or failures in the implementation of IRCA. The bill identified separate tracks for family and nonfamily immigrants, called for increased total legal immigration, tipped the ratio of independent to family-related immigrants, and separated refugees from family-related immigrants. It called for establishing an eligibility for entrepreneurs who created at least ten new jobs, investing at least $1 million in the new jobs. The bill created separate avenues of entrance for immigrants with needed job skills and more than doubled such visas from 54,000 to 150,000, aimed at drawing more-skilled and better-educated workers.

The Kennedy-Simpson bill was a slightly modified version of one passed by the Senate in 1988 but not voted on in the House, a bill sponsored by Sen. Paul Simon (D.–Ill.). Simon's bill addressed some problems associated with the implementation of IRCA and contained an amendment to end direct federal benefits to undocumented immigrants and a provision to grant stays of deportation to immediate relatives of persons in the process of legalizing under IRCA. In response to the repression of the pro-democracy movement in mainland China, the bill allowed for an increase in the annual immigration level from Hong Kong, from 2 percent to 3.5 percent of the worldwide total, and let Chinese students already in the United States remain for four years and qualify for legal residency (Bean, Vernez, and Keely 1989, 106–107).

Sen. Dennis DeConcini (D.–Ariz.) introduced a bill halting the deportation of Salvadorans and Nicaraguans, a companion bill to one in the House sponsored by Rep. Joseph Moakley (D.–Mass.). Senator DeConcini and Representative Moakley launched their antideportation bills during the struggle to enact IRCA, but their provisions were deleted in the compromises of the conference committee. The manner in which IRCA was implemented aggravated the problems of Salvadorans and Nicaraguans. This led Senator DeConcini to sponsor the new Senate bill to deal with the situation (Church World Service 1987, 131–132).

Representative Berman introduced a companion bill to that introduced by Senators Simpson, Kennedy, and Simon. The Berman bill also exempted immediate relatives of permanent residents from the current family-preference limit. Under the 1965 law, the maximum visa allotment per country was 20,000. The Senate version set that at 7 percent of the total, and the Berman bill set it at 22,000 (Bean, Vernez, and Keely 1989, 102).

Another proposal to reform legal immigration was sponsored by Representatives Rodino and Mazzoli. Their measure differed from the Kennedy-Simpson-Simon Senate bill in that it neither imposed a ceiling on annual admissions of immediate relatives of U.S. citizens nor offset such admissions against other family-sponsored immigration (Benda 1989, 72).

Congress enacted several laws slightly modifying the fringes of existing immigration law. In 1987, it passed the Amerasian Homecoming Act, which was an appropriations bill providing for the admission of children born in Vietnam between specified dates to Vietnamese mothers and American fathers, together with their immediate relatives. Though admitted as nonquota immigrants, they received refugee-program benefits.

In 1988, as part of the U.S.-Canada Free Trade Agreement Implementation Act, Congress facilitated temporary entry of Canadians on a reciprocal basis with Canada accepting U.S. emigrants. In November of that year, it amended the Immigration and Nationality Act of 1965 by providing for the extension of stay for certain nonimmigrant H-1 nurses, and in another appropriations bill, the Foreign Operations Act of 1989 (*Statutes at Large* 1989b, 3908), Congress adjusted to permanent resident status certain Soviet and Indochinese nationals who were paroled into the United States between certain dates after denial of refugee status. Finally, in December 1989, Congress amended the Immigration and Naturalization Act of 1965 as the Immigration Nursing Relief Act of 1989, adjusting to permanent resident status without numerical limitations certain nonimmigrants employed as registered nurses for three years.

Congress revised legal immigration and plugged some IRCA-related loopholes when it enacted, on November 29, 1990, the Immigration Act of 1990. This act was the culmination of the efforts to reform legal immigration begun with SCIRP, and it contained elements of virtually all the bills discussed above. Its major authors in the Senate were Kennedy, Simpson, and Simon; and its chief author in the House was Rep. Bruce Morrison (D.–Conn.). Its major provisions are summarized here:

- It increased total immigration under a flexible "cap" of 675,000 beginning in 1995. The 675,000 immigrants were to consist of 480,000 family-sponsored immigrants, 140,000 employment-based immigrants, and 55,000 "diversity" immigrants.

- It revised grounds for exclusion and deportation.
- It authorized the attorney general to grant temporary protected status to undocumented alien nationals from designated countries subject to armed conflict or natural disaster.
- It revised nonimmigrant admission categories by redefining the H-1B temporary-worker category and creating new temporary-worker admission categories, revised and extended to 1994 the Visa Waiver Pilot Program, and revised naturalization authority by transferring jurisdiction from the courts to the attorney general and amending substantive requirements for naturalization.
- It revised enforcement activities in several ways, including by broadening the definition of "aggravated felony" and imposing new legal restrictions on aliens convicted of crimes, it revised employer-sanctions provisions of IRCA, and it authorized funds to increase by 1,000 the personnel level of the Border Patrol.
- It revised criminal and deportation provisions by recodifying thirty-two grounds for exclusion into nine categories and revising or repealing some grounds for exclusion (including some health grounds).
- It established a commission to do mandatory regular and continued study of immigration.

The bill passed in the House by a vote of 264 to 118 and in the Senate by a vote of 89 to 8, with 3 not voting.

The 1996 Acts

Although hailed as the most extensive reform of immigration law since 1965, the 1990 act hardly solved all the problems nor marked the end of demands for reform of immigration. The annual studies mandated by the 1990 act further documented the effects of the push side of the immigration process. Attempts to cope with drug smuggling and human trafficking added to the sense of a need for bilateral and multilateral agreements and pressured U.S. immigration policy toward a multinational approach.

In 1993, Congress passed the North American Free Trade Agreement (NAFTA), which was clearly seen as a step in that direction. Proponents of NAFTA emphasized that its benefits to the Mexican economy would have a beneficial impact on illegal immigration pressures.

To the extent that the Mexican economy expanded, jobs were created, and Mexicans' standard of living rose, a corresponding reduction in pressure to emigrate north was evident. Even NAFTA's proponents estimated that the treaty would cause up to 500,000 jobs to drain south of the border, conceding that point.

A recession in the U.S. economy in 1991–1993 contributed to calls for further action. The resulting federal budget crisis meant that authorization to substantially increase the Border Patrol's personnel and budget would remain unfunded. The Border Patrol continued to suffer from poor training, high turnover, little supervision, and a fortress mentality. The INS came under fire by allegations of discrimination, mismanagement, misconduct, and gross ineptitude. In 1993, the Clinton administration proposed legislation to significantly restructure the INS.

Sen. Dianne Feinstein (D.–Calif.) advocated a controversial $1-per-person border-crossing fee to fund improvements to the Border Patrol. The IMMACT's study commission proposed merging the INS, the Border Patrol, U.S. Customs, and certain divisions of the Departments of the Treasury and Health and Human Services into one federal agency responsible for admitting, processing, and resettling immigrants (Caulen 1993, 49).

Asylum problems continued to fester, and a tremendous rise in the number of asylum cases created backlogs the INS could not handle. The asylum issue was highlighted in 1993 when several boatloads of Chinese attempting to enter the United States illegally were seized off the shores of both California and New York. The renewed visibility of the influx of illegal aliens and the highly publicized cases of attempts to smuggle asylum seekers in fueled public opposition to immigration. As the economic picture improved in late 1993, the Clinton administration proposed new spending and new measures to tighten defense against undocumented aliens, including proposals for quick settlement of asylum cases, a beefed-up Border Patrol, and prosecution of alien smuggling rings under the racketeering laws. It proposed funding those measures by a $5 to $6 international airport inspection fee and by increasing fees for various benefits such as naturalization adjustment of immigrant status.

States receiving the largest numbers of both legal and illegal immigrants, such as California, Florida, and Texas, sued the federal government in their respective federal district courts for the estimated billions of dollars they were having to bear for costs related to illegal immigrants and their children. In 1994, California attempted to legislate a solution, in part to reduce the strain on its economy and in part to send a message to Congress to do more about the issue. It passed an anti-immigration measure by initiative: Proposition 187.

California Governor Pete Wilson was running for reelection in 1994. The state was slow in emerging from the recession, and Governor Wilson initially trailed his Democratic challenger, Kathleen Brown, by a wide margin in the polls. Although as a U.S. senator in the 1980s Pete Wilson had favored guest-worker programs and similar measures designed to ensure a supply of cheap agricultural labor, he was fighting for his political life in his 1994 reelection bid, and he seized on the anti-immigration sentiment and the "Save Our State" initiative (Proposition 187) as the horse to ride back into the governor's mansion. He became the leading spokesman for the Proposition 187 initiative. The measure declared that citizens of the state suffered economic hardship from the presence of illegal aliens in the state and were suffering injury and damage by the criminal conduct of such illegal aliens. In order to protect themselves from such illegal immigration, the initiative required all state and local government agencies, with the federal government, to establish a system for identifying suspected illegal aliens and denying them benefits or public services in California. The measure dealt with the manufacturing, distribution, or sale of false citizenship or resident-alien documents; it criminalized and increased the penalty for using such false documents; required law enforcement cooperation with the INS; denied education, public health, and social service benefits to all persons who could not verify their legal status; and excluded illegal aliens from postsecondary educational institutions.

The initiative was passed with more than 60 percent of the voters approving it, and Governor Wilson was easily reelected. Opponents of Proposition 187 argued that it was unconstitutional. Proponents argued that it was constitutional and that in any case, it would "send a strong message" to Congress that something had to be done about the illegal alien problem. The provisions of Proposition 187 anticipated a federal court challenge as to its constitutionality. It was immediately brought to court by the League of United Latin American Citizens (LULAC).

In a November 1995 ruling, the federal district court ruled

that most of Proposition 187 was unconstitutional (*LULAC et al. v. Wilson et al.* [908 F. Supp. 755 (C.D. Cal. 1995): 787–791]). District Judge Marianna Pfaelzer held that (1) the classification, notification, cooperation, and reporting provisions of the measure had a direct and substantial effect on immigration and were preempted by federal immigration law; (2) the initiative's denial of public benefits based on federal determinations of immigration status was impermissible regulation of immigration; (3) the provision excluding illegal aliens from public elementary and secondary schools was preempted by federal law as being prohibited by the equal protection clause of the Fourteenth Amendment; (4) the verification components of the measure prohibiting postsecondary education were permissible; (5) the provisions concerning the criminalizing of the manufacture, distribution, and use of false documentation were permissible; (6) the provisions denying public social services were preempted by federal law; (7) the provisions denying postsecondary education were not preempted by federal law; and (8) the criminal penalties on the manufacture, sale, and distribution of false documents to conceal immigration status were not preempted by federal law. The judge granted in part and denied in part the petition of the plaintiffs (LULAC). Many of the provisions most clearly aimed at discouraging illegal immigrants from coming to California because services would be denied them were overturned. But the forces urging voter approval of Proposition 187 were right in that its approval in the popular vote (59 percent) and Governor Pete Wilson's easy margin of victory in his reelection bid did not go unnoticed by the U.S. Congress.

In 1996, Congress passed and President Bill Clinton signed into law two measures that essentially enacted the provisions of Proposition 187. Congress enacted a welfare reform act that contained several immigrant-related provisions concerning both legal and illegal immigrants that had aspects similar to those contained in Proposition 187. Congress then cleared a measure dealing with illegal immigration and some aspects of legal immigration by folding its provisions into the omnibus fiscal 1996 spending bill.

The 1996 welfare reform measure, the Personal Responsibility and Work Opportunity Act of August 22, 1996, contained several immigration-related provisions:

- *Restrictions.* The act restricted the federal benefits for which illegal aliens and legal nonimmigrants (such as travelers and students) could qualify, denying the use of federal funds for any grant, contract, loan, professional or commercial license, or retirement, welfare, disability, food assistance, or unemployment benefits.

- *Exceptions.* It allowed legal and illegal immigrants to receive emergency medical assistance (but denied coverage for prenatal care or for delivery assistance that was not an emergency); short-term, noncash emergency disaster relief; immunizations and testing for treatment of communicable diseases; noncash programs identified by the attorney general, such as soup kitchens, counseling, and short-term shelter; certain housing benefits; license and benefits directly related to work for which a nonimmigrant had been authorized to enter the United States; and certain Social Security retirement benefits protected by treaty or statute.
- *State and local programs.* It prohibited states from providing state or local benefits to most illegal aliens, except that illegal aliens who were eligible for free public education under state or local law were entitled to school lunch or breakfast programs, and it permitted a state to opt to provide certain other benefits related to child nutrition and emergency food assistance.
- *Current immigrants.* It made most legal immigrants ineligible for Supplemental Security Income (SSI) and food stamps until they became citizens, except for refugees and those granted asylum whose deportation was being withheld, those who had worked in the United States for ten years, veterans, or those on active duty and their spouses and unmarried children.
- *Future immigrants.* It barred legal immigrants arriving after the 1996 law from receiving most federal benefits for low-income persons for five years, with some exemptions.
- *State options.* It allowed states to deny benefits from the welfare block grants, Medicaid, and social service block grants to most legal immigrants, with exemptions for the SSI and food stamps; future immigrants would be subject to the five-year ban as for federal benefits.
- *Sponsors.* It expanded the circumstances under which an immigrant's sponsor would be financially responsible for that individual.

- *Reporting and verifying.* It required agencies that administer SSI, housing assistance, and welfare block grants to report quarterly to the INS the names and addresses of people they knew were unlawfully in the United States.

Conclusion

The Illegal Immigration Reform and Immigrant Responsibility Act (IIRIRA) was passed September 30, 1996, as immigrant provisions on the Omnibus Spending Bill. The IIRIRA enacted more than sixty provisions; some of the major ones are highlighted here.

- It authorized a doubling of the Border Patrol (from 5,000 to 10,000 agents) by 2001.
- It authorized funding of 900 additional INS agents to investigate and prosecute cases of smuggling, harboring, or employing illegal aliens and 300 new agents to investigate visa overstayers.
- It authorized a three-tier border fence along a fourteen-mile strip of the U.S.-Mexican border south of San Diego and required that INS border-crossing cards include a biometric identifier and that future cards use devices such as retina scanners.
- It granted increased wire-tap authority to the Justice Department for immigration document fraud, increased the penalties for smuggling, and granted broad authority to the INS to conduct underground operations to track organized illegal immigration rings.
- It increased the penalties for document fraud from five to ten years and created a criminal penalty of up to five years for falsely claiming U.S. citizenship and up to one year in prison for unlawfully voting in a federal election.
- It allowed courts to seize the assets of immigration law violators, greatly revised detention and deportation provisions by expanding the authority of the attorney general in such proceedings, and created a pilot program to use closed military bases as INS detention centers.
- It modified employment-verification programs and ordered the attorney general to create three pilot programs and to develop a program to use machine-readable documentation.

- It made it harder for the government to sue employers who use immigration laws to discriminate against certain workers or job applicants.
- It included a dozen provisions concerning public benefits, amended certain parole and asylum provisions, and denied visas to immigrants whose intent was to attend public elementary or secondary schools for more than one year.
- It made female genital mutilation a crime punishable by prison.
- It required the INS to report by the end of 1996 whether or not the United States had an adequate number of temporary agricultural workers.
- It required the Social Security Administration to develop a prototype tamper-proof identity card.

By 2000, however, when the economy improved, the Clinton administration proposed softening some of the more controversial of the denial-of-benefit provisions of the 1996 act.

Such softening on immigration policy, however, was short-lived. The attacks on the World Trade Center in New York City and the Pentagon in Washington, D.C., on September 11, 2001, led to sweeping changes in the law, changes aimed at combating international and domestic terrorism but with significant implications for immigration policy. Passage of these laws signal what might be called the era of "Fortress America" in immigration policy. The USA Patriot Act (the Uniting and Strengthening America by Providing Appropriate Tools Required to Intercept and Obstruct Terrorism Act), despite being 288 pages long, passed after no debate and nearly unanimously in October 2001. It granted powers to the attorney general and the Justice Department that restricted the civil liberties of U.S. citizens, broadened the terrorism-related definitions in the 1965 Immigration and Naturalization Act, expanded grounds of inadmissibility to include aliens who publicly endorse terrorist activity, and gave the government broad powers to monitor students and resident aliens and to detain and expedite the deportation of noncitizens suspected even of links to terrorist organizations—that is, of those whom the attorney general certifies as threats to national security on whatever grounds. Critics charged that the act legalized the racial profiling of Middle Easterners. Parts of the act are reprinted in Chapter 6. About a year later, on November 19, 2002, Congress passed the Homeland Security Act establishing the

Figure 1.1
Legal Immigration: Fiscal Years 1901–2001

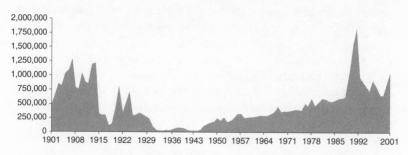

Source: U.S. Department of Justice, "Legal Immigration, Fiscal Year 2001," *Annual Report* (August 2002)

Department of Homeland Security. The act radically restructured the INS, and many of its provisions dramatically changed the way immigration policy is conducted. It is partially reprinted in Chapter 6.

References and Further Reading

Allen, Leslie. 1985. *Liberty: The Statue and the American Dream.* New York: Statue of Liberty–Ellis Island Foundation.

Anderson, James. 1979. *Public Policymaking.* New York: Holt, Rinehart and Winston.

Bean, Frank, Georges Vernez, and Charles B. Keely. 1989. *Opening and Closing the Doors.* Santa Monica, CA: Rand Corporation; Washington, DC: Urban Institute.

Benda, Susan. 1989. "The Unfinished Business of Immigration Reform." In Lydio Tomasi, ed. *In Defense of the Alien,* vol. 12. New York: Center for Migration Studies, 70–72.

Bennett, Marion T. 1963. *American Immigration Policy: A History.* Washington, DC: Public Affairs Press.

Brubaker, William Roger, ed. 1989. *Immigration and the Politics of Citizenship in Europe and North America.* New York: University Press of America; German Marshall Fund of the United States.

Caulen, Brae. 1993. "San Diego Burning." *California Lawyer,* August: 44–49.

Chiswick, Barry, ed. 1982. *The Gateway: U.S. Immigration Issues and Policies.* Washington, DC: American Enterprise Institute.

Church World Service. 1987. *Fulfilling the Promise: Church Orientation Guide to the New Immigration Law.* New York: Church World Service.

Guide to the New Immigration Law. New York: Church World Service.

Congressional Record. 1990. 101st Congress, 2nd Session, Vol. 136, No. 149, Part IV, October 26. H-13203–13240.

Divine, Robert A. 1957. *American Immigration Policy, 1924–1952.* New Haven: Yale University Press.

Ferris, Elizabeth G., ed. 1985. *Refugees and World Politics.* New York: Praeger Publishers.

General Accounting Office (GAO). 1990. *Immigration Reform: Employer Sanctions and the Question of Discrimination.* Washington, DC: U.S. Government Printing Office.

Gorman, Robert F. 1994. *Historical Dictionary of Refugee and Disaster Relief.* Metuchen, NJ: Scarecrow Press.

Ingraham, Patricia W. 1987. "Towards a More Systematic Consideration of Policy Design." *Policy Studies Journal* 15, no. 4: 610–628.

Jones, Maldwyn Allen. 1960. *American Immigration.* Chicago: University of Chicago Press.

Kennedy, John F. 1986. *A Nation of Immigrants.* Rev. ed. New York: Harper and Row. Original edition, 1958.

LeMay, Michael. 1994. *Anatomy of a Public Policy: The Reform of Contemporary American Immigration Law.* New York: Praeger Publishers.

———. 1989. *The Gatekeepers: Comparative Immigration Policy.* New York: Praeger Publishers.

———. 1987. *From Open Door to Dutch Door: An Analysis of U.S. Immigration Policy Since 1820.* New York: Praeger Publishers.

LeMay, Michael, and Elliott Robert Barkan. 1999. *U.S. Immigration and Naturalization Laws and Issues: A Documentary History.* Westport, CT: Greenwood Press.

Loescher, Gil, and Ann Dull Loescher. 1994. *The Global Refugee Crisis.* Santa Barbara, CA: ABC-CLIO.

Montero, David. 1979. *Vietnamese Americans.* Boulder, CO: Westview Press.

Muller, Thomas, and Thomas Espanshade. 1985. *The Fourth Wave.* Washington, DC: Urban Institute.

Papademetriou, Demetrios, and Mark J. Miller, eds. 1984. *The Unavoidable Issue.* Philadelphia: Institute for the Study of Human Issues.

Perotti, Rosanna. 1989. "Resolving Policy Conflict: Congress and Immigration Reform." Ph.D. diss., University of Pennsylvania.

Pitkin, Thomas M. 1975. *Keepers of the Gate.* New York: New York University Press.

Select Commission on Immigration and Refugee Policy (SCIRP). 1981. Final Report. Washington, DC: U.S. Government Printing Office.

Tomasi, Lydio, ed. 1989. *In Defense of the Alien.* Vol. 11. New York: Center for Migration Studies.

Truman, David. 1951. *The Governmental Process.* New York: Knopf.

U.S. Statutes at Large. 1987. Vol. 101, p. 1329. Amerasian Homecoming Act.

———. 1988. Vol. 102, p. 1876. U.S.-Canada Free Trade Agreement Implementation Act.

———. 1989a. Vol. 103, p. 3908. Foreign Operations Act.

———. 1989b. Vol. 103, p. 2099. Immigration Nursing Relief Act.

2

Domestic Policy

When proponents and opponents of reforming assimilation law battle over particular bills, such as those discussed in Chapter 1, they often describe the conflict as a battle to once and for all solve an immigration problem or talk as if passage of the bill would result in some sort of national calamity. As the historical review presented in Chapter 1 demonstrates, however, conflict over immigration reform is never really over, never finally won or lost, and never without unanticipated consequences.

Why is the struggle over achieving an immigration policy that satisfies national needs and effectively "resolves" whatever is viewed as the current "immigration problem" so constant? Why is a true resolution such an illusion? To a great extent, the answer to those questions lies in the *intermestic* nature—that is, inherently weaving together international and domestic policy-making considerations—of immigration policy, but it also lies in the desire to balance the following four elements (1) the impact immigration has on the nation's economy, (2) how immigration affects the very nature of the mix of race and ethnicity that makes up the American people, (3) how that flow affects nationalism, the composite sense of "peoplehood," and (4) considerations affecting national perceptions of foreign policy needs. Conditions in the policy environment change. No sooner are some international problems or foreign policy considerations regarding immigration dealt with than the world changes. U.S. national policymakers simply cannot resolve all the world's international conflicts, nor can they set policy for other nation-states. In the global environment, what other nations choose to do or fail to do affects the dynamics of immigration and worldwide migration flows. Failure to achieve a sound economy in other nations pushes their citizens to emigrate. Foreign civil wars and domestic strife renew mass refugee movements. Events such as natural disasters and epidemics compel tens or even hundreds of thousands to migrate elsewhere. Conditions change globally, and each such change affects immigration flows to the United States. The flow changes in its overall size or in its origin. Such changes are simply beyond the control of national policymakers.

Domestic conditions likewise are in constant flux. The balance achieved at one time soon tips out of balance as citizens reassess how much value they place on one or another of the four elements. The political influence of some groups declines while that of others rises, renewing pressure to readdress the balance previously achieved. New problems are perceived. Old problems are viewed in new ways, and demands for a change in the balance are once again registered in the political and public policymaking arenas.

This chapter reviews what are considered the new or current issues in immigration in the domestic policy arena. No sooner is an immigration reform bill passed than one hears a call for some new law. The very implementation of yesterday's law often generates demands for some new adjustment to yesterday's "balance." What, then, are the concerns at the turn of the twenty-first century? Most involve aspects of issues already reviewed in Chapter 1. They are, at best, attempts to pour new wine into old wineskins. This chapter examines seven such policy issues of domestic concern.

Amnesty and Legalization Issues for Current Undocumented Aliens

The continuous arrival of illegal aliens periodically gives rise to calls for a new amnesty or legalization program. Currently, and typically, the proposal to legalize the estimated 6 million illegal immigrants in the nation is being sponsored by Democrats. Former House minority leader Richard Gephardt (D.–Mo.) sponsored a measure that would legalize immigrants who have lived in the United States for five years and have worked in the country for two years. Both Republicans and Democrats split their vote for the last large-scale amnesty program, a provision of IRCA discussed in Chapter 1, which legalized about 3 million previously illegal aliens. Democrats voted 196 (65 percent) in favor of IRCA to 88 (45 percent) against it. Republicans voted 105 (35 percent) in favor to 109 (55 percent) against the measure (LeMay 1994, 53). Democrats typically sponsor legalization measures. Republican legislators are more likely to advocate more restrictionist immigration reforms and provisions for guest-worker programs.

Democratic sponsors of legalization argue, as did Minority Leader Gephardt at a July 2002 meeting in Miami of the National Council of La Raza, a Hispanic civil rights group, that the program "will bring undocumented immigrants out of the shadows and into the light of accountability and greater cooperation in our fight against terrorism." Proponents contend that there are millions of immigrants in the United States who have done everything asked of them: They work hard, stay out of trouble, obey the law, and help their families, and they would like the opportunity to legalize their status. Democratic advocates refer to the measure as "earned legalization" and contend it would not be an incentive for new immigration. Interest groups supporting the new proposal include Hispanic groups like La Raza, the United Farm Workers Union, El Movimiento Estudiantil Chicano de Aztlan (MECHA), and LULAC.

The administration of President George W. Bush opposes legalization, favoring instead achieving some migration accord with Mexico and perhaps an expanded guest-worker program. Opponents of the measure contend it will spark increased immigration, spur population growth, thus placing increased strain on development and more stress on overcrowded schools, and exacerbate water shortage problems in the Southwest. Public opinion, especially since September 11, 2001, opposes legalization.

Recent estimates place annual increases in illegal immigration at more than 200,000 people per year. The INS estimates that about 60 percent of illegal immigrants come across the borders, mostly from Mexico, and that about 40 percent enter legally but overstay their visas. California is home to an estimated 40 percent of illegal aliens. Two magnets drawing illegal aliens are jobs and family reunion.

The typical Mexican worker earns about a tenth of what his or her North American counterpart earns, and numerous U.S. businesses welcome and even rely on such workers, who are seen as cheap, compliant labor. Community networks among recently arrived legal immigrants help establish systems used by illegal aliens and draw more to the United States by helping provide jobs, housing, and entry to the United States for their illegal relatives and compatriots (Center for Immigration Studies News Backgrounder, April 2002). Throughout the 1990s, more than a million immigrants, counting both legal and estimated illegals, entered the United States annually. The Census Bureau projects that immigration will help swell the total U.S. population from its present 280 million to more than 400 million. As discussed in Chapter 1, legal immigration fluctuated between 700,000 and 900,000 each year during the 1990s. It is estimated an additional 420,000 illegal aliens settle in the United States annually. Their numbers are reduced by death, out-migration, and legalization, leaving an estimated net growth of 275,000 illegal aliens per year. The immigrant population, however, is growing six and a half times faster than the native-born population. The more than 10 million immigrants who arrived between 1990 and 2000 represent 42 percent of the increase in total U.S. population since 1990. Recent studies estimate that California has the most undocumented aliens, about 2 million. Table 2.1 presents the estimated number of illegal aliens in the United States by country of origin for the top twenty sending nations and lists the top twenty states in which they settled. Five sets of data were used to arrive at these estimates. The table, then, presents estimates of the undocumented alien population who might seek to be legalized should a legalization proposal be enacted by Congress and not vetoed by President Bush. These projections are based on the most reliable data available, but they do have their limitations and are truly "best guestimates."

Figure 2.1 presents the data on the number of aliens apprehended at the borders by the INS for fiscal years 1951 to 1996. Note the slight dip in apprehensions after enactment of IRCA in 1986 and the steady rise in numbers since 1988. In 1996, almost all of those caught and deported were Mexicans (97 percent), 99 percent of whom were so-called entries without inspection (EWIs). INS estimates that in 1999, for every illegal alien apprehended at the borders, two to three evaded capture and made it through. One must remember, however, that the INS counts apprehensions, not individuals, and many persons apprehended and repatriated to Mexico return to the border to try to cross again.

In 1996, the Border Patrol apprehended about 1.6 million persons nationwide, of whom 1.5 million were Mexicans crossing along the 1,952-mile southwestern border. The INS estimates that 93 percent of Mexicans who entered without documentation came to work, many even with a job waiting. The Border Patrol caught 122,233 aliens who were smuggled into the country, and it seized about $1.2 billion worth of narcotics (INS Statistical Year-

Table 2.1
INS Estimates of Undocumented Aliens in the United States, October 1996, By Top Twenty Nations of Origin and Top Twenty States of Residence

Country of Origin	Population	State of Residence	Population
All Countries	5,000,000	All States	5,000,000
1. Mexico	2,700,000	1. California	2,000,000
2. El Salvador	335,000	2. Texas	700,000
3. Guatemala	165,000	3. New York	540,000
4. Canada	120,000	4. Florida	350,000
5. Haiti	105,000	5. Illinois	290,000
6. Philippines	95,000	6. New Jersey	135,000
7. Honduras	90,000	7. Arizona	115,000
8. Poland	70,000	8. Massachusetts	85,000
9. Nicaragua	70,000	9. Virginia	55,000
10. Bahamas	70,000	10. Washington	52,000
11. Colombia	65,000	11. Colorado	45,000
12. Ecuador	55,000	12. Maryland	44,000
13. Dominican Republic	50,000	13. Michigan	37,000
14. Trinidad/Tobago	50,000	14. Pennsylvania	37,000
15. Jamaica	50,000	15. New Mexico	37,000
16. Pakistan	41,000	16. Oregon	33,000
17. India	33,000	17. Georgia	32,000
18. Dominica	32,000	18. District of Columbia	30,000
19. Peru	30,000	19. Connecticut	29,000
20. Korea	30,000	20. Nevada	24,000
All other	740,000	Other	330,000

Source: http://www.ins.usdoj.gov/graphics/aboutins/statistics/illegalalien/index.htm.

Figure 2.1
Aliens Apprehended Fiscal Years 1951–1996

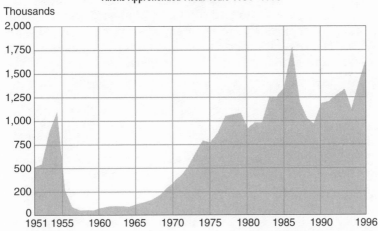

Source: Statistical Yearbook of the Immigration and Naturalization Service, 1996, Washington, DC: U.S. Department of Justice, 1997.

book 1996). The increased crackdown, especially on Mexican migrants, makes crossing the border riskier, which fuels the growing use of smugglers. Immigrants' rights groups charge that the new crackdown, dubbed Operation Gatekeeper, is increasing demand for smugglers and putting more migrants at peril. An estimated 800 have perished since 2000 (Sanchez 2002, 17).

Assimilation and the Incorporation of Immigrants and Their Children

A concern closely related to the issue of amnesty and legalization is the issue of the assimilation of immigrants and their children into U.S. society. With each new wave of immigrants from new or different nations of origin came a corresponding rise in anxiety about their ability to be absorbed. That pattern holds true today. Since 1965, the sources of immigration to the United States have shifted from largely northwestern European nations to Latin American and Asian nations. The change in immigration flow renewed concerns about the newcomers' ability to incorporate into U.S. cultural, economic, political, and social systems.

The shift in the sources of immigration is demonstrated in Table 2.2. Table 2.2 lists the number of legal immigrants to the United States by region for fiscal years 1990–2000 and the percent of the total legal immigration from that region. Because immigration from Mexico is such a predominant portion of that from the North American region, its figures are included in the table as well.

The graphs in Figure 2.2 show the numbers of persons naturalized, by decades and selected region of birth, for fiscal years 1961–1996. They illustrate the dramatic shift in region of origin from Europe to the Western Hemisphere and Asia.

Of perhaps even greater concern to critics of immigration is the projected impact the trend to such increased numbers of both legal and illegal immigrants from Mexico, South and Central America, and Asia will have on the racial makeup of the U.S. population. Critics fear this trend is changing the very face of the United States. Figure 2.3 presents a graphic image of that impact by showing bar graphs for the percent distribution of net immigration, by race and Hispanic origin, from 1995 to 2050, according to Census Bureau projections.

Although current immigration trends are undeniably reshaping the racial composition of the United States and indeed

Table 2.2
Legal Immigrants Admitted to the United States by Region of Origin, Fiscal Years 1990–2000
(rounded to 1,000)

Region	1990	1991	1992	1993	1994	1995	1996	1997	1998	1999	2000
Total	1,536	1,827	974	904	804	720	916	798	654	646	850
Europe	112	135	145	158	161	128	147	120	91	93	132
(% total)	(7)	(7)	(15)	(17.5)	(20)	(17.8)	(16)	(15)	(13.8)	(14.3)	(15.6)
Asia	338	358	357	358	292	268	308	266	220	199	265
	(22)	(19.6)	(36.6)	(39.6)	(36)	(37)	(33.6)	(33.3)	(33.5)	(30.8)	(31.2)
Africa	36	36	28	27	42	53	48	47	41	37	45
	(2)	(2)	(2.7)	(3)	(3.3)	(5.8)	(5.7)	(5.9)	(6.2)	(5.6)	(5.2)
North America	958	1,200	384	301	272	232	341	307	253	271	345
	(62.3)	(66.3)	(39.4)	(33.3)	(33.8)	(32.1)	(37.1)	(38.5)	(38.6)	(41.9)	(40.5)
Mexico	679	946	214	127	111	90	164	147	132	148	174
	(44)	(51.8)	(21.9)	(14)	(13.8)	(12.4)	(17.8)	(18.4)	(20.1)	(22.8)	(20.4)
Caribbean	115	140	97	99	105	97	117	105	76	72	88
	(7.5)	(7.6)	(10)	(11)	(13)	(13.4)	(12.7)	(13.2)	(11.5)	(11.1)	(10.3)
Central	146	111	58	58	40	32	44	44	36	43	66
America	(9.5)	(6)	(6.1)	(6.4)	(4.9)	(4.4)	(4.8)	(5.4)	(5.4)	(6.6)	(7.8)
South	86	80	55	54	47	46	62	53	45	42	56
America	(5.5)	(4.3)	(5.6)	(5.9)	(5.8)	(6.3)	(6.7)	(6.6)	(6.9)	(6.4)	(6.5)
% Male	53.3	66.4	51.0	46.9	46.3	46.3	46.2	45.8	45.8	44.9	44.5

Figure 2.2

Persons naturalized by decade and selected region of birth, fiscal years 1961–98

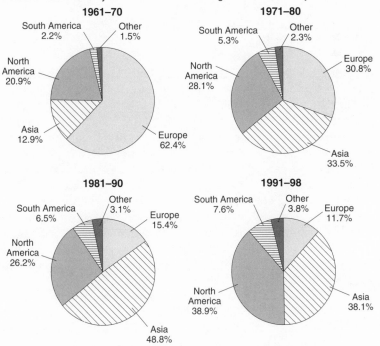

1961–70
South America 2.2%
Other 1.5%
North America 20.9%
Asia 12.9%
Europe 62.4%

1971–80
South America 5.3%
Other 2.3%
North America 28.1%
Europe 30.8%
Asia 33.5%

1981–90
Other 3.1%
South America 6.5%
Europe 15.4%
North America 26.2%
Asia 48.8%

1991–98
South America 7.6%
Other 3.8%
Europe 11.7%
North America 38.9%
Asia 38.1%

Source: "Chart O: Persons Naturalized by Decade and Selected Region of Birth: Fiscal Years 1961–1998," in *Statistical Yearbook of the Immigration and Naturalization Service, 1998,* Washington, DC: U.S. Department of Justice, 2000.

Figure 2.3

Percent Distribution of Net Immigration by Race and Hispanic Origin: 1995–2050 (Middle series beyond 1990)

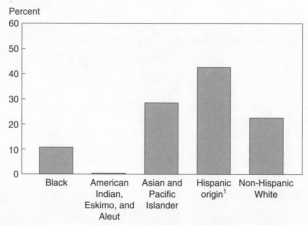

[1]Persons of Hispanic origin may be of any race. The information on the total and Hispanic population shown in this report was collected in the 50 States and the District of Columbia and, therefore, does not include residents of Puerto Rico.

Source: Population Projections of the United States by Age, Sex, Race, and Hispanic Origin: 1995–2050, Washington, DC: Bureau of the Census, 1996.

changing the very way "Americans" look, are these newest immigrants any less able to incorporate into the United States than did immigrants of the past?

By most measures available at this time, such fears seem to be more xenophobic than grounded in reality. In large measure, how quickly an immigrant assimilates into society is influenced by his or her age. The median age of recent immigrants was twenty-eight years (INS, *1997 Statistical Yearbook,* Table 3.10). This influx of young people is particularly important because the U.S. population, with its relatively low birthrate among native-born citizens, is aging rapidly, and by 2025, when about 20 percent of the population will be more than sixty-five years old, more working people will be needed to support them and maintain the Social Security system through payroll taxes.

One indication of assimilation of immigrants themselves is their rate of naturalization. Naturalization is the conferring of U.S. citizenship, by any means, upon a person after birth. A person who becomes a naturalized citizen pledges allegiance to the United States and renounces allegiance to his or her former country of nationality. The candidate must meet certain general requirements: A

Figure 2.4

Number of Persons Naturalized, Fiscal Years 1908-2001

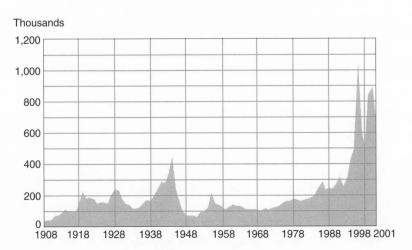

Source: U.S. Department of Justice, "Legal Immigration, Fiscal Year 2001," *Annual Report* (August 2002).

person must be eighteen years old or older, must have been legally admitted to the United States for permanent residence, and must have lived here continuously for at least five years. He or she must demonstrate the ability to speak, read, and write English, know how the U.S. government works, have a basic knowledge of U.S. history, and be of good character. In 1996, 96 percent of the immigrants who became naturalized citizens met those requirements. The other 4 percent were persons admitted under special provisions of the naturalization law that exempted them from one or more of those general requirements. Figure 2.4 shows the number of persons naturalized for fiscal years 1908–2001.

The post-1970 cohort of immigrants, especially those arriving since 1986, have naturalized in nearly unprecedented rates. Immigrants who are young adults when they arrive, those who come from more distant parts of the world, such as Africa or Asia, and those who were admitted as refugees or in professional categories are the most likely to naturalize. Asian immigrants are

Table 2.3
Median Years of Residence at Year of Naturalization, By Region of Birth, Fiscal Years 1965–1996

Region of birth	1996	1990	1985	1980	1975	1970	1965
Persons naturalized	9	8	8	8	7	8	7
Europe	8	10	9	10	8	9	7
Asia	7	7	7	7	6	6	6
Africa	7	7	7	7	6	6	6
Oceania	10	10	8	8	7	9	8
North America	11	11	13	11	9	7	9
South America	9	9	8	9	10	7	7

Source: *Statistical Yearbook of the Immigration and Naturalization Service, 1996*, Immigration and Naturalization Service, U.S. Department of Justice, Washington, D.C. 1997

more likely to become citizens: They have come great distances, often through very difficult conditions, requiring a strong commitment. The distance makes it harder to maintain contacts with their mother country. Many emigrants from China and Vietnam left for political reasons, having rejected the political systems of their native countries, and there may no longer be a possibility of return. In contrast, Mexicans and Canadians, living so close to their countries of origin, may easily keep in contact with families and travel back and forth. Most have come for economic reasons and have not necessarily rejected the political systems of their native lands. Likewise, people with high-status occupations, for example, in the medical professions or engineering, have the highest naturalization rates. Those without a substantial attachment to the labor force, such as homemakers and retired or unemployed persons, have the lowest rates.

Table 2.3 shows the median years of residence by year of naturalization and region of birth for fiscal years 1965–1996. Clearly, Europeans simply do not naturalize substantially faster than those from Asia, Africa, or South America. Those from North America (mostly Mexico and Canada) are the slowest to naturalize, though not in any way unusually so.

Critics of current immigration policy fear that the level and makeup of today's immigration flow makes efforts at "Americanization" more difficult. As we have seen above, the 1990s witnessed the largest number of immigrants in U.S. history. The foreign-born population now numbers about 27 million, twice the level of 1910. Immigrants are more concentrated, with the top four immigrant receiving states accounting for a 20 percent larger share of that population than did the top four states in 1975. Critics fear the new immigrant flow is less varied than in the past, with more than 50 percent of the post-1970 immigrants coming from Spanish-speaking countries, representing what they feel is a degree of ethnic concentration unprecedented in U.S. history. They also feel the mass immigration rate is hindering the economic assimilation of immigrants, and they offer evidence that immigrant wages are falling behind those of native workers, causing a steady rise in immigrant poverty.

Finally, critics feel that current immigration policy is anti-assimilationist. They are worried that the nation may not have the self-confidence and resolve needed to sustain an Americanization campaign. Multiculturalism, bilingualism, and changes in communications and transportation, critics fear, make it more difficult to do so. They contend that most immigrants only undergo a superficial assimilation. These critics hold that Americanization is more than just learning English or getting a job. For them, the development of a visceral, emotional attachment to the United States and its history is a "patriotic assimilation" that they fear is unlikely to occur when the schools and the general culture is skeptical, even hostile, to patriotism and when communication technology enables immigrants to maintain strong psychological and even physical ties to their countries of origin (Center for Immigration Studies News Backgrounder, June 2002).

A recent spate of carefully constructed social science studies of immigrants and their children has looked at their rates of incorporation. The studies provide evidence that the claim that the newest immigrants will be unable or less able to assimilate or will be significantly slower to do so than were the immigrants of, for example, the pet-door era is clearly questionable. Indeed, recent studies of the rate of incorporation of immigrants and their children demonstrate quite a different case. The findings of several studies show that their respondents reverse the conventional expectations, a result that has potential for long-term political consequences. These studies offer a different theoretical view or model of the assimilation process than that traditionally held. In place of viewing immigration as a homogeneous, linear process, these scholars argue it is better seen as a highly segmented, nonlinear process that does not always lead to "amalgamation." Biculturalism and pluralism are as evident as is traditional assimilation (see, for example, Portes and Rumbaut 2001a).

Of concern to most scholars of immigration is the language ability and adaptation of immigrants. A 1989 Current Population

Study examined immigrants arriving between 1987 and 1989 and who therefore had had little time to learn English in the United States. It found that about half of the recently arrived immigrants spoke English "well" or "very well" (Jasso et al. 2000). There is considerable variation between immigrant groups in English-language ability, depending on the language of the nation of origin and on the educational backgrounds and occupational categories of the immigrants. For example, among immigrants entering through "employment" provisions, more than 40 percent speak English very well. Among those coming to join spouses or close relatives, and particularly among those entering as refugees or asylees, only a small percent (from 2 percent to less than 20 percent) speak English very well. Post-1965 immigrants are less likely than immigrants during the middle 1900s to have entered the United States with high levels of proficiency in English (Stevens 2001, 186–187). As one scholar notes,

> Although nativism is a complex phenomenon that varies over time, one common feature is the use of cultural and racial criteria to identify the foreigners as different and un-American. An increase in the numbers of new immigrants from non-English-speaking countries means an increase in the number of foreign-born persons who have not yet had the time and opportunities to learn English and therefore an increase in the proportion of non-English speakers among the foreign-born population. . . .

Research based on historic and contemporary data show that immigrants and their children quickly become more proficient in English the longer they live in the United States (e.g., Espenshade and Fu 1997; Labov 1998; Stevens 1999).

Yet recent immigrants in general have been vilified as not setting the learning of English as a high priority, and Hispanic immigrants have been singled out as particularly unwilling to learn English (Lamm and Imhoff 1985, 99–124).

Census 2000 data, however, shows that the children of immigrant families quickly become the family's English translators, and this function helps their own assimilation and their self-images (see Obsatz 2002c).

Since there is no national policy on the incorporation of immigrants to encourage their learning of English, immigrants' pursuit of competence in English is ad hoc, pertains to particular contexts, and is highly variable across local and state areas and over time. Although twenty-five states have "official English" laws, twenty-five do not. California's Proposition 227, passed in 1998, undermined the provision of bilingual education programs, and several other states have or are considering enactment of similar measures. This patchwork of public and political responses to the language skills, or lack thereof, of these newest immigrants reflects the difficulties and benefits of welcoming newcomers to a nation that prides itself on being a nation of immigrants, even though national policy does not identify English as the language of the United States (Stevens 2001, 188–189).

What about other aspects of incorporation beyond speaking English? An extensive study of political participation by immigrants in New York State found that nativity, indeed, had an independent, direct influence on political participation. Foreign birth moderately depresses registering for actual voting, even when socioeconomic status is controlled. Naturalized citizens were less likely to register and to vote in the 1994 state elections than were native-born citizens, but their turnout rate in the federal elections of 1996 were similar to those reported by native-born citizens. When organizational affiliations, which serve as mobilization variables, are factored in, membership in organizations and inclusion in networks that are politically engaged emerged as important factors influencing the levels of political participation. The foreign-born do not appear to be less connected to voluntary organizations fostering participation in society than are the native-born. Mobilization variables were found to be more important than socioeconomic status, confirming the priority given to civic life in understanding political participation. Membership in specifically political organizations plays an important role in mobilizing both foreign-born and native-born citizens to participate in politics (Minnite, Holdaway, and Hayduk 2001, 220–223).

And what of the incorporation of immigrants' children? Immigrant children and the U.S.-born children of immigrants are now the fastest growing segment of the U.S. child-age population, accounting for more than 20 percent of all children in the United States. That proportion is likely to increase as a result of continued immigration and the higher birthrates among immigrant parents than among native-born parents. The "immigrant stock"—first-generation foreign-born persons and second-generation U.S.-born persons with at least one foreign-born parent—now exceeds 60 million people. The Children of Immigrants Longitudinal Study

(CILS) is a multifaceted examination of the educational performance and the social, cultural, and psychological adaptation of children of immigrants. It is the largest study of its kind to date in the
United States (Rumbaut 2001; Portes and Rumbaut 2001b).

The CILS found that although more than 90 percent of these
children of immigrants lived in homes in which a language other
than English was spoken, 73 percent preferred to speak English instead of their parents' native tongue. Within three years, the proportion of these children who preferred English had risen to 88
percent. Even among the group most likely to retain the mother
tongue, Mexican youth living in San Diego, California, with its
large Spanish-speaking population and many Spanish-language
radio and television stations, the 32 percent preferring English
originally had risen to 61 percent by three years later. Among
Cuban-origin youth in Miami, the shift was even more dramatic.
There, 95 percent of both the foreign-born and the native-born preferred English by three years later (Rumbaut 2000, 237).

The study found a somewhat lower but similar shift in identity in the second generation as well, where the U.S.-born children
of foreign-born parents were one-quarter as likely to identify themselves by their parents' national origins than were the foreign-born
children. The CILS study found an overall picture of resilient am-
bition and noteworthy achievement (Rumbaut 2000, 242–257).

The incorporation of immigrants' children into the economy
is also evident. An examination of the 2000 census data published
in *American Demographics* revealed that nearly half of all the foreign-born population (42 percent of the men, 37 percent of the
women) have middle income levels, and 29 percent earn more
than $50,000 annually. Among the newest immigrants, those in
the United States less than ten years, 31 percent of the men and 25
percent of the women are middle class. Asian immigrants lead the
foreign-born group in median income at $42,900 (above the na-
tional average) in 1996. Among them, 36 percent worked in managerial or professional roles. Among Canadian-born immigrants,
46.5 percent were professional, as were 37.8 percent of European-
born newest immigrants. Indeed, the median incomes in immigrant households from Europe, Africa, South America, and North
America are all more than $30,000. These immigrants understand
the U.S. economic market, and the percentage who have personal
computers in their homes is similar to that percentage in the total
population (Wellner 2000, 58–64).

Immigrant adaptation to U.S. culture, politics, and society is,
of course, a time-related process. Table 2.4 shows the results of

Table 2.4
Immigrants' Adaptation: Time-Related Processes

Years in U.S.	0–4	5–9	10–14	15–19	20–24	25–29	30+
Adaptation Processes							
% Speak English Well or Very Well (LASUI):							
1. Chinese	15.9	29.1	30.5	48.2	38.9	47.6	61.1
2. Korean	9.8	12.0	20.9	33.9	33.3	66.7	66.7
% Using English All or Most of the Time (LNPS):							
3. Mexican	5.3	2.8	4.9	4.4	16.7	22.6	16.0
4. Puerto Rican	2.7	0	0	8.4	14.3	10.7	17.2
5. Cuban	0	0	2.0	0	4.7	8.5	8.0
% Who have developed racially diverse social networks (LASUI):							
6. Chinese	4.6	9.6	7.1	3.5	12.8	0	19.0
7. Korean	1.9	1.9	3.4	3.3	9.4	0	25.0
% Attendance at Non-Latino Social Event (LNPS):							
8. Mexican	62.0	59.0	59.5	53.7	70.4	73.6	72.5
9. Puerto Rican	80.6	68.0	79.4	71.7	80.8	86.3	87.0
10. Cuban	48.1	76.1	50.2	73.8	71.0	84.9	83.3
% Who have returned to country of origin for more than 3 months (LASUI):							
11. Chinese	8.3	13.8	12.6	12.8	17.9	9.1	4.8
12. Korean	1.9	4.6	4.6	6.7	3.1	33.3	25.0
% Who plan to return permanently to country of origin (LNPS):							
13. Mexican	28.2	11.6	8.4	4.7	7.8	0	6.0
14. Puerto Rican	53.6	34.8	44.8	38.9	27.1	32.4	20.9
15. Cuban	12.0	10.3	12.2	2.0	3.7	0	6.3
% Who return to country of origin at least once every two years (LAT):							
16. Chinese	50.8	35.2	28.0	19.0	27.2	16.7	21.8

Source: Table by author, adapted from Wong, 2000: 137, Table 7.

some interesting studies on the effects of the length of residence on immigrants' political involvement. This table uses data from the 1994 Los Angeles Survey of Urban Inequality (LSUI), the Latino National Political Survey (LNPS) of 1990, and a 1997 *Los Angeles Times* poll of Chinese Americans living in southern California (LAT). It demonstrates a mixed picture of immigrants' adaptation over time depending on the immigrant group. Overall, however, it indicates significant degrees of assimilation after a few decades.

Asylum and Adjudication Processing Issues

Asylum and adjudication processing issues are something of a constant among criticisms of the INS. Just a few headlines from recent Center for Immigration Studies news releases illustrate the point: "INS to Enforce Address Change Rules," "La Raza Objects to INS Enforcement of Laws," "Immigrant Complaint Draws Support for INS Bill," "Detention Center for Illegal Aliens Draws Criticism," "INS Chief Visits Detained Haitians," "More on Four Illegal Alien Students Facing Deportation," "Fewer Judges, Less Justice," and "INS Proposes Adjustment of Status Rules for Certain Indochinese Aliens."

Processing delays by the INS keep families separated or in a sort of legal limbo, often for years on end. These problems further impede the educational progress of their children and can prevent potential wage earners from supporting their families. In part, the issue of backlogs reflects the sheer volume of immigrants. Immigrants and their children make up 20 percent of the population. Among children, 9 percent have at least one noncitizen parent, and 10 percent live in mixed-status-family households. The issue reflects the results of the 1996 reform act.

The backlog of paperwork at the INS is notorious. Some of the backlog is undoubtedly the result of the sheer volume of paperwork. Given its current resources and applicable computer technology, the INS is simply incapable of keeping up. A recent INS report, for example, noted that applications for citizenship between October 1, 2001, and May 31, 2002, had increased 65 percent over the same period the year before—a total of 519,523 applicants. In May 2002 alone, the agency received 48,378 applications—a 121 percent increase over the May 2001 total. The INS's efforts to weed out potential terrorists in the post–September 11, 2001, context means it will take longer to approve applications and the backlogs will grow.

Some of the backlog is just as undoubtedly the result of the INS's chronic ineptitude. In August 2002, for example, the INS admitted that it had recently "found" 2 million unfiled documents sent in by foreign residents, documents that the agency had apparently misplaced or forgotten, including 200,000 change-of-address forms required by the INS that had been piling up for years in a warehouse complex near Kansas City, Missouri (Interpreter Releases 2002b). Immigration experts and civil rights groups charge that the INS's failures are an embarrassment to the government and an affront to the foreigners who play by the rules. An ACLU critic noted, "The agency's own record-keeping and information systems are completely inadequate, yet it so often turns around and punishes law-abiding immigrants when the agency's own shoddy record keeping is at fault" (quoted in Associated Press 2002a). Yet, ironically, Attorney General John Ashcroft announced the INS issue of a proposed rule on July 26, 2002 that (1) would require every alien applying for immigration benefits to acknowledge having received notice that he or she is required to provide a valid current address to the INS, including any change of address within ten days of the change; (2) stated that the INS would use the most recent address provided by the alien for all purposes, including the service of notices to appear if the INS initiates removal proceedings; and (3) stated that if the alien has changed his or her address but failed to provide the new address to the INS, he or she would be held responsible for any communications sent to the most recent address provided by the alien. In reaction to the news of the "found" cache of 2 million documents, an immigration attorney, William Bernstein, said, "It's outrageous. It at least raises the possibility that there could be innocent people who were deported on bogus charges" (Associated Press 2002a; see also "INS Should Put Its House in Order" 2002).

Currently, there are more than 35 million family members of U.S. citizens and legal permanent residents whom the INS has approved for family-based immigrant visas and who are languishing in backlogs. Another substantial number, an estimated 5 million, are undocumented persons living in the United States as "unlawfully present," who thereby face a three-to-ten-year bar to "admission." In 1999, the INS removed more than 176,000 persons. Immigration judges ordered another 72,000 to "depart voluntarily." In 1999, the INS removed more than 62,000 immigrants with criminal convictions, and in 1998, it detained more than 153,500, a figure that could easily double due to the Illegal Immigration Reform and Immigrant Responsibility Act of 1996 "mandatory detention" provision. As many as 5,000 immigrants on any given night languish in "indefinite" INS custody because their country of birth will not accept their return and the INS will not release them (Kerwin 2001, 108–109).

Delays in processing visa applications routinely run from two to eight months for "immediate relatives" and to more than two years in other cases, depending on which INS service station is handling the applications. Backlogs in visa-preference categories are another major delay in the family immigration process. A Mexican adult son or daughter of a legal permanent resident faces a wait of eight and a half years, as do similar nationals from other high-immigration-source countries, such as India or the Philippines. Such backlogs fuel pressures for illegal entry. Children whose applications are caught in the backlog often face the problem of "aging out" of their preference category if, during the delays, they change from being under eighteen years old (a minor child), to more than eighteen years of age (putting them into a new category of "adult children"). In 1997, the Department of State estimated the number of visa-backlogged persons at more than three and a half million (Kerwin 2001, 112).

The process to adjust one's status takes an average of 52 months, with projected delays varying from 4 months in Baltimore, Maryland, to 128 months in San Diego. In 1998–1999, even while the application fee for permanent residence increased from $130 to $220 to help defray the costs of increased staff to process them, pending adjustment cases increased to more than 1 million. In 1994, the adjustment backlog was just over 121,000 cases. In the last quarter of 1999, the INS received 172,566 adjustment applications but only processed 82,498 of them. The INS reports that by the end of 1999, the naturalization backlog had decreased to 1,317,348. Nonetheless, nationally, processing times still average more than one year. This delay compounds family-related problems. Because legal permanent aliens cannot become U.S. citizens in a timely manner, their eligible family members likewise cannot become legal permanent residents for years on end (Kerwin 2001, 114).

Likewise, asylum seekers must file an asylum application and obtain U.S. government approval. The approval process is likely to take longer and be less fairly conducted since the Department of Justice, responding to national security issues after September 11, 2001, abolished the Board of Immigration Appeals.

Another asylum-processing and due-process issue involves the "expedited removal" process. Originally called "expedited expulsion," the process was a reaction to persons claiming asylum upon arrival at a port of entry. Proponents of the process, such as Rep. Bill McCollum (R.–Fla.), led a thirteen-year effort to pass "summary exclusion," giving the U.S. attorney general wide latitude to exercise expedited removal (ER) of aliens. Their first success at enactment of the concept was the April 1996 passage of the Antiterrorism and Effective Death Penalty Act of 1996. The act was poorly drafted in that it gave INS inspectors sweeping authority to expel arriving aliens based on "on-the-spot" determinations as to the "credible fear" status of asylum seekers. Before its provisions could go into effect, they were superseded by the Illegal Immigration Reform and Immigrant Responsibility Act of 1996 (IIRIRA). This act contained provisions that became effective on April 1, 1997, and are now better known as ER. It emphasized asylum reform: preventing, defeating, or deterring the cynical use of asylum by claimants who had destroyed or hidden their identity in order to get past border screening and then disappear into the country. This act has proven to be primarily an overall border-control and antifraud tool. Most arrivals subjected to it never plead a "fear of return or of persecution." ER subjects clearly fraudulent violators to a more efficient removal order than before and lays the legal groundwork for more severe sanctions should such persons attempt illegal entry at a later date.

Most of the expedited removal orders issued to date have not involved asylum cases. The 1996 law mandated a GAO review process. The GAO made its first report, after seven months' experience with the provision, in 1998. It found that in that period, 29,170 aliens were processed under ER procedures, with 5 percent, 1,396, being referred for a "credible fear" review. Of those, 79 percent were found to have a credible fear. The GAO report also found that 47 percent of those referred to an ER removal procedure for attempting to enter without proper documents or through fraud or misrepresentation were *not* found to be inadmissible into the United States on the basis of those charges (Wolchok 2000, 185).

Asylum applications present the most sensitive questions, since the consequences of an erroneous decision can be extreme, even fatal. The 1996 law mandates a review by an immigration judge, expressly specifying "an opportunity for the alien to be heard and questioned by a judge, either in person or by telephonic or video connection," within seven days of the asylum officer's decision (Martin 2000, 162–173).

David Martin has argued that the ER provision should be retained with some key modifications to enhance its due process. He recommends that the ER procedures should

1. Assure humane treatment of persons going through secondary inspection
2. Improve internal monitoring of secondary inspection
3. Provide for carefully designed outside monitoring
4. Limit ER to persons with fraudulent documents or no documents
5. Improve consultation arrangements
6. Avoid backsliding on key protections
7. Resist the temptation to apply ER to "entrants without inspection"
8. Use ER for persons caught during or after an observed entry between points of entry
9. Improve conditions and times of detention of asylum seekers (Martin 2000, 174–180)

Expedited removal power is exercised by about 4,500 INS officers at nearly 300 ports of entry to U.S. land borders, at both international airports and seaports. About 77,000 removal orders were issued in fiscal year 1998, following which 3,000 people were referred to the asylum corps for "credible fear" interviews.

Critics of the ER process—such as human rights advocates, legal organizations, and refugee-service organizations—fear that admissible individuals are being denied entry and that refugees fleeing persecution may not make it through the inspection process to a "credible fear" interview. They maintain that the secrecy surrounding the ER process, anecdotal evidence of mistreatment by INS inspectors, and the drop in asylum applications by arriving aliens indicate that these processes are being misused behind closed doors. They argue for independent researchers to monitor and report on the process (Wolchok 2000, 185).

Critics of ER have raised questions about the future of ER and about how the process may be expanded as the process becomes institutionalized in the INS, particularly in light of the post–September 11 homeland-security measures and subsequent announcements by Attorney General Ashcroft. Those questions are summarized here:

1. Will there be an expansion of the ER program between ports of entry?
2. Will "inspections" be treated as an enforcement function if the INS is split into two agencies or separated into an enforcement and a service component?
3. Will asylum seekers who have passed the "credible fear" screening process be eligible for release from detention, and if so, who will make that determination? Today there are 16,000 detention beds available to the INS, 60 percent of which are rented from state and local jails.
4. Will asylum officers be authorized to grant asylum to eligible individuals at their "credible fear" interviews?
5. Will litigation resolve some of the implementation issues?
6. Is further legislation likely?

Given the concerns raised by nongovernmental human rights, legal, and refugee organizations over the ER process, the Bush administration's consideration of legislation dubbed "Patriot Act II," and its efforts to reform ER provisions rather than to repeal them, expedited removal will probably remain a contested issue for the foreseeable future.

Border Control and Management Issues

The perennial proposals for immigration reform all speak to another ongoing concern: Does the United States have adequate control over its borders? The political battles over control of illegal immigration, now three decades long, reflect the view of many that the nation has lost control of its borders. The 1986, 1990, and 1996 laws all involved some provisions to "beef-up" or "reform" the Border Patrol. These concerns were exacerbated by the September 11, 2001, attacks, resulting in two laws that address the issue (the USA Patriot Act of 2001 and the Homeland Security Act of 2002) and in ongoing proposals to further revise and strengthen "homeland security." This is no small task. The United States shares 5,525 miles of border with Canada and 1,952 miles with Mexico. Ocean borders include 95,000 miles of shore and a 3.4-million-square-mile exclusivity zone. Annually, more than 500 million persons cross the borders, among whom some 350 million are noncitizens. They enter through no fewer than 350 official ports of entry. Managing the borders, securing transportation systems by sea and air, and controlling international airports and seaports are inseparable tasks.

The USA Patriot Act, passed nearly unanimously by Congress with great emotion and little debate, grants the attorney general and the Department of Justice sweeping new powers for domestic surveillance, powers largely unchecked by judicial review. On May 8, 2002, the House of Representatives overwhelmingly approved establishment of the new Department of Homeland Security (DHS). The vote in the House was 411 in favor, none opposed, and two House members voting present but neither in favor nor opposed to the bill. On April 18, 2002, the bill to establish the new department passed in the Senate by a vote of 97 to 0. The final version of the law (HR 5005) was passed on November 19, 2002. The DHS has four divisions: Border and Transportation Security; Emergency Preparedness and Response; Chemical, Biological, Radiological, and Nuclear Countermeasures; and Information Analysis and Infrastructure Protection.

The DHS restructures the INS by moving the Border Patrol from the Justice Department to the new Department of Homeland

Security. These actions reflect a consensus that the United States faces a severe problem of control or management of its borders. If the cliché "If it ain't broke, don't fix it" has any validity, then a corresponding old saw applies here: "If it's obviously broken, then it needs a major overhaul, not some minor tinkering."

The debate over how best to control or manage the borders has traditionally hinged on arguments posited as zero-sum, no-win trade-offs, as "rights versus rights." Strong enforcement is pitted against service. Greater control is opposed to civil liberties. Group interest, identity, and diversity are balanced against shared national goals. Balancing such polarized arguments involves inevitable trade-offs deeply ingrained in fundamental constitutional principles and hence seems to be a never-ending quest (Bach 2000, 239–240).

The new DHS, through its Border Patrol, the U.S. Customs Service, or the Department of Agriculture, encounters, processes, and daily makes decisions about more than 1 million border crossers. In fiscal year 1998, the INS alone conducted 503 million transactions involving cross-border travelers. With globalization, the economies of the United States and the world depend more and more on such border crossings for increased trade, business, mobility, and tourism. The Border Patrol remains the primary agency responsible for the control of U.S. borders. Its biggest problems occur along the 1,952-mile U.S.-Mexican border, although illegal aliens also enter as stowaways on ships or enter through airports. Figure 2.5 shows the thirty-six land ports operated by the INS along the U.S.-Mexican border.

Past attempts to beef up the border at problematic areas simply resulted in a temporary increase in apprehensions there, followed by a shift in the flow of illegal traffic. In 1994, for example, the Border Patrol allocated additional personnel to San Diego and El Paso, Texas. In 1993, those two areas had accounted for 68 percent of all southwestern border apprehensions. During 1997, apprehensions there were less than half the rate of 1993 (33 percent). Illegal alien traffic had moved to other sectors. New agents were allotted to Tucson, Arizona, and to Del Rio, Laredo, and McAllen, Texas. In 1996, Congress approved adding 1,000 agents a year for the next five years. Although 1,148 agents were hired in 1998, only 200 to 400 were trained to be hired in fiscal year 2000 (Information Plus 1999, 96).

The IIRIRA of 1996 further required the attorney general to install additional physical barriers to prevent illegal crossings in sectors that experience high levels of illegal entry. In San Diego,

Figure 2.5
INS Land Ports of Entry along U.S.-Mexican Border

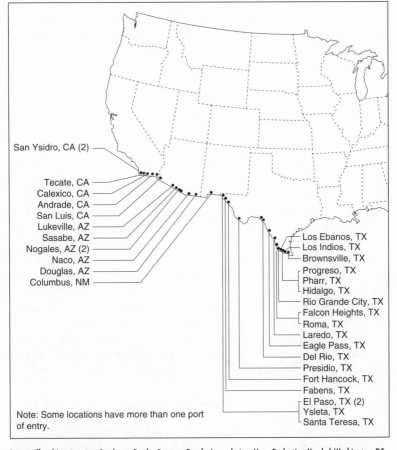

Note: Some locations have more than one port of entry.

Source: Illegal Immigration: Southwest Border Strategy Results Inconclusive; More Evaluation Needed, Washington, DC: U.S. General Accounting Office, 1997.

thirty-two miles of bollard-type fencing was added to the previously existing fourteen miles of reinforced-steel fencing.

In 1995, an international advocacy group for human rights, Human Rights Watch, issued a highly critical report alleging abuses committed by the Border Patrol, including the use of excessive force. Then INS Commissioner Doris Meissner signed a Non-Deadly Force Policy, but Human Rights Watch insisted the policy was too broad and permitted the use of force in too many circumstances. The Border Patrol countered that its officers often come into contact with human and narcotics smugglers prepared to use all means, including violence, to enter the United States. Such smugglers are dangerous, and Border Patrol agents are not as well armed as they would like to be. Pressure to increase the Border Patrol capabilities rose dramatically after the terrorist attacks of September 11, 2001. Individual citizens, mostly ranchers whose lands abut the Mexican border, have formed vigilante groups. They arm themselves with lethal weapons and patrol border areas looking for human smugglers and bands of illegal aliens crossing the border.

Airline companies are responsible for screening passengers and preventing those without proper documentation from boarding an airplane. They are required to provide the INS with a list of all departing and arriving passengers. They are held responsible for bringing in passengers without documents, whether or not such documents were verified before departure, and can be fined $3,000 per illegal passenger and bear the cost for alien detentions. Sometimes such costs, which include hotel and twenty-four-hour security guards for months, are very high—an estimated $9 million a year. Delta Airlines maintains a motel exclusively for detainees near JFK Airport in New York City. At some high-risk airports, carriers photocopy visas and passports prior to departure, collect and hold documents, or take other precautions to screen out document-flushers and to establish that the passenger is not a stowaway.

Border management is complicated by high volume. Increased security results in cross-border exchanges that are slow, and at the current rate of flow and with the rather primitive technology available to manage it, the risk to public safety and the potential for illegal entry are high. Ports of entry often do not present would-be illegal entrants with any credible risk of apprehension, and the ability of smugglers and traffickers to adapt their techniques and tactics at border crossing increases the law enforcement problem.

Improving border patrol and management service requires better enforcement, and to speed up traffic, security must be increased, not decreased. But how do policymakers accomplish those seemingly contradictory aims? Future innovations and processes must alter the past zero-sum, either-or approaches. One INS Associate Commissioner, Robert Bach, has suggested the broad outlines for better border management (Bach 2000, 242–250). Such a new approach would rely on new technology and better use of information:

1. At airports, advanced passenger-information systems

would relay biographical data collected from passengers to inspectors at the port of entry. INS and customs officers could then analyze these data while the passengers are in flight and would then be able to spend less time with passengers at inspection booths on ground.

2. Dedicated commuter lanes have been shown to work well at both the Canadian and Mexican borders. These rely on improved service and facilitation that enhance law enforcement control of the traffic at the ports of entry. Participants using such lanes are pre-registered and prescreened.

3. The INS began to test an information system that matches information on passengers as they arrive and depart. Non-U.S. citizens now use the system on U.S. Airways flights between Frankfurt, Munich, Philadelphia, and Pittsburgh. Travelers are automatically provided an electronic I-94 form with their boarding passes. Upon arrival, their biographical data is already in the INS computers, having been transmitted electronically from aboard. When the person departs, the form is collected and read electronically, better enabling the INS to track how many travelers overstay their visa conditions. By analyzing these data, the INS should be able to improve enforcement and security.

4. The IIRIRA of 1996 requires the implementation of an enforcement system at land borders that is simply not feasible with current technology or with the investment dollars necessary to build the new infrastructure at ports of entry. Whether or not post–September 11 security concerns will increase the priority sufficiently to develop that technology and to justify those expenditures is still an open question.

5. Current reform discussions emphasize four perspectives with very different assessments of the problems:

   a. The first seeks to harden the borders. This perspective argues that one terrorist who crosses the border undetected is one too many. As long as drugs, guns, and even persons are smuggled across the border, no law enforcement person and no community can feel comfortable under the level of scrutiny necessary to achieve a perfectly closed border. Enforcement strategies responding to this perspective involve tightening inspections of each person and vehicle, which means stopping traffic long enough to open every trunk and interview every passenger. This approach trades much-decreased efficiency for increased enforcement.

b. A second perspective stresses technology and the capacity to automate inspection activities. Strategies corresponding to this perspective include attempts to develop high-volume processing of documents. Such processing emphasizes service in which a certain degree of error and risk is expected and considered normal. Law enforcement, of course, is correspondingly less emphasized. Hope for the future in the technology approach relies on the use of biometrics to ensure that a person's identity and documents match. Technology using a traveler's fingerprints is becoming the more common solution in this approach. Retinal and photographic profiling and scanning are also under experimental development.

c. A third approach focuses on creating exceptions to rules for particular groups of passengers in order to speed their processing at ports of entry. Proposals include exempting first-class passengers from long inspection lines, visa waivers for preferred nationalities, special procedures for certain occupational groups, and even facilitated entry for vacationers who also own property. Such improved services for these groups comes at a cost to the general public and an increased security risk.

d. A fourth approach seeks comprehensive transformation of the principles of border management. The goal is to reduce some of the pressures at the border because ports of entry are among the weakest locations to achieve either efficient facilitation or effective enforcement. This approach hinges on regional cooperation.

In November 1997, then U.S. Attorney General Janet Reno and the Canadian minister of citizenship and immigration formed a new working partnership on migration issues. The focus was to create a new Border Vision to set long-term priorities and directions. The two governments agreed that they faced common problems arising from illegal immigration, including international human smuggling. Law enforcement agencies in both countries were to work together to define problems as regional problems and to seek regional solutions, including efforts to disrupt international networks of organized human smuggling and alternate approaches to strengthening law enforcement that require less dependence on screening all travelers and more on developing common standards, procedures, and processes for both countries for inspections at airports and seaports. This approach emphasizes overseas interdiction, including training and document control. Pre-inspection and preclearance arrangements hold potential for transferring the locus of immigration enforcement overseas, where it can often do the most good and the least harm. Such overseas inspection occurs when the inspectors have more time, where security is greater, and under circumstances where the government has the upper hand. Such a regional framework means a shared set of rules for cross-border activity (Bach 2000, 244–248).

A more difficult set of trade-offs involves the enforcement of immigration laws within the United States. The failures of IRCA's employer-sanctions approach led to calls for new strategies that bring people together rather than pitting them against each other. Again, INS Commissioner Bach suggests four such strategies:

1. Enforcement should target criminals, who should be imprisoned and removed.
2. It should target smuggling operations and rally all interest groups to the realities of modern-day trafficking in humans.
3. It should target work-site enforcement by increasing the impact of INS enforcement on the labor market and on individual firms and their unauthorized workers. The appropriate tactics would dismantle the labor-market mechanisms, such as recruitment schemes between employers and labor contractors, that encourage smuggling. Such improvement would involve increasing the ability of the Department of Labor and the Equal Employment Opportunity Commission to enforce laws against those employers.
4. A fourth priority involves visa and document abuse. In fiscal year 2000, the INS completed 4.7 million adjudications and issued almost 16 million documents.

> Controlling fraud is essential to providing better
> services (Bach 2000, 248–250).

Post-September 11 concerns led Attorney General Ashcroft to propose a program, the Terrorism Information and Protections System (TIPS), that would have citizens alert law enforcement to "suspicious behavior." Critics, such as the ACLU, alleged this approach would turn citizens into spies on one another and would probably lead to many more false accusations than to terrorists caught. House Majority Leader Dick Armey (R.–Tex.) broke with the administration on this issue and sponsored a bill to prevent citizens spying on one another. In mid-July 2002, the House rejected TIPS by passing the 200-page Armey bill by a 295 to 132 vote. The law establishing the Department of Homeland Security did not include a provision for TIPS, and therefore the House vote killed the proposal, at least for the immediate future. A June 2002 ABCNEWS poll, however, found that 64 percent of the public favored expanding FBI surveillance powers, even if such expanded powers were to intrude on privacy and necessitate a reduction in civil liberties.

The Cost of Immigration

Controversy over immigration centers on whether immigration is of overall benefit to the nation or a huge drain on resources. The anti-immigration sentiment, and particularly sentiment against illegal aliens, that is registered in public opinion polls emphasizes such aliens' use of public educational, health, and welfare services or the added costs to the criminal justice system caused by illegals. These costs are viewed as a drain on the citizen taxpayers and a strain on state and local governments. Critics maintain that illegal immigrants take jobs away from native-born citizens. State governments, especially in those states with high immigration-receiving rates, are concerned that federal immigration laws have imposed huge financial burdens on them. Others, however, dispute the "burden" argument. Pro-immigration advocates contend that the United States, in the long run, benefits economically, culturally, and socially from immigration, whether legal or illegal. Immigration brings workers, and workers create wealth. These advocates point out that the United States benefits greatly from the brain drain from other nations, wherein highly talented persons come from developing nations to the United States, bringing their talents with them. Immigrants add workers to the labor force, and with their higher birthrates, they continue to add to the employee base upon which an increasingly older native-born population depends for the continued solvency of Social Security and Medicare. This controversy is unlikely to be resolved soon because the two perspectives use different measures in their assumptions to assess both the costs and the benefits of immigration.

The "cost debate" over immigration first came to national attention in 1993 when the economist Donald Huddle completed a report for the Carrying Capacity Network, an environmental group concerned over rapid population growth (Huddle 1993). Huddle calculated that for every 100 unskilled immigrants who were working, 25 unskilled U.S.-born workers were displaced from jobs. In 1992, Huddle placed the net costs of immigration at $42.5 billion. In 1997, he estimated such net costs had risen to $68 billion.

An Urban Institute study by Jeffrey Passel disputed Huddle's findings (Passel 1994). Passel maintained that Huddle had neglected to account for the positive economic impact of immigrant business and consumer spending. Passel claimed that Huddle had overstated costs and displacement effects. He calculated that immigrants pay more than $70 billion in taxes, $50 billion above Huddle's estimate.

Because the different approaches to measuring the cost-benefit ratio of immigration use different assumptions in their calculations, it is difficult to assess which is more accurate. Their estimates of economic gains and losses differ substantially. The GAO, in a 1995 report, examined three national studies of costs and benefits associated with illegal aliens. All three concluded that illegal aliens cost more than they generated in revenues to federal, state, and local governments. They found that the estimates of that cost ranged from $2 billion (the Urban Institute study) to about $19 billion (Huddle's updated estimates in 1993) (GAO 1995). Estimates of the primary fiscal benefits of immigrants focus on their positive impact on the Medicare and Social Security systems. A study by Stephen Moore noted that although immigrants pay into the Medicare and Social Security systems, their own parents are not collecting benefits. This creates a one-generation windfall to the Social Security system (Moore 1998). Immigration will help ease the financial hardship projected for the system by the baby-boom generation (about 40 million people), who will begin collecting retirement benefits in 2011. A 1998 Social Security *Board of Trustees Report* projects that if net immigration remains at 800,000 over the next twenty-five, fifty, and seventy-five years, working immigrants will contribute an estimated $19.3 billion, $22.3 billion, and $25.8 billion, respectively, to the Social Security Trust Fund (SSTF) benefit (SSTF 1998). Moore estimates that in 1997, the total immigrant income was $390 billion, generating $133 billion in taxes (Moore 1998). A 1996 Census Bureau study found that families with a member who is a naturalized citizen pay an average of $6,580 in federal taxes, whereas those with U.S. citizen members pay an average $5,070.

The cost-benefit effects of immigration, legal and illegal, are hotly contested. Immigration supporters, such as the Urban Institute, emphasize the need to take into consideration the revenues generated by immigrants. George Borjas, a Cuban immigrant and professor of public policy at the John F. Kennedy School of Government at Harvard University, believes immigration is harming the country, claiming that the lower educational levels of the more recent immigrants mean that they remain at an economic disadvantage and in the long run will result in greater use of welfare (Borjas 1994).

The National Research Council (NRC), in a 1997 report, concluded that immigration had little negative effect on the wages and job opportunities of most native-born Americans and that the estimates of immigrants' costs to state and local taxpayers may be inflated (NRC 1997).

The Guest-Worker Issue

Another recurring immigration issue since the end of the Bracero Program in 1964 is a program allowing for guest workers. Guest workers are temporary immigrants who are legally admitted to the United States for a given period of time (for example, nine months of a fiscal year). Typically in guest-worker programs, the temporary workers are assigned to specific jobs, often to a particular employer, and are legally or practically unable to change the terms of their employment or to switch employers. Historically, most such programs have been associated with agricultural work. American growers import such workers through the H-2A program. Congressmembers associated with the growers have consistently sought to expand H-2A. Since 1990, the computer, electronic, and similar high-tech industries have lobbied successfully for an increase in the annual allotment of H-1B visas for high- or special-skilled workers.

In 1980–1981, there were approximately 44,000 guest workers admitted into the United States. By 1990, that number had increased to 139,000, and by 1996, to 227,000 (Center for Immigration Studies n.d.). Although growers argue that their sector of the economy could not survive without either illegal aliens or guest workers, critics contend that the artificial inflation of the low-skilled agricultural labor market simply encourages farmers to use more labor-intensive crops and harvesting processes, thereby retarding the progress of U.S. agriculture.

The H-1B visa program was established with the 1990 IM-MACT in reaction to a labor shortage that was projected but never occurred. This program allows for 65,000 temporary visas, good for up to six years, for people in specialty occupations and tied to a specific employer. The drawing card of the H-1B visa is that the employer sponsors the "green card." Government audits have identified the program as being rife with abuse. The current system allows unscrupulous employers to exploit workers and retaliate against them if they try to assert labor or workplace rights (Goldstein 2001). In the 1990s, the guest-worker programs were aimed at filling a narrower range of vacancies in the labor market, such as foreign nurses in areas with few medical personnel. The 1990 act was a response to an anticipated need for more scientists and engineers. It was established just as the Cold War was ending, leading to a layoff of many such professionals. The number was capped at 65,000 a year, with a maximum of 300,000 such H-1B workers being employed at any given time. In 1997, employers lobbied for an increase in the 65,000 cap; the lobbying was led by the computer industry, which convinced Congress more foreign professionals were needed. The program has been controversial. Then Labor Secretary Robert Reich, in the Clinton administration, testified against it, stating that industry was using it to replace skilled U.S. workers with cheaper foreign workers.

The American Competitiveness and Workforce Improvement Act of 1998 increased the number of H-1B visas available by 142,500 over three years. It imposed two employer requirements, however, for those seeking H-1B workers: The employer must pay a $500 fee per applicant; these funds were to support scholarships for Americans studying computer and related fields. And employers with 15 percent or more of such workers in their labor force had to certify that U.S. workers were not laid off to make room for the H-1Bs ninety days before or after the H-1B workers arrived at the workplace. The Department of Labor estimated that about 50,000 employers filed 250,000 applications in 1999.

About 44 percent of H-1B workers admitted are from India, and most are computer programmers (Martin 2001, 49).

In 2001, another bipartisan Senate bill was introduced to further increase the H-1 cap.

The proposed American Competitiveness in the Twenty-First Century Act (ACTFCA) would raise the visa cap for H-1B to 195,000 for three years. A similar House bill sets the total at 200,000.

H-2As are certified foreign guest workers; that is, the employer seeking H-2A workers must certify the need through the Department of Labor. Growers have been trying to obtain guest workers without going through a certification process. A bill to do such passed the House in 1984, and the Senate approved a measure authored by then Sen. Pete Wilson (R.–Calif.) in 1985. Congress approved a Replenishment Worker Program in 1986, and the Senate approved a revision of the H-2A program, called Agjobs, in 1988 (Martin 2001, 50). Agjobs were in a proposed pilot project and introduced the concept of farmworker registries, lists of farmworkers whom local employment service offices have screened and determined to be legally authorized to work in the United States. Growers liked that feature because if farmers requested 5,000 workers and only 1,000 were listed in the local registry, they would get almost automatic approval to have 4,000 more admitted. Critics contended that Agjobs would make it too easy for farmers to reject qualified U.S. workers; would in effect eliminate the Adverse Effect Wage Rate, a government-set minimum wage designed to offset the wage-depressing effects of foreign workers; and would eliminate the requirement that employers provide housing to the workers. Though the Agjobs program was not enacted, growers continue to press for some similar guest-worker program.

There are pros and cons to the guest-worker program approach. Foreign-born farmworkers earning low wages by U.S. standards are still earning better wages than they could earn at home. However, they, and U.S.-born farmworkers, then find it hard to get work at wages above the poverty-level farm earnings. U.S. farmers are better off, enjoying higher profits. U.S. consumers pay less for fresh produce and other commodities. The critical policy choice is, which is more valuable to U.S. society, cheaper food or higher farm wages? Another policy choice involves the time frame used to assess the impact of a guest-worker program: today, or over some time into the future? (Martin 2001, 53–54). Advocates of programs like the H-1B argue that the

United States needs such programs to find the skilled labor it must have if it is to stay competitive with its trade partners who do have such programs, especially Australia, Canada, and the United Kingdom. They argue that although such programs are small, these workers fill a vital niche in the global economy and global workforce (Shotwell 2001, 56).

A final and related issue to the guest-worker program is the special visa categories for spouses of professional workers employed in the United States. Spouses of H1-B visa immigrants may be able to use one of a couple of special-category employment visas: The L-1 visa is an option for spouses who have been employed abroad by a multinational organization; the E visa relies on a treaty of trade or commerce between the United States and the spouse's country of nationality; and the O visa is available to "individuals of extraordinary ability in sciences, arts, education, business, or athletics" (the individual must be able to supply evidence that he or she has risen to the very top of his or her field of endeavor—by having won a Nobel Prize, the Tour de France or an Olympic Gold Medal, an Academy of Science Award, and so on). Finally, there is the J-1 visa, covering work experience through specialized training. Similar types of programs are available in countries including Argentina, Australia, Canada, Hong Kong, the Netherlands, Sweden, and the United Kingdom (Sharp 2000, 62–63).

Restructuring the INS

Many, if not most, of the issues discussed above involve criticism of the INS. Calls for its restructuring go back to legislative proposals that predate the enactment of IRCA. Some in Congress called for restructuring the INS during the Carter administration, when the INS could not establish even how many Iranian students were living in the United States. More carefully considered proposals have emerged since 1990. The IMMACT of 1990 established a Commission on Immigration Reform (CIR). The CIR issued a report in 1997 calling for a restructuring of the INS (Meissner 2000, 3; Gardner 2000, 7–8).

Over five years, the Jordan Commission, as the CIR came to be known, held hearings, consultations, and roundtable discussions. It defined four core functions of government in implementing immigration policy: (1) enforcement of laws at the border and in the interior, (2) adjudication and administration of immigration and citizenship benefits, (3) work-site enforcement of labor standards, and (4) administrative review of agency decisions. It felt the current system had two major systemic flaws in carrying out those functions: mission overload and fragmentation and diffusion of responsibility. Its final recommendations for structural reform included the following:

1. Immigration enforcement and investigations within a new Bureau of Immigration Enforcement remaining within the Department of Justice
2. Immigration and citizen services with the State Department under a new Undersecretary for Citizens, Immigration, and Refugees
3. Work-site enforcement of immigration-related standards within the Wage and Hour Division of the Department of Labor
4. Administrative review of all immigration-related decisions within a newly created Independent Agency for Immigration Review (Gardner 2000, 17–21)

In 1998, after the Jordan Commission issued its report, several representatives introduced variations to restructure the INS, but these measures were put on hold when the House Judiciary Committee undertook its impeachment referral. In 1999, a new bill was introduced by Representatives Mike Rogers (R.–Mich.) and Silvestre Reyes (D.–Tex.) and the chairman of the House Subcommittee on Immigration and Claims, Lamar S. Smith (R.–Tex.). This bill called for creating two bureaus, a Bureau of Immigration Services and a Bureau of Immigration Enforcement. Each bureau would be headed by a director appointed by the president with the Senate's consent, and each would report directly to the attorney general.

If this bill had been passed, it would have transferred from the INS commissioner to the new director of the Bureau of Immigration Services all functions, personnel, infrastructure, and funding provided to support adjudications of nonimmigrant and immigrant visa petitions, of naturalization petitions, and of asylum and refugee applications; adjudications performed at service centers; and all other adjudications under the Immigration and Nationality Act now performed by the INS. It would have transferred to the director of the Bureau of Immigration Enforcement all functions, personnel, infrastructure, and funding in support of the Border Patrol, the Detention and Deportation program, the Intelligence program, the Investigations program, and the Inspections program, and it would have created in each bureau a chief financial officer (Ries 2001, 101).

Another perspective and proposal to restructure the INS came from the International Migration Policy Program of the Carnegie Endowment for International Peace (Papademetriou, Aleinikoff, and Meyers 1999). There were several areas of consensus among the proposals by the INS itself, by the Jordan Commission, and by the Carnegie Endowment report. All agreed on the need for a dramatic structural change of the INS. All agreed on the need for a separation of enforcement and service functions and chain of command. All agreed on the need for drastic improvement in management. Finally, all agreed that the detention and asylum functions need to be separated from other functions. The Carnegie plan proposed two options: either to establish an independent agency, along the lines of the Environmental Protection Agency, with separate enforcement and service divisions, or to elevate INS functions within the Department of Justice (Aleinikoff 2000, 22–27).

The Carnegie plan for a new independent agency would combine the immigration work of the Justice Department (the visa, passport, and most of the asylum and refugee functions), the immigration functions of the State Department, the labor-certification functions of the Labor Department, and the refugee functions of the Department of Health and Human Services. The establishment of such an agency would, for the first time ever, fully focus the resources of the executive branch on the important and difficult issues of immigration and citizenship.

The Carnegie Endowment's second option, in the event that Congress rejected the proposal for a separate agency, proposed to elevate the immigration functions within the Department of Justice by establishing an Office of the Associate Attorney General for Immigration. All functions performed by the INS would be folded into the Department of Justice, with separate chains of command: The Executive Office for Immigration Review and the Office of Immigration Litigation were each to report directly to the attorney general. This concept would keep separate the service and enforcement activities but would place them higher within the hierarchy of the Department of Justice. Such restructuring would enable an upgrading in pay and benefits for immigration officers, spark much-needed agency cultural change in the way immigration laws are implemented and enforced, and yet enable substantial cost savings and increased efficiency by eliminating several layers of overlapping bureaucracy (Aleinikoff 2000 27–31).

The terrorist attacks of September 11, 2001 made all these proposals moot, although many of these ideas were incorporated into the DHS law. The INS's failure to prevent the terrorists from entering the country, especially combined with the announcement, some six months after the attack, that visa applications had been approved for several of the hijackers to come to the United States to attend flight-training schools, raised the level of rhetoric and the political support for change, and indeed, the demand that something be done. The Bush administration developed and announced a plan to establish a new cabinet-level Department of Homeland Security. As enacted, the establishment of the new department involves the most extensive reorganization of the executive branch in decades. On November 19, 2002, President Bush signed the law establishing the new DHS. It moved twenty-two agencies and 190,000 employees into the new department, the most massive reorganization since the Department of Defense was established after World War II. The Congressional Budget Office placed the number of affected workers at 225,000, out of a federal civilian workforce of 1.7 million, and pegged the cost of creating the department at $3 billion just for the reorganization, not including the increased cost of additional security technology and so on. The new department's budget for 2003–2004 was authorized at $38 billion. Scholars at the Brookings Institution warned that with such a massive reorganization, the new department's top management will for some time be concerned with the integration of the agencies into a new management and budget system. The twenty-two agencies being moved have varied financial management systems and 100 personnel systems, and the new department managers have to negotiate contracts with eighteen labor unions. Some of the agencies moved to the DHS have admirable reputations as being among the nation's best-performing organizations (the Coast Guard, Federal Emergency Management Agency [FEMA], the Secret Service), but also among the twenty-two are some that are widely viewed as being among the worst-run agencies (the Customs Service, the INS, and the Border Patrol, in particular). INS investigators and Border Patrol agents are notoriously undertrained, overworked, and overstressed, and as discussed above, the INS's information management system is abysmal (Light 2002; Interpreter Releases 2002a).

Congressional debate before passage of the measure generally followed party lines, with a majority of House Democrats voicing concerns about the bill on the grounds that it gutted civil service protection for employees, seriously limited civil liberties, and gave

Figure 2.6
Organization of the Department of Homeland Security

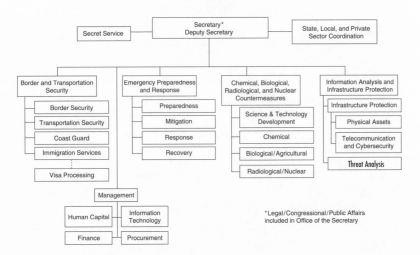

companies involved in homeland security excessive protection from legal liability. They also wanted airport security guards to be federal employees rather than private-sector employees under contract with airport authorities or airline companies.

Among the twenty-two agencies transferred to the new department are the Coast Guard, the Customs Service, the Border Patrol, the Secret Service, the Transportation Security Administration, and the FEMA. Figure 2.6 presents a diagram of the new department. As in the earlier proposals to restructure the INS advocated by the Bush administration, the new Department of Homeland Security separates the visa processing, immigration services, and Border Patrol (now called Border Security) functions as bureaus within the new department.

References and Further Reading

Aleinikoff, T. Alexander. 2000. "Reorganizing the U.S. Immigration Function." In *In Defense of the Alien*, ed. Lydio Tomasi, vol. 22, 22–32. New York: Center for Migration Studies.

Allen, James Paul, and Eugene Turner. 2002. *Changing Faces, Changing Places: Mapping Southern Californians*. Los Angeles: Center for Geographical Studies.

Associated Press. 2002a. "INS Is Years Behind in Processing Records." Washington, DC, August 5.

———. 2002b. "House Panel Approves Homeland Security Agency." Washington, DC, July 20.

———. 2002c. "More Seek Citizenship, but Fewer Get It." Washington, DC, July 17.

Bach, Robert L. 2000. "Looking Forward: New Approaches to Immigration Law Enforcement." In *In Defense of the Alien,* ed. Lydio Tomasi, vol. 22, 239–251. New York: Center for Migration Studies.

Borjas, George J. 1994. "The Economics of Immigration." *Journal of Economic Literature* 32: 1667–1717.

"Bush Signs Homeland Measure." 2002. Riverside, CA, *Press-Enterprise,* November 26, A-1, A-5.

Calavita, Kitty. 1992. *Inside the State: The Bracero Program, Immigration, and the INS.* New York: Routledge.

Camarota, Steve A. 1999. *Immigrants in the United States—1998: A Snapshot of America's Foreign-Born Population.* Washington, DC: Center for Immigration Studies.

Center for Immigration Studies News Backgrounder. June 2002. Washinton, DC: Center for Immigration Studies.

———. N.d. "Guestworkers." On-line; available: www.cis.org/topics/guestworkers.html; accessed July 14, 2003.

Chang, Gordon H., ed. 2001. *Asian Americans and Politics: Perspectives, Experiences, Prospects.* Palo Alto, CA: Stanford University Press.

Chen, Shehong. 2002. *Being Chinese, Becoming Chinese American.* Champaign: University of Illinois Press.

Cohen, Steve, Beth Humphries, and Ed Mynott, eds. 2001. *From Immigration Controls to Welfare Controls.* New York: Routledge.

Cordero-Guzman, Hector, Robert C. Smith, and Ramon Grosfoguel, eds. 2002. *Migration, Transnationalization, and Race in a Changing New York.* Philadelphia: Temple University Press.

Daniels, Roger. 1998. *Not Like Us: Immigrants and Minorities in America, 1890–1924.* Lanham, MD: Ivan R. Dee.

DeSipio, Louis. 2000. "The New Urban Citizen: Political Participation and Political Attitudes of the Newly Naturalized." Paper presented at the American Political Science Association Meeting, Boston, 2000. In *In Defense of the Alien,* ed. Lydio Tomasi, vol. 22, 79–100. New York: Center for Migration Studies.

Dummett, Michael. 2001. *On Immigration and Refugees*. New York: Routledge.

Eggen, Dan. 2003. "Big Brother on Campus?" *Washington Post National Weekly Edition*, February 3–9, 29.

Espenshade, T. J., and H. Fu. 1997. "An Analysis of English-Language Proficiency among U.S. Immigrants." *American Sociological Review* 62: 288–305.

Freeman, Gary P. 2000. "Democratic Politics and Multilateral Immigration Policy." In *In Defense of the Alien*, ed. Lydio Tomasi, vol. 22, 223–235. New York: Center for Migration Studies.

Gardner, Robert. 2000. "Restructuring the INS: Draft Design Proposal." In *In Defense of the Alien*, ed. Lydio Tomasi, vol. 22, 6–10. New York: Center for Migration Studies.

General Accounting Office (GAO). 1995. *Illegal Aliens: National Cost Estimates Vary Widely*. Washington, DC: U.S. Government Printing Office.

Goldstein, Bruce. 2001. "Recent Temporary Worker Proposals in Agriculture." In Lydio Tomasi, ed., *In Defense of the Alien*, vol. 23. New York: Center for Migration Studies, 69–85.

"Homeland Security Gets OK." 2002. Riverside, CA, *Press-Enterprise*, November 20, A-1, A-5.

Huddle, Donald. 1993. *The Costs of Immigration*. Washington, DC: Carrying Capacity Network.

Immigration and Naturalization Service (INS). 1997. *INS Statistical Yearbook, 1996*. Washington, DC: Government Printing Office.

———. 1998. *INS Statistical Yearbook, 1997*. Washington, DC: Government Printing Office.

———. 2002a. Interpreter Releases. "Homeland Security Debate on Hold." August 5.

———. 2002b. Interpreter Releases. "INS Proposes Requiring Aliens to Acknowledge Advance Notice of Change of Address Requirements: 200,000 Cards Remain Unfiled." August 5.

———. 2002c. "Legal Immigration, Fiscal Year 2001: Annual Report, Office of Policy and Planning, Statistics Division." Washington, DC: INS, no. 7, August.

Information Plus. 1999, 2001. *Immigration and Illegal Aliens: Burdens or Blessing?* Wylie, TX: Information Plus.

"INS Should Put Its House in Order." 2002. *Atlanta Journal-Constitution*, August 9. Available on-line: www.cis.org; accessed August 12, 2002.

Jasso, G., D. S. Massey, M. R. Rosenzweig, and J. P. Smith. 2000. "The New Immigrant Pilot Survey (NIS-P): Overview and New Findings about U.S. Legal Immigrants at Admission." *Demography* 37: 127–138.

Kerwin, Donald. 2001. "Family Reunification and the Living Law: Processing, Delays, Backlogs, and Legal Barriers." In *In Defense of the Alien*, ed. Lydio Tomasi, vol. 23, 107–116. New York: Center for Migration Studies.

Labov, T. 1998. "English Acquisition by Immigrants to the United States at the Beginning of the Twentieth Century." *American Speech* 73: 368–398.

Lamm, R. D., and G. Imhoff. 1985. *The Immigration Time Bomb.* New York: Truman Tally Books.

LeMay, Michael. 1994. *Anatomy of a Public Policy.* Westport, CT: Praeger.

———. 2001. "Assessing Assimilation: Cultural and Political Integration of Immigrants and Their Descendants." In *In Defense of the Alien*, ed. Lydio Tomasi, vol. 23, 163–176. New York: Center for Migration Studies.

Light, Paul C. 2002. *Homeland Security Will Be Hard to Manage.* Brookings Institution's Center for Public Service, Washington, DC, August 25.

Lopez-Garza, Marta, and David R. Diaz, eds. 2001. *Asian and Latino Immigrants in a Restructuring Economy: The Metamorphosis of Southern California.* Palo Alto, CA: Stanford University Press.

Martin, David. 2000. "Expedited Removal, Detention, and Due Process." In *In Defense of the Alien*, ed. Lydio Tomasi, vol. 22, 161–180. New York: Center for Migration Studies.

Martin, Philip. 2001. "Temporary Workers at the Top and Bottom of the Labor Market." In *In Defense of the Alien*, ed. Lydio Tomasi, vol. 23, 44–55. New York: Center for Migration Studies.

McCarthy, Kevin F., and Georges Vernez. 1997. *Immigration in a Changing Economy: California's Experience.* Santa Monica, CA: Rand Corporation.

McConnell, Eileen Diaz, and Felicia B. Leclere. 2002. "Selection, Context, or Both? The English Fluency of Mexican Immigrants in the American Midwest and Southwest." *Population Research and Policy Review* 21, no. 3 (June): 159–178.

Meissner, Doris. 2000. "Management Challenge and Program Risks." In *In Defense of the Alien*, ed. Lydio Tomasi, vol. 22, 1–5. New York: Center for Migration Studies.

Minnite, Lorraine, Jennifer Holdaway, and Ronald Hayduk. 2001. "The Political Participation of Immigrants in New York." In *In Defense of the Alien*, ed. Lydio Tomasi, vol. 23, 192–228. New York: Center for Migration Studies.

Mintz, John, and Christopher Lee. 2003. "The Homeland Security Wish List." *Washington Post National Weekly Edition,* February 3–9, 31.

Moore, Stephen. 1998. *Fiscal Impact of the Newest Americans.* Washington, DC: National Immigration Forum, Cato Institute.

Mosisa, Abraham T. 2002. "The Role of Foreign-Born Workers in the U.S. Economy." *Monthly Labor Review* (Washington, DC, U.S. Department of Labor) 125, no. 5 (May): 3–14.

National Research Council (NRC). 1997. *The New Americans: Economic, Demographic, and Fiscal Effects of Immigration.* Washington, DC: NRC; National Academy Press.

Nevins, Joseph. 2001. *Operation Gatekeeper.* New York: Routledge.

Obsatz, Sharyn. 2002a. "INS Says Foreigners Required to Register." Riverside, CA, *Press-Enterprise,* December 7, B-5.

———. 2002b. "Vandals Turn Desert Deadly." Riverside, CA, *Press-Enterprise,* September 14, A-1, A-10.

———. 2002c. Obsatz, Sharyn. "Between Two Worlds." Riverside, CA, *Press-Enterprise,* August 27, A-1.

O'Harrow, Robert Jr. 2002. "Who's Minding the Passengers?" *Washington Post National Weekly Edition,* September 16–22, 29.

Papademetriou, Demetrios, Alexander Aleinikoff, and D. W. Meyers. 1999. *Reorganizing the U.S. Immigration Function: Toward a New Framework for Accountability.* Washington, DC: Carnegie Endowment for International Peace.

Passel, Jeffrey. 1994. *Immigration and Taxes: A Reappraisal of Huddle's 'The Cost of Immigration.'* Washington, DC: Urban Institute.

Passel, Jeffrey S., and Rebecca L. Clark. 1994. *How Much Do Immigrants Really Cost?* Washington, DC: Urban Institute.

Podesta, John, and Peter Swire. 2002. "Speaking Out about Wiretaps." *Washington Post National Weekly Edition,* September 9–15, 27.

Portes, Alejandro, and Ruben G. Rumbaut. 2001a. *Legacies: The Story of the Immigrant Second Generation.* New York: Russell Sage Foundation.

———, eds. 2001b. *Ethnicities: Children of Immigrants in America.* New York: Russell Sage Foundation.

Razin, Assaf, Efraim Sadka, and Phillip Swagel. "Tax Burden and Migration: A Political Economic Theory and Evidence." *Journal of Political Economics* 85 (August): 167–190.

Ries, Lora. 2001. "An Update from Capitol Hill." In *In Defense of the Alien,* ed. Lydio Tomasi, vol. 23, 99–103. New York: Center for Migration Studies.

Rumbaut, Ruben G. 2001. "Transformations: The Post-Immigrant Generation in an Age of Diversity." In *In Defense of the Alien*, ed. Lydio Tomasi, vol. 23, 229–259. New York: Center for Migration Studies.

Rumbaut, Ruben G., and Alejandro Portes. 2001. *Ethnicities: Children of Immigrants in America.* Berkeley and Los Angeles: University of California Press; New York: Russell Sage Foundation.

Sanchez, Rene. 2002. "Deadly Smuggling at the Border." *Washington Post Weekly Edition,* August 19–25, 17.

Sharp, Nancy A. 2000. "International Assignments and the Immigration Issues Surrounding Spousal Employment." In Lydio Tomasi, ed., *In Defense of the Alien*, vol. 22. New York: Center for Migration Studies, 59–63.

Shotwell, Lynn Frendt. 2001. "Comparison of the H-1B Bills." In *In Defense of the Alien*, ed. Lydio Tomasi, vol. 23, 87–95. New York: Center for Migration Studies.

Simcox, David. 1997. *Measuring the Fallout: The Cost of the IRCA Amnesty after Ten Years.* Washington, DC: Center for Immigration Studies.

Singh, Jaswinder, and Kalyani Gopal. 2002. *Americanization of New Immigrants.* Lanham, MD: University Press of America.

Social Security Trust Fund (SSTF). 1998. *Board of Trustees Report.* Washington, DC: U.S. Government Printing Office.

Stevens, Gillian. 2001. "U.S. Immigration Policy and the Language Characteristics of Immigrants." In *In Defense of the Alien*, ed. Lydio Tomasi, vol. 23, 177–191. New York: Center for Migration Studies.

———. 1999. "Age at Immigration and Second Language Proficiency among Foreign-Born Adults." *Language in Society* 28: 555–578.

Wellner, Alison Stein. 2000. "The Money in the Middle." *American Demographics* 22 (April): 58–64.

Wolchok, Carole Leslie. 2000. "Where Do We Go from Here? The Future of the Expedited Removal Process." In *In Defense of the Alien*, ed. Lydio Tomasi, vol. 22, 181–192. New York: Center for Migration Studies.

Wong, Janelle E. 2000. "The Effects of Length of Residence and Community Context on Political Attitude Formation and Participation among Asian and Latino Immigrants." In *In Defense of the Alien*, ed. Lydio Tomasi, vol. 22, 123–157. New York: Center for Migration Studies.

3

Global Issues

Given the intermestic nature of immigration policy, it is not surprising that many of the issues and concerns facing domestic policymakers, discussed in Chapter 2, are similar to the concerns faced by other immigration-receiving nation-states and by the organizations of the international community. Because mass migration is a global phenomenon, the policy issues involved are likewise global in nature.

Amnesty, or "Regularization," Issues

Virtually every major immigrant-receiving nation has experienced some degree of illegal immigration. Several, like the United States, have enacted or are considering some sort of amnesty program to legalize the status of undocumented or otherwise illegal resident aliens. Australia, Canada, France, Italy, the Netherlands, Spain, and the United States have all experienced legalization programs, which in Europe are more usually referred to as "regularization" programs.

France has had several legalization programs, instituted by successive governments, between 1972 and 1998. The French legalization programs and the most recent large-scale U.S. immigrant-legalization program, of more than 3 million immigrants as a result of IRCA, provide examples of what seem to be some elements common to all such amnesty efforts:

1. Generally, immigrant-receiving nations consider legalization after some period of time during which they tolerate illegal immigration, unauthorized

73

employment, or some temporary guest-worker program that has become an entrenched part of their labor markets.

2. Legalization programs are promoted by a particular political party, as the Democratic Party did in the United States and the Socialist Party did in France and other European states.

3. Most legalization programs have involved some degree of the carrot-and-stick approach, wherein amnesty is balanced by increased enforcement in the labor market against employers who encourage or exploit illegal aliens.

4. Legalization programs have been successful only when backed by a coalition of interests: trade unions, the Catholic church or other religious organizations, a plethora of immigrant assistance, mutual aid, and welfare groups, and so on. In the French *régularisations*, in 1981 and 1983, protesters brought pressure to bear on the government. The National Assembly and the Senate never debated the programs. The programs were authorized by the government after protest campaigns succeeded in mounting sufficient pressure. In the U.S. experience, both with IRCA and with current calls for a legalization program, there have been no public protests demanding amnesty; rather, lobbying with Congress went on behind the scenes.

5. Legalization programs have generally sparked anti-immigrant reflexes, evident both in France and in the United States.

6. All such programs have experienced a degree of fraudulent applications. They are difficult to administer and implement.

7. These programs have not resolved the illegal immigration influx problem to which they were, in part, addressed. Critics argue and marshal evidence to show that such programs induce further illegal immigration. Whatever their shortcomings, such programs have allowed significant numbers of illegal resident aliens to gain legal status, and they diminish to some degree sociopolitical concerns arising from the illegal status of long-term resident aliens. Observers contend that illegally resident and employed populations have grown after such programs—in the United

States, as we have seen, to an estimated 5 million or more. In France, the 1981 and 1983 programs were followed by several additional "specialized" legalizations directed at applicants for asylum, at those who had been turned down in the 1981 and 1983 programs, and at those who had been "wrongfully denied" legal status by conservative governments. The most recent regularization in France ended on December 31, 1998. It legalized some 80,000 applicants, most of whom had family members in France, out of some 130,000 applicants in all. This represents a higher success rate than those during the 1981 and 1983 procedures. (Miller 2000, 259–269)

Both France and the United States have experienced anti-immigrant backlashes to their respective amnesty programs, but one cannot rule out future recourse to the process even in a political period of stricter immigration control. Amnesty programs provide a symbolic counter to stricter immigration control by expressing solidarity with a vulnerable and often exploited foreign population who provide what many see as much-needed services in the labor market in relatively affluent democracies. Amnesty programs offer humane and practical solutions to what are enormously complex problems that resist easy solutions. They endow rights and privileges that facilitate the social and political incorporation of those foreign-born populations.

Drawbacks to such programs include the following: (1) They undercut legal immigration processes, (2) they seem to reward "lawbreakers," (3) they violate equity by rewarding a group or class of aliens with special consideration, and (4) they fuel anti-immigrant backlash.

As various nation-states worldwide struggle with amnesty proposals, it is clear that whether or not such legalizations will be enacted or otherwise authorized depends on a complex calculus of interest-group interaction and bargaining, electoral considerations that often affect political party coalitions for decades, and the impact of such programs on foreign policy concerns.

Control of Illegal Immigration

Amnesty programs are closely tied to another perplexing global concern: how to control illegal immigration. Table 3.1 lists more

Table 3.1
Coping with Illegal Immigration—From A to Z

Australia	European Union	Italy	Poland
Austria	Fiji	Japan	Portugal
Basotho	France	Lethoso	Russia
Botswana	Gambia	Malaysia	Saudi Arabia
Brunei	Germany	Malta	South Africa
Burma	Georgia	Mexico	South Korea
Cambodia	Greece	Morocco	Spain
Canada	Guatemala	Netherlands	Switzerland
Caribbean	Hong Kong	New Zealand	Taiwan
China	India	Norway	Turkey
Costa Rica	Indonesia	Pakistan	Ukraine
Cyprus	Ireland	Peru	Uganda
Denmark	Israel	Panama	UAE
Dominican Republic	Iran	Philippines	Zambia

than fifty countries whose illegal alien problems received attention in articles on the CISNews site in just a few days of mid-July 2002.

Problems associated with illegal alien streams in these countries echo those facing the United States: undocumented persons entering for jobs, human trafficking or smuggling, and visa overstayers.

Several countries listed in Table 3.1 experience problems of illegals who are passing through on their way to more preferred nations for more permanent residency. In short, they are "stepping-stone" countries in the flow of illegal aliens; such countries include, for example, the Dominican Republic, Georgia, Hong Kong, Ireland, Mexico, Poland, and Turkey. The European Union recently approved a plan to help fund Poland's efforts to tighten immigration controls on its eastern border. The EU governments were concerned that Poland would become a gateway for trafficking in humans, drugs, arms, and prostitution. Under the agreement, Poland will hire 5,300 extra border guards by 2006, a 50 percent increase in staff, and build more border stations and buy new equipment, such as helicopters and infrared detection devices. These measures are needed to crack down on the trafficking of women for prostitution and to curb the flow of illegal immigrants from east Asia and poor Communist countries who seek better lives in western Europe (IOM 2002).

The German Migration Council, a nongovernmental body, projects that 5 million immigrants will move from the east to western Europe by 2020. As the former Soviet-bloc nations improve economically, there will be more opportunity at home and less pressure to leave. The Czech Republic, Slovenia, and Hungary—the three richest of the central European republics—have few emigrants, and many former migrants have returned home. But the current trend is to the central and western nations: Ukrainians are often seen in the Czech Republic and Poland; Romanians serve as farm labor on Hungarian farms. In Hungary, the fourth-largest foreign community comprises more than 10,000 Chinese. EU immigration rules are getting tougher as border areas in eastern Germany and Austria attract more unskilled laborers and see increased cross-border commuting.

Every year, thousands of Africans seeking work and attempting to escape war and grinding poverty at home try to enter Spain. Many of them sail west from Morocco to the Canary Islands, and still others cross the Strait of Gibraltar and seek to enter Spain at its southern tip.

Recent news reports reveal examples of this illegal alien influx. For example, at the end of August 2002, Turkish police detained two vans jammed with seventy-one illegal immigrants who had each paid $800 to be smuggled across Turkey and over the border into Greece. Turkey is under considerable pressure from EU nations, such as Greece, to clamp down on the thousands of illegal aliens who use Turkey's borders and coasts every year for illegal entry.

In France, the same day, 400 illegal aliens occupied a famous basilica in a northern Paris suburb where they had sought refuge for ten days, and they were demanding legal papers to live and work in France. An anti-immigrant group calling itself the Committee of Saint Louis is believed to be behind a false bomb threat that forced the immigrants to evacuate the basilica.

Malaysian authorities have been enforcing new immigration-restriction laws that allow whipping, imprisonment, and large fines for illegal workers found there. Immigration officials in Malaysia estimate that there are up to 600,000 illegal workers present in the country because that wealthy nation has become a magnet to migrants from nearby, poorer Southeast Asian neighbors. Dozens of illegals have been sentenced to prison terms and to beatings with a rattan cane. An estimated 300,000 illegal immigrants fled Malaysia during a prosecution amnesty before the August 2002 deadline. The foreign minister of the Philippines protested the crackdown and treatment of its citizens, who make up much of the illegal alien population in Malaysia, calling the conditions in detention centers unduly harsh and the congestion appalling. In Indonesia, another major source of the illegal alien population, demonstrators burned a Malaysian flag in protest against the crackdown. Some 60,000 Filipinos returned from Malaysia in 2002, and 4,000 more are awaiting deportation. An estimated 180,000 Filipinos are estimated to be staying illegally in Malaysia's state of Sabah.

These cases illustrate a major concern about the mass movement of illegal aliens and refugees: protecting their basic human rights. As one scholar of the issue, Jorge Bustamente, put it,

> The number of international migrants moving around the world estimated by the UN Population Agency of approximately 120 million is bound to increase. This trend and the problem of their vulnerability as subjects of human rights . . . imply a spectrum of instability and conflict as one of the most serious problems of the twenty-first century, negatively affecting peaceful relations in the community of nations. (Bustamante 2002, 354)

Global Refugee Issues

Pressures for illegal migration often result from mass migration movements of refugees, some of whom attempt illegal entry into other countries. Refugee movements are generated by civil war or strife, ethnic conflicts, war, political persecution or repression that often follows regime changes, and such natural disasters as famine, floods, earthquakes, hurricanes, and outbreaks of epidemic disease. Mass refugee movements happen when thousands of persons conclude it is a matter of life or death that they depart their home or native country.

In the international context, the term "refugee" is defined in the UN Convention Relating to the Status of Refugees of July 1951, which established the Office of the High Commissioner for Refugees (UNHCR) based on the statute adopted by the UN General Assembly on December 14, 1950, and refined by the Multilateral Protocol and Convention Relating to the Status of Refugees adopted on January 31, 1967, which took effect October 4, 1967. To date, 130 nations have signed the convention or the protocol. The convention defines "refugee" as

> any person who is outside any country of such person's nationality, or, in the case of a person having no nationality, is outside any country in which such person habit-

ually resided, and who is unable or unwilling to return to, and is unable or unwilling to avail himself or herself of the protection of that country because of persecution or a well-founded fear of persecution on account of race, religion, nationality, membership in a particular social group, or political opinion.

This convention and related protocols are occasionally updated by the UNHCR, such as by the Guidelines on Applicable Criteria and Standards Relating to the Detention of Asylum Seekers, agreed upon in Geneva in February 1999.

Estimates of the number of refugees worldwide as of 2002 approached 20 million. The UN estimated there were 4 million Afghan refugees abroad, and 1.7 million refugees returned to Afghanistan from Pakistan alone by the end of 2002. The flood of refugees returning to Afghanistan was overwhelming the UN budget for refugees. By regional area, the UN estimated that the number of persons of concern (asylees and refugees) who fell under the mandates of the UNHCR as of January 1, 2002, were Asia, 8,820,700; Europe, 4,855,400; Africa, 4,173,500; North America, 1,086,800; Latin America and the Caribbean, 765,400; and Oceania, 81,300, for a total of 19,783,100.

The Organization for Economic Cooperation and Development of the European Union estimates that there are 3 million eastern European refugees in the European Union, about 2 million of whom are refugees from the former Yugoslavia. Others are Poles, Romanians, and Albanians.

Asylees and refugees under the mandate of the UNHCR are hosted in 150 nations around the world. Space does not permit listing all of those countries and their numbers of refugees. But Table 3.2 does list those countries in which 100,000 or more refugees reside.

Table 3.3 presents the number of applications for asylum in the twenty-eight most industrialized nations submitted from January 2001 to June 2002, according to the UNHCR, and the nation of origin from the top twenty source nations.

The desperation driving mass refugee movements often leads refugees to use exceedingly dangerous means of travel. New Zealand, for instance, recently agreed to take in 136 refugees rescued from a sinking boat. They were to be transferred from Auckland to the Managere Refugee Resettlement Centre. They were to be part of an annual quota of 750 refugees that New Zealand has accepted under convention by the UNHCR. They came from

Table 3.2
Refugees By Host Country

Host Country: Number of Refugees/Asylees, Returned Refugees, or Internally Displaced

Afghanistan	1,226,098	France	166,152	Pakistan	2,199,379
Algeria	169,497	FYR Macedonia	168,953	Russian	1,139,842
Angola	228,280	Georgia	272,214	Saudi Arabia	345,502
Armenia	264,339	Germany	988,533	Sierra Leone	103,105
Azerbaijan	587,317	Guinea	179,318	Sri Lanka	683,347
Bosnia/Herzegovina	570,221	India	169,756	Sweden	164,091
Burundi	125,775	Iraq	130,503	Thailand	111,059
Canada	175,028	Iran	1,868,011	Turkmenistan	200,518
China	295,326	Kazakhstan	119,543	United Kingdom	187,950
Colombia	720,389	Kenya	251,816	Tanzania	691,438
Congo	122,251	Kuwait	139,335	United States	911,730
Cote d'Ivoire	128,563	Liberia	253,424	Yugoslavia Fed.	777,104
Dem. R. of Congo	366,917	Nepal	130,957	Zimbabwe	284,671
Ethiopia	161,922	Netherlands	230,888		

Source: UNHCR.Governments, 6 June 2002. Visited 7/30/2002.

Table 3.3
Asylum Applications, 28 Industrialized Countries, January 2001–June 2002

Country of Asylum	Jan.–June 2001	July–Dec. 2001	Jan.–June 2002
Austria	14,991	15,144	17,075
Belgium	12,372	12,176	9,029
Bulgaria	1,090	1,337	2,055
Czech Republic	8,907	9,130	4,622
Denmark	5,856	6,547	3,310
Finland	773	878	1,400
France	23,258	24,005	24,761
Germany	40,786	47,577	38,259
Hungary	3,842	5,712	3,120
Ireland	4,769	5,555	5,085
Liechtenstein	39	73	35
Luxembourg	321	368	394
Netherlands	17,137	15,442	11,135
Norway	4,050	10,734	8,153
Poland	2,195	2,338	1,789
Portugal	116	118	117
Romania	1,292	1,008	609
Slovakia	2,417	5,734	3,351
Slovenia	1,057	451	258
Spain	4,342	4,877	3,798
Sweden	8,753	14,760	14,607
Switzerland	9,308	11,450	11,854
United Kingdom	42,800	47,500	51,500
Canada	20,954	21,792	15,633
United States	32,078	29,632	32,441
Australia	7,138	5,228	3,284
New Zealand	879	722	541
Total	272,683	304,715	268,498
Europe	211,634	247,341	216,599
EU-14	177,437	199,284	180,753

Source: UNHCR, Governments, June 2002. Accessed 7/30/2002.

Table 3.3, continued

Asylum Seekers, Top Twenty Nations of Origin

Origin	Applications
Iraq	22,833
Afghanistan	15,514
Turkey	14,540
Federal Republic of Yugoslavia	14,522
China	13,024
Russian Federation	8,398
Colombia	7,104
Mexico	6,448
Democratic Republic of the Congo	6,422
India	6,027
Nigeria	5,956
Iran (Islamic Republic of)	5,405
Somalia	5,322
Algeria	5,301
Sri Lanka	5,191
Pakistan	5,172
Armenia	4,713
Angola	4,503
Georgia	4,150
Bosnia and Herzegovina	3,910

Source: UNHCR, Governments, June 2002. Accessed 7/30/2002.

Tampa, Manus (an island of Papua New Guinea), and Nauru. These boat people were originally from Afghanistan, Iraq, and other countries, and they had been sent to Pacific islands to have their refugee claims processed. These 136 refugees were the first that New Zealand had accepted whose claims had been determined by Australia, but a spokesperson for the Immigration Ministry noted that "the quality of their [Australia's] determination is equal to our own and the UNHCR. I am satisfied that they are genuine refugees." More than a thousand asylum seekers remain in Australia's Pacific detention centers, where their applications for refugee status are being processed (Associated Press 2002c).

Border-Management Issues

The massive, worldwide migrations of refugees and illegal immigrants have strained the resources of all the major receiving countries. They all struggle with border-management issues. Among the preferred receiving nations of this flow are Australia, Canada, France, Germany, the Netherlands, New Zealand, and the United Kingdom. Each has its own general pattern in terms of the source of the flow and each has its own particular management issues. Each has a comparatively strong economy and borders areas of developing or weak economies; the migration to find labor is thereby enhanced and often difficult to manage. Australia, New Zealand, and the United Kingdom share a common heritage, flows dominated by persons from the former British Commonwealth of nations, and island geographies that enable them to better control their borders. Their management issues primarily concern visa overstayers and persons smuggled into the country. France, Germany, and the Netherlands, which have land borders with sending sources, have additional border management concerns. They also struggle with illegals who came initially as guest workers and then overstayed their time or smuggled in family members. These countries have one distinct advantage over the United States with respect to their border-management concerns: Because they face a much smaller flow of migration, border-management efforts are easier to finance. Most of these countries charge special exit stamps or fees to visitors, and that funding supports the border-management efforts. These nations are better computerized and seem better able to track the flow of immigrants, and they manage the information and record keeping far better than does the INS in the United States.

On September 7, 2002, Mexico began issuing *matricula consular* (identification) cards for Mexican and other nationals who travel through Mexico and into the United States. Guatemala has begun issuing such cards, and El Salvador and Honduras are planning to issue similar ID cards, following Mexico's example.

The cards are considered helpful in preventing fraud. Mexican ID cards are accepted by banks and nearly 1,000 police departments in the United States. They resemble a California driver's license. They can be used to cash checks and are accepted by police departments to establish identity and Mexican citizenship. Anti-immigrant groups contend that acceptance of the ID cards provides a quasi-legal status to Mexican citizens who are in the United States illegally and that they are virtually a "mini-amnesty." Mexico has issued 500,000 such cards in its first year of using them (Associated Press 2002a).

Migration and Development Issues

The push and pull of international migration is another important global issue. Many countries in the developing world are sending nations. The emigration they experience often results in a brain drain. A significant portion of their talented population emigrates to immigration-receiving countries.

Sometimes even more-developed countries experiencing economic difficulties struggle with this issue. South Africa, for example, is currently experiencing emigration outflow and brain-drain problems. The causes of the exodus include such factors as the uncertainties of majority rule, fears about rising crime, the AIDS pandemic, massive unemployment, the government's policy of affirmative action favoring black South Africans, corruption, and declining standards of health care and education. Violent crime is cited by an estimated 60 percent of emigrants leaving the country as a major reason for their decision. Others leave for better opportunities available since South Africa's reintegration into international business after the long period of isolation associated with apartheid policy. Because salaries are paid in rands, South African labor is cheap to hire, and the falling value of the currency has increased white middle-class anxiety about their future spending power in relation to the European and United States middle classes. Favored destinations for South Africans are Australia, New Zealand, Canada, the United States, and the United Kingdom. As many as 800,000 South Africans hold British passports and are thereby able to enter the United Kingdom to work. Others can extend their stay in the United Kingdom on the strength of having British ancestry. They are able to gain permanent-resident status after four years, and in six years they may claim a British passport. South Africa is shedding skilled labor at a worrying rate in comparison to its global economic competitors.

Similarly, there are more than 1 million Moroccan nationals who are officially resident in fifteen member states of the European Union, according to a Push and Pull Migration Study research project of the Netherlands Interdisciplinary Demographic Institute and the statistical office of the European Commission.

Thailand struggles with controlling the pull its economy exerts on nearby nations such as Myanmar (formerly known as Burma). Thailand's comparatively booming economy acts like a magnet for foreign workers, and a significant illegal flow is both dangerous and highly exploited. Hundreds of thousands of

Myanmar migrants have fled to Thailand to escape their impoverished and military-ruled homeland, and Laotians and Cambodians join them. The Thai government has registered 400,000 immigrants, allowing them to work, but tensions along its 1,300-mile border remain high. Thai officials estimate that there are more than 250,000 illegal Myanmar workers in the country. Migrants pay smugglers $100 to $250 to get them into the country, where they are employed in factories, on farms, in the fishing and construction industries, or as domestic workers. Some work as prostitutes, by choice or by coercion. Amnesty International reports indicate that most were paid less than Thailand's legal minimum wage. Typically, farmworkers were paid as little as $1.25 per day. In construction, immigrants do the dirtiest, most dangerous, and most difficult jobs. Thailand has no systematic protection against the abuse and prejudice they encounter. In March 2002, the bodies of thirteen immigrants, including women and children, were discovered in a waste dump. They had suffocated while packed under vegetables in a truck being used to smuggle them into the country, and the smuggling gang admitted to having dumped the corpses there. In February 2002, twenty ethnic Myanmars were found along a trail used for smuggling. In July, an eighteen-year-old girl died shortly after being found north of Bangkok. Before her death, she told Thai police she had been working as a maid at the house of a factory owner who kept her a virtual prisoner. He accused her of stealing a gold necklace. She denied the charge and was beaten up, taken away, doused with gasoline, and set afire (Associated Press 2002b).

Emigration has emerged as among the greatest of challenges to postapartheid South Africa. South African skilled workers are eagerly snapped up abroad. The emigration flow is seriously undermining the country's efforts to rise above a 3 percent economic growth rate. An estimated 39,000 South Africans left in 1999, joining some 1.6 million South Africans living abroad. One study found that 70 percent of skilled South Africans are considering emigrating, and an estimated 20 percent have already left. The brain drain costs South Africa about 2.5 billion rands ($250 million dollars) annually. Each skilled professional leaving the country costs it as many as ten unskilled jobs, according to a University of South Africa study (Lamont 2002).

Southeast Asia loses many of its more skilled workers to Malaysia or to Europe, Australia, Canada, and the United States. In Australia, for instance, in the current immigration flow, some two-thirds of work visas are granted to applicants from Africa, the Middle East, and Southeast Asia. The Australian immigration minister said the country's migrant intake for fiscal year 2001–2002 was the largest in a decade and the most skilled ever, numbering over 93,000. Per capita, Australia had a greater net overseas migration than any other comparable country. As the immigration minister put it, "What you've got is 53,520 highly skilled and educated young people and their families bringing their energy and their skills and knowledge, and their experience to Australia and helping our economy to grow" (quoted in Ruddock 2002).

Canada also benefits from the brain-drain flow. Its immigration minister, Denis Coderre, released a major proposal to encourage new immigrants to come to Canada and settle in the country's smaller urban centers. The plan intends to put a million newcomers into the nation's less populated regions by 2011, and if accomplished, it would constitute the most dramatic effort to channel immigrants since the settlement of western Canada during the early decades of the twentieth century. Under the plan, only skilled workers, who make up about 60 percent of the current inflow, would be eligible to sign a social contract under which they would agree to reside in the Atlantic provinces, the Prairie provinces, or rural areas of Ontario, Quebec, and British Columbia provinces for three to five years. In advocating the program, Coderre noted,

> It's not complicated. You know why? It's everybody's business and everybody participates in the process. Because immigration is not just a port of entry. By bringing them to a specific place, first of all it's economic, it's a matter of quality of life because it provides services to the citizens living there, and thirdly, it sends a clear sensitivity to a regional approach that Canada is the country to come to and that it is serious about plans to encourage settlement in all its regions and that people from Flin Flon or North Bay or Kelowna have a right to have the same services. There's no such thing as a second-class citizen. (Quoted in Curry 2002)

Canada has good reason to welcome tradesmen from Italy, medical doctors from India, and similar skilled workers from around the globe who fill jobs and pay taxes. They ease Canada's significant demographic crunch. Canada is experiencing a tumbling birthrate among its current population precisely as its baby-boom generation readies to retire. By 2020, an estimated 1 million jobs will go unfilled—a projection with huge implications for government revenues, for businesses seeking employees, and even for retirees, who will rely on taxpayers to fund health care and government pensions.

Ireland, too, is experiencing a long economic boom and its first-ever wave of immigration. Long considered one of the major sending nations, particularly to Australia, Canada, New Zealand, and the United States, Ireland is now attracting immigrants to its growing economy. Current census figures show a population surge that is at the highest level in modern history. Since 1996, the Republic of Ireland (which excludes British North Ireland) has seen an 8.2 percent increase in its population, which has reached nearly 4 million. It, too, benefits from the brain drain flow (Associated Press 2002d).

The Economics of Emigration

When developing countries are close to countries with booming or even relatively healthy economies, the migration flow is virtually unstoppable. Sending countries rely on emigration to relieve economic, social, and political pressures. Receiving countries enjoy a source of cheap and easily exploitable labor. Migrants, both legal and illegal, send support to their families at home, significantly enhancing the economies of the sending countries. Recently, for example, the Banco de Mexico reported that during the first half of 2002, Mexicans living and working in the United States sent a record $4.753 billion dollars in remittance, a nearly 11 percent increase over the previous year. Competition among banks and wire-money transfer services over the lucrative business increased when the banks agreed to accept the identification cards issued by Mexico to verify Mexican citizenship. With these ID cards, Mexicans can open accounts at banks in the United States, and their family members can use ATMs with corresponding banks in Mexico to withdraw funds at lower costs and with immediate access, thus making it easier to "send" money home. The Mexican economy is highly susceptible to economic trends in the United States. An old Mexican saying states, "When the U.S. economy sneezes, the Mexican economy catches a cold." The current U.S. recession has given Mexico a case of economic pneumonia. Unemployment and underemployment have reached epidemic proportions, forcing more Mexicans to seek employment in the United States to send money home and thus vastly increasing the flow of remittances to help out. As discussed above, similar flows are noted to EU nations from the Middle East and to Thailand from nearby Southeast Asian countries.

Regional Approaches to Migration Issues

The worldwide refugee crisis is but one issue illustrating an increasingly important trend in worldwide migration movements: the effort to cope with problems generated by such mass migrations with a regional governmental or even nongovernmental organization (NGO) approach.

Regional or multilateral agreements have been forged as a better way to cope with several migration issues: antitrafficking strategies to deal with human smuggling across national borders; migration and its impact on development; the human rights afforded or guaranteed to migrants, especially refugees and asylees; the right to return of migrants; how nation-state policy interacts with cooperative or multilateral links; and technical cooperation. As Amy Freedman notes,

> The global and regional contexts within which immigration and refugee policies are made are changing in ways that produce pressures for states to forego their traditional practices of devising and executing autonomous immigration policy and increasingly to participate in more coordinated, jointly-produced, multilateral policies fashioned in participation with their neighbors and the governments of the countries from which immigrants come. (Freedman 2000, 223)

For example, one international migration issue that benefits from the multilateral approach is trafficking in human beings. Trafficking in human beings is defined as a process involving the recruitment, transportation, harboring, sale, or receipt of persons through the use of deceit, fraud, coercion, force, or abduction for the purpose of placing such persons in conditions of near-slavery, including forced prostitution, bonded sweatshop labor, domestic servitude, or other debt bondage (Helton and Jacobs 2001, 120–121).

Trafficking in men, women, or children poses relatively few risks and promises significant financial rewards to the traffickers.

The United Nations estimates that 4 million persons are trafficked around the world each year and estimates that the profit to criminal syndicates perpetrating the traffic is about $7 billion dollars annually (UN Centre for International Crime Prevention Website n.d.). In 2000, an estimated 50,000 women and children were smuggled into the United States for bonded sweatshop and domestic servitude. Men are also brought in to forced labor. This problem prompted Rep. Christopher Smith (R.–N.J.) to sponsor, in November 1999, the Trafficking Victims Protection Act, which provides up to 5,000 T visas, for humanitarian relief of those so abused, to enter the United States annually (Helton and Jacobs 2001, 122).

The United Nations has touched on the issue in several ways: agreements and protocols based on the Universal Declaration of Human Rights, passed by the UN General Assembly in 1948, and on the International Covenant on Civil and Political Rights, passed by the UN General Assembly in December 1966. The UNHCR has issued suggested guidelines for dealing with aspects of the issue, for example, Guidelines on Policies and Procedures in Dealing with Unaccompanied Children Seeking Asylum (Geneva, Switzerland, 1997), Guidelines on Applicable Criteria and Standards Relating to the Detention of Asylum Seekers (Geneva, 1999), and, most importantly, the UN Protocol on Human Trafficking and Immigrant Smuggling (Palermo, Italy, July 2002). This last protocol has been signed by 141 countries. To date, fifteen countries have ratified it. It must receive forty ratifications to become effective.

This issue is well illustrated by a case reported by the Associated Press on July 24, 2002. According to the report, a Greek court convicted a British yacht captain of smuggling seventy-two Iraqi and Syrian illegals, including nine children, from Turkey to Greece. Each illegal alien had paid $2,000 to be smuggled into Greece. The captain was sentenced to ten years for smuggling (Associated Press 2002c).

Although the United Nations is undoubtedly the largest and most important international organization addressing international policy on dealing with worldwide migration, it is not alone. Several regional approaches are highlighted here.

The Central American region has developed multilateral approaches, mostly in response to the massive emigration of refugees from El Salvador, Guatemala, and Nicaragua fleeing their civil wars of national liberation. Ten countries formed what has become known as the Puebla Group (after a 1996 conference in Puebla, Mexico): Belize, Canada, Costa Rica, El Salvador, Guatemala, Honduras, Mexico, Nicaragua, Panama, and the United States. The Puebla Group's Regional Conference on Migration has developed into an ongoing cooperative mechanism, with representatives of the participating nations meeting annually to discuss common problems and to try to develop mutual approaches and solutions. They deal specifically with irregular (that is, illegal) immigration, migrant trafficking, cross-border labor issues, and human rights issues. The Regional Conference on Migration (RCM) seeks migration management strategies across the region. In recent years the conference has invited participation by NGOs involved in refugee assistance. Mostly religious NGOs from the United States and Canada are joined by Mexican and Central American activists in relief efforts on behalf of refugees. In 1989, a coalition of such groups formed the Conference for Central American Refugees (CIREFCA, from its initials in Spanish) and later the National Coordination of NGOs to Assist Refugees (CONONGAR, from its initials in Spanish). Although those organizations largely ceased to exist after the civil strife declined in the mid-1990s, they developed the Asociacion Regional para las Migraciones Forzedas (ARMIF; the Regional Association on Forced Migration). This regional network operates currently and cooperates with the RCM. In 1998, the RCM representatives, meeting in Ottawa, Canada, formally invited the NGOs to participate in the annual conference. Another related group of NGOs involved in the issue, the Heartland Alliance for Human Needs and Human Rights, was formed as a communication network in 1995. It is a Chicago-based NGO for binational and regional coalitions (Gzesh 2000, 207–222).

ARMIF was formed in January 1999 after Hurricane Mitch devastated the Central American region. ARMIF attended the RCM meeting held in San Salvador and helped form the International Organization for Migration, which successfully advocated for the Nicaraguan and Central American Relief Act, in which the U.S. Congress approved a program to give Salvadorans and Guatemalans the same opportunity to adjust their status as was offered to Nicaraguans. The Puebla Group also deals with intraregional migration.

South-to-south migration affecting the area is exemplified by large-scale and mostly illegal immigration from Colombia to Panama and from Nicaragua to Costa Rica.

Regional cooperation in Europe to address both the legal and the increasing illegal immigration flows is exemplified by the EU

Dublin Convention on Refugees and Asylees and by the United Kingdom's Empire Settlement Scheme. Several EU member states have ratified the UN's Palermo, Italy, protocol outlawing the trafficking in women and children for forced labor sweatshops or for "sex slavery." Involvement by organized crime in human trafficking is one of the most serious transnational threats the EU nations face.

Illegal immigration for purposes of employment is a larger and more contentious issue, and one over which the European Union has yet to develop a consensual approach (Miller 1994). Moreover, since the mid-1990s, migration between eastern and western Europe has become much more fluid, with movements into the European Union often being nearly offset by movements back to the ex-Communist states. The Organization for Economic Cooperation and Development is an EU-based organization established, in part, to deal with the issue.

References and Further Reading

Al-Ali, Nadje, and Khalid Koser, eds. 2001. *New Approaches to Migration: Transnational Communities and the Transformation of Home.* New York: Routledge.

Associated Press. 2002a. "Consulates to Issue ID Cards Following Mexican Success." *Los Angeles Times*, September 7, B-4.

———. 2002b. *Riverside Press-Enterprise*, September 1, A-24.

———. 2002c. "More Refugees to Arrive from Pacific Island Camps." Available on-line at www.cisnews.org. Accessed July 26, 2002.

———. 2002d. "Irish Population Soars above 3.9 Million." Dublin, Ireland, July 24.

Bauer, Thomas, and Klaus F. Zimmerman. 1998. "Looking South and East: Labor Market Implications of Migration in Europe and Developing Countries." In *Globalization of Labour Markets, Challenges, Adjustment and Policy Response in the European Union and the Less Developed Countries*, ed. Olga Memodovic, Arie Kuyvnhoven, and Wilhelm T. M. Molle, 75–103. Dordrecht: Kluwer Academic Publishers.

Bauer, Thomas, Pedro T. Pereira, Michael Volger, and Klaus F. Zimmerman. 2002. "Portuguese Migrants in the German Labor Market: Selection and Performance." *International Migration Review* 36, no. 2 (Summer): 467–491.

Brettell, Caroline B., and James F. Hollifield, eds. 2000. *Migration Theory: Talking across Disciplines.* New York: Routledge.

Bustamante, Jorge A. 2002. "Immigrants' Vulnerability as Subjects of Human Rights." *International Migration Review* 36, no. 2 (Summer): 333–354.

Castles, Stephen, and Alastair Davidson, eds. 2000. *Citizenship and Migration: Globalization and the Politics of Belonging.* New York: Routledge.

Curry, Bill. 2002. "Immigrants Coming to Flin Flon." (Canada) *National Post*, accessed on-line at www.nationalpost.com August 27, 2002.

Freedman, Amy L. 2000. *Political Participation and Ethnic Minorities: Chinese Overseas in Malaysia, Indonesia, and the United States.* New York: Routledge.

Gallogher, Stephen. 2002. "Towards a Common European Asylum System: Fortress Europe Redesigns the Ramparts." *International Journal* 57, no. 3 (Summer): 375–394.

Guiraudon, Virginie, and Christian Joppke, eds. 2001. *Controlling a New Migration World.* New York: Routledge.

Gzesh, Susan. 2000. "Advocacy for Human Rights in an Intergovernmental Forum: The Puebla Process from the Perspective of Non-governmental Organizations." In *In Defense of the Alien*, ed. Lydio Tomasi, vol. 22, 207–222. New York: Center for Migration Studies.

Helton, Arthur, and Eliana Jacobs. 2001. "Combating Human Smuggling by Enlisting the Victims." In *In Defense of the Alien*, ed. Lydio Tomasi, vol. 23, 119–128. New York: Center for Migration Studies.

Hughes, Helen. 2002. *Immigrants, Refugees, and Asylum Seekers: A Global View.* New Providence, Australia: Center for Independent Study.

International Organization for Migration (IOM). 2002. *Trafficking in Women and Prostitution in the Baltic States: Social and Legal Aspects.* Washington, DC: IOM.

Karim, H. Karim, ed. 2002. *Diaspora and Communication: Mapping the Globe.* New York: Routledge.

Kennedy, Paul, and Victor Roudometof, eds. 2002. *Communities across Borders: New Immigrants and Transnational Cultures.* New York: Routledge.

Kofman, Eleonore, Annie Phizucklea, Ravati Raghuarn, and Rosemary Sales. 2001. *Gender and International Migration in Europe.* New York: Routledge.

Lamont, James. 2002. "Skilled South Africans Leave to Find Fortune." *Financial Times*, July 23. Accessed on-line at www.cisnews.org August 26, 2002.

Miller, Mark J. 1989. "Continuities and Discontinuities in Immigration Reform in Industrial Democracies." *International Review of Comparative Public Policy* 1: 131–151.

———. 1994. *Strategies for Immigration Control: An International Comparison.* Thousand Oaks, CA: Sage.

———. 2000. "Legalization and the Capacity of Democratic States to Prevent Illegal Alien Residency and Employment: French and American Experiences." In *In Defense of the Alien,* ed. Lydio Tomasi, vol. 22, 259–272. New York: Center for Migration Studies.

Morris, Lydia. 2003. *Managing Migration: Civic Stratification and Migrants Rights.* New York: Routledge.

Ruddock, Philip. 2002. "Immigration Figures Show High Skilled Intake." Associated Press, Sydney, July 24.

Sharp, Nancy. 2001. "International Assignments and the Immigration Issues Surrounding Spousal Employment." In *In Defense of the Alien,* ed. Lydio Tomasi, vol. 23, 59–63. New York: Center for Migration Studies.

Sorenson, Ninna, and Karen Fog Olwig, eds. 2001. *Work and Migration: Life and Livelihoods in a Globalizing World.* New York: Routledge.

UN Centre for International Crime Prevention Website. N.d. Available: www.uncjin.org/CICP/cicp.html; accessed June 2000.

Zimmerman, Klaus F. 1995. "Tackling the European Migration Problem." *Journal of Economic Perspectives* 9: 45–62.

Zolberg, Aristide, Astri Suhrke, and Sergio Aguayo. 1989. *Escape from Violence: Conflict and the Refugee Crisis in the Developing World.* New York: Oxford University Press.

Zucker, Norman L., and Naomi Flink Zucker. 1987. *The Guarded Gate: The Reality of American Refugee Policy.* San Diego: Harcourt Brace Jovanovich.

4

Chronology

The Open-Door Era: Foundation–1880

1740   A British naturalization law enacted to systematize procedures and encourage immigration to the American colonies sets the pattern followed by the colonies and later by the U.S. government after independence.

1789   The U.S. Constitution is adopted. Article 1, Section 8 empowers Congress "To establish a uniform Rule of Naturalization."

1790   As one of its very first actions, Congress establishes a uniform rule of naturalization, imposing a two-year residency requirement for aliens who are "free white persons" of good moral character.

1802   Congress revises the Naturalization Act of 1790 to require a five-year residency and renunciation of allegiance and fidelity to foreign powers.

1813   Congress reaffirms the five-year residency period in the Five-Year Residence Act.

1819   Congress passes an act requiring shipmasters to deliver a manifest enumerating all aliens transported for immigration and requiring the secretary of state to inform Congress annually of the number of immigrants admitted.

1848   The Treaty of Guadalupe Hidalgo guarantees citizenship to Mexicans remaining in the territory ceded by Mexico to the United States.

1855   Castle Garden becomes New York's principal point of entry.

1862   Congress enacts the Homestead Act, which granted up to 160 acres of free land to settlers who would develop the land and remain on it for five years, spurring much immigration.

1868   The Fourteenth Amendment is ratified, guaranteeing that all persons born or naturalized in the United States and subject to its jurisdiction are citizens and stating that no state may abridge their rights without due process nor deny them equal protection of the law. The amendment ensures the citizenship rights of the former slaves and thereby changes the "free white persons" phrase on citizenship to include blacks.

1870   Congress enacts a law granting citizenship to persons of African descent.

The Door-Ajar Era: 1880–1920

1882   Congress enacts the Chinese Exclusion Act barring the immigration of Chinese laborers for ten years and denying Chinese eligibility for naturalization. The act will be reenacted and extended in 1888, 1892, and 1904.

Congress passes an act to regulate immigration, specifying some restrictions on who may immigrate (for example, excluding convicts or persons likely to become public charges).

1885   Congress passes an act making it unlawful for laborers to immigrate to the United States under contract with a U.S. employer who in any manner prepays passage to bring the laborer to the United States.

1886   *Yick Wo v. Hopkins* overturns a San Francisco ordinance against Chinese laundry workers as discriminatory and unconstitutional on the grounds that the Fourteenth Amendment prohibits state and local governments from depriving any person (even a noncitizen) of life, liberty, or property without due process.

1888   Congress expands the Chinese Exclusion Act by rescinding reentry permits for Chinese laborers and thus prohibiting their return (also known as the Scott Act).

1889   *Chae Chan Ping v. United States* upholds Congress's right to repeal the certificate of reentry as contained in the 1888 Chinese Exclusion Act (and thereby ex post facto exclude Chinese immigrants).

1891   Congress expands the classes of individuals excluded from admission, forbids the soliciting of immigrants, and creates the position of superintendent of immigration.

1892   The Ellis Island reception station is opened; it quickly becomes the leading port of entry.

1894   Congress extends the Chinese Exclusion Act and establishes the Bureau of Immigration within the Treasury Department.

1896   The U.S. Supreme Court decides *Plessy v. Ferguson*, establishing the legal principle of "separate but equal" and giving a constitutional basis to legal segregation based on race.

1897   In *In re Rodriquez*, the federal district court in west Texas affirms the citizenship rights of Mexicans based on the 1848 Treaty of Guadalupe Hidalgo and notwithstanding that such persons may not be considered to be "white."

1898   *Wong Kim Ark v. United States* rules that a native-born person of Asian descent is indeed a citizen of the United States despite the fact that his or her parents may have been resident aliens ineligible for naturalization.

The Spanish-American War establishes U.S. control over Guam, Puerto Rico, the Philippines, and Cuba.

The United States annexes Hawaii.

1903   Congress passes a law making immigration the responsibility of the Department of Commerce and Labor.

1906   The Basic Naturalization Law codifies a uniform law for naturalization. With some amendments and supplements, it forms the basic naturalization law thereafter.

1907   Congress adds important regulations regarding the issuing of passports and the expatriation and marriage of U.S. women to foreigners. The act continues to stir controversy until Section 3 of the act is repealed in 1922.

President Theodore Roosevelt issues an executive order stating the Gentleman's Agreement with Japan, by which Japan agrees to restrict the emigration of laborers from Japan and Korea (then under Japanese jurisdiction). Picture brides are permitted to emigrate.

Congress enacts the White-Slave Traffic Act forbidding importation of any woman or girl for the purpose of prostitution or similar immoral purposes.

1911   The Dillingham Commission issues its report. Its recommendations form the basis of the quota acts of the 1920s.

1915   The Americanization/100 Percentism campaign begins as both a government and a private enterprise. These social movements represent the first attempt at "forced assimilation" encouraging the adoption of the English language and social customs. After World War I, its perceived failure will contribute to the disillusionment that set the stage for the quota acts of the 1920s.

1917   The United States enters World War I in April.

Congress enacts an immigration law that includes a literacy test for all immigrants and bars immigration from a specified area, the Asian barred zone.

The Departments of State and Labor issue a joint order requiring passports from all aliens seeking to enter the United States and requiring that would-be entrants be issued visas by American consular officers in their country of origin rather than seeking permission to enter the United States only when arriving at the port of entry.

Puerto Ricans are granted U.S. citizenship.

1918   Congress gives the president sweeping powers to disallow the entrance or departure of aliens during time of war. Similar presidential proclamations are used in virtually all periods of war thereafter.

1919   Congress enacts a law granting honorably discharged Native Americans citizenship for their service during World War I.

In the summer, the Red Scare following the Bolshevik revolution leads to the deportation of certain specified "radical" aliens deemed a threat to security.

The Pet-Door Era: 1920–1965

1921   Congress passes the first Quota Act. The quota for immigration from a particular country is set at 3 percent of the foreign-born population from that country according to the 1910 census.

1922   Congress enacts the Cable Act, stating that the right of any woman to become a naturalized citizen of the United States shall not be abridged because of her sex or because she is a married woman, unless she is wed to an alien ineligible for citizenship. The latter provision will later be repealed.

1923   The U.S. Supreme Court rules in *United States v. Bhagat Singh Thind* that "white persons" means those persons who appear and would commonly be viewed as white. Thus, East Asian Indians, although Caucasians, are not "white" and are therefore not eligible for citizenship.

1924   Congress enacts an Immigration Act, known as the Johnson-Reed Act, setting the national-origin quota for a particular country at 2 percent of the foreign-born population from that country as of the census of 1890. This new sys-

1924, tem dramatically shifts the sources of European immigra-
cont. tion from south, central, and eastern Europe to northwestern Europe. The act bars the admission of most Asians, who are classified as "aliens ineligible for citizenship."

Congress passes an act granting citizenship to those Native Americans who had not already received it by allotments under the 1887 Dawes Act or by military service during World War I.

1925 Congress establishes the Border Patrol.

1929 President Herbert Hoover proclaims new and permanent quotas, in which national-origin quotas are based for European immigrants on the proportion of those nationalities in the total population as determined by the 1920 census. The total number of immigrants to be admitted is lowered to just over 150,000.

1929– The Great Depression significantly depresses worldwide
1939 emigration and slows U.S. immigration dramatically.

1940 Congress declares that the third Sunday of May is to be celebrated as Citizenship Day.

Congress passes the Registration Law, requiring noncitizens to register their address annually. The process remains in effect until 1980.

Congress passes the Nationality Act of 1940, codifying and consolidating all previous nationality laws dealing with the naturalization process.

1941 President Franklin D. Roosevelt issues a proclamation to control persons entering or leaving the United States based on congressional passage of the first War Powers Act.

1942 President Roosevelt issues Executive Order 9066, leading to the evacuation, relocation, and internment of Japanese and Japanese Americans into relocation camps.

1943 In *Hirabayashi v. United States*, the U.S. Supreme Court rules that the executive orders for curfews and evacuation programs are constitutional based upon "military necessity."

1944   The U.S. Supreme Court decides *Korematsu v. United States,* again affirming the constitutionality of the executive orders excluding Japanese Americans from remaining in certain "excluded zones."

The Court also rules in *Ex Parte Mitsuye Endo* that the internment program is an unconstitutional violation of the habeas corpus rights of U.S. citizens, namely, the Nisei.

1945   Congress enacts the War Brides Act.

1946   In *Girouard v. United States,* the U.S. Supreme Court rules that an applicant may be admitted to naturalization despite his or her conscientious-objector status.

Congress passes a law allowing for the naturalization of Filipinos and Asian Indians.

1948   Congress enacts the Displaced Persons Act, beginning a process of modifying the quota law by enacting exceptions to enable a greater number of immigrants to enter.

1949   Congress passes the Agricultural Act, which has a provision to recruit temporary farmworkers from Mexico: the Bracero Program.

1952   Congress passes the Immigration and Nationality Act (also known as the McCarran-Walter Act), which recodifies immigration and naturalization law, maintains the quota system, sets up a quota for the Asian-Pacific Triangle, and removes all racial and national-origin barriers to U.S. citizenship.

1953   The President's Commission on Immigration and Naturalization issues its report, *Whom Shall We Welcome?* It presents a stinging criticism of the 1952 act, calls for an end to the quota system, and severely criticizes naturalization laws and procedures. Its recommendations become the basis for many of the reforms and amendments to the 1952 act passed in 1965 and thereafter.

1954   Ellis Island, the nation's largest and primary immigrant-receiving station, is closed.

1956   President Dwight D. Eisenhower establishes a parole system for Hungarian freedom fighters. Two years later, Congress endorses the procedures, passing an act to admit Hungarian refugees.

1959   Congress amends the Immigration and Nationality Act of 1952 to allow unmarried sons and daughters of U.S. citizens to enter as nonquota immigrants.

1960   Congress enacts a program to assist the resettlement of refugees from Communist countries (mostly Cubans) who have been paroled by the attorney general.

         Sen. Philip Hart (D–Mich.) introduces the Hart bill on January 15.

The Revolving-Door Era: 1965–2001

1965   Congress passes the Immigration and Naturalization Act. It amends the 1952 act by ending the quota system, establishing a preference system emphasizing the reunification of families and the meeting of certain skill goals, standardizing admission procedures, and setting limits of 20,000 per country for Eastern European nations, with a total of 170,000. The first ceiling on Western Hemisphere immigration, of 120,000, is set.

1966   Congress amends the 1965 act to adjust Cuban refugee status.

1967   In *Afroyim v. Rusk*, the U.S. Supreme Court rules that a citizen who holds dual citizenship with Israel does not lose his citizenship by the act of voting in an Israeli election. It establishes in strong language how limited the government is in taking away citizenship once granted by birthright or by naturalization.

1968   The Bilingual Education Act is passed.

President Johnson issues a proclamation on the UN Protocol on the Status of Refugees, basically endorsing the U.S. commitment to the multinational protocols.

1972   The House passes but the Senate kills a bill that would have made it illegal to knowingly hire an illegal alien.

Illegal aliens begin arriving on the East Coast, mostly in Florida, by boat from Haiti. Detention camps are set up in Miami for the Haitians.

1975   The fall of Saigon and then the rest of South Vietnam along with Cambodia and Laos precipitates a massive flight of refugees to the United States from Indochina.

President Jimmy Carter establishes and Congress funds the Indochinese Refugee Resettlement Program.

Jews begin fleeing the Soviet Union in large numbers. Civil war in El Salvador leads to the beginning of their refugee movement. Haitians continue arriving in large numbers.

1976   Congress amends the 1965 Immigration and Naturalization Act by extending the per-country limits of visa applicants on a first-come, first-served basis to Western Hemisphere nations as regulated by the preference system.

In *Mathews v. Santiago Diaz et al.*, the U.S. Supreme Court rules that an alien has no right to Social Security or Medicare benefits.

President Gerald R. Ford's administration establishes a cabinet-level committee to study immigration options.

1978   President Carter and Congress set up the Select Commission on Immigration and Refugee Policy (SCIRP).

1979   SCIRP begins its work.

An influx of boat people, refugees from Vietnam and Southeast Asia, begins.

1980   Congress passes the Refugee Act to systematize refugee policy and incorporates the UN definition of refugee, allowing the admittance of 50,000 persons annually who have a "well-founded fear" of persecution based on race, religion, nationality, or membership in a social or political movement. The act provides for the first time for the admission of "asylum seekers," set at 5,000.

On March 1, the SCIRP issues its final report, recommending many changes in policy that will form the basis of the Immigration Reform and Control Act (IRCA) of 1986 and other subsequent reform acts.

President Ronald Reagan establishes the Task Force on Immigration and Refugee Policy, which issues its report in July.

1982   A federal district judge rules that the detention of Haitians is unconstitutional and orders the release of 1,900 detainees.

A major bill to amend the 1965 Immigration and Naturalization Act is introduced into the House.

1983   An immigration-reform bill is reintroduced into Congress.

In *INS v. Chadha et al.*, the U.S. Supreme Court rules that the use by the House of Representatives of the legislative veto to overturn certain INS deportation proceedings, rules, and regulations is unconstitutional.

1984   An immigration-reform bill passes in different versions in both chambers but dies in conference.

1985   Sen. Alan Simpson (R.–Wyo.) reintroduces what becomes known as the Simpson-Mazzoli-Rodino bill.

1986   In *Jean et al. v. Nelson*, the U.S. Supreme Court rules on an INS denial of parole to undocumented aliens.

Congress enacts IRCA, and its employer sanctions/legalization approach grants amnesty to about 1.5 million illegal aliens and more than 1 million special agricultural workers.

1987   In *INS v. Cardoza-Fonseca,* by a vote of 6 to 3, the U.S. Supreme Court rules that the government must relax its standards for deciding whether aliens who insist that they will be persecuted if they return to their homelands are eligible for asylum.

1988   The Senate passes but the House kills the Kennedy-Simpson bill, which later passes in 1990.

The U.S.-Canada Free Trade Agreement Implementation Act is signed.

Congress amends the 1965 Immigration and Naturalization Act regarding H-1 category use by nurses.

1990   Congress passes a major reform of the laws concerning legal immigration, setting new ceilings for worldwide immigration, redefining the preference system for family reunification and employment, and setting up a new category of preference called "the diversity immigrants." It enacts special provisions about Central American refugees, Filipino veterans, and persons seeking to leave Hong Kong. Significant changes to naturalization procedures are included.

1993   Congress ratifies the North American Free Trade Agreement (NAFTA).

1994   California passes Proposition 187, the "Save Our State" initiative.

Congress enacts the Violent Crime Control and Law Enforcement Act, also known as the Smith Act, giving the attorney general more authority to issue visas, the S visas.

Congress passes Violence Against Women Act (VAWA), which includes a provision to grant special status to immigrant women through the cancellation of removal and self-petitioning provisions.

1995   In *LULAC et al. v. Pete Wilson et al.,* a federal district court for California rules that many of Proposition 187's provisions are unconstitutional.

1996   In June, the Board of Immigration Appeals (*In re Fauziya Kasinga*) grants the first asylum on the basis of gender persecution (female genital mutilation).

Congress enacts the Personal Responsibility and Work Opportunity Act (welfare reform), which has numerous immigration-related provisions. Congress essentially enacts aspects of Proposition 187, regarding welfare and other public benefits, that had been overturned.

Congress passes the Illegal Immigration Reform and Immigrant Responsibility Act (IIRIRA), the more than sixty immigration-related provisions of the Omnibus Spending Bill. It denies other welfare and economic benefits to illegal aliens and to some legal resident aliens.

The Antiterrorism and Effective Death Penalty Act of 1996 is passed. Among its provisions, it gives INS inspectors the power to make on-the-spot determinations of asylum seekers' "credible fear." It takes effect April 1, 1997, as part of the IIRIRA reforms beginning then.

1997   The Jordan Commission on immigration reform, set up by the IIRIRA, recommends in its final report that the INS be restructured.

The expedited enforcement rules of the IIRIRA take effect at U.S. land borders, international airports, and seaports allowing the issuing and enforcement of expulsion orders. At 300 ports of entry, 4,500 INS officers are added.

1998   President Bill Clinton sends another immigration bill to Congress, seeking, in part, a restructuring of the INS.

The Agriculture Job Opportunity Benefits and Security Act establishes a pilot program for 20,000–25,000 farmworkers.

1999   The Carnegie Endowment for International Peace presents its International Migration Policy Program. Twenty-one nongovernmental organizations concerned with immigration call for the restructuring of the INS, the separation of enforcement from visa and naturalization functions, and the transfer of some immigration functions to the Departments of Labor and Health and Human Services. INS provides Border Patrol adjudication.

In *INS v. Aguirre-Augirre,* the U.S. Supreme Court unanimously rules that aliens who have committed serious nonpolitical crimes in their home countries are ineligible to seek asylum in the United States regardless of their risk of persecution when returned to their countries.

Rep. Christopher Smith (R.–N.J.) introduces the Trafficking Victims Protection Act of 1999.

With a restored economy, President Clinton's administration restores some of the benefits stripped from legal aliens by the 1996 acts.

On November 22, 1999, Elian Gonzalez is rescued off the Florida coast.

2000   Negotiations in the Elian Gonzalez case begin.

In April, Attorney General Janet Reno approves a Justice Department "raid" on a Miami home to return Elian Gonzalez to his father in Cuba.

In May 2000, Sen. Sam Brownback (R.–Kans.) introduces a bill to establish the T visa.

On June 1, in *Gonzalez v. Reno,* the U.S. Court of Appeals for the Eleventh Circuit rules that only the father of Elian Gonzalez can speak for the boy.

The Storm-Door Era? 2001–Present

2001   On September 11, terrorists attack the World Trade Center Twin Towers in New York City and the Pentagon in Washington, D.C. Calls for a crackdown on terrorists begin immediately.

On October 24, Congress passes the USA Patriot Act, granting sweeping new powers to the attorney general, the FBI, and the Department of Justice with regard to immigrants and granting the authority to detain "enemy combatants" involved in or suspected of terrorism.

2002   The INS reports that several of the hijackers had been given permission to enroll in U.S. flight-training programs. Calls for the restructuring of the INS, to remove its Border Patrol functions, result immediately.

Congress establishes a cabinet-level Department of Homeland Security. The attorney general is granted sweeping new powers for the expedited removal of aliens. As of March 2003, the INS is abolished and its functions are extensively restructured as part of the new department. The undersecretary for border and transportation security begins oversight of immigration enforcement and of Citizenship and Immigration Services.

References and Further Reading

Electronic Privacy Information Center (EPIC) Website. Available: http://www.epic.org/privacy/terrorism/hr3162.html; accessed April 20, 2003.

Information Plus. 1999, 2001. *Immigration and Illegal Aliens: Burden or Blessing?* Wylie, TX: Information Plus.

LeMay, Michael, and Elliott Robert Barkan. 1999. *U.S. Immigration and Naturalization Law and Issues: A Documentary History.* Westport, CT: Greenwood Press. Available: http://www.usdhs.gov; accessed April 20, 2003.

5

Biographical Sketches

This chapter is only a partial list of the individuals who have been or are key players in the arena of immigration reform. Individuals cited here include executive branch officials, including several U.S. presidents; legislative branch officials; and nongovernmental actors, including important advocates for and against immigration as well as scholars, or think-tank actors, who have had particular impact on the debates over immigration-policy reform.

The chapter presents brief biographical sketches for the two most recent attorneys general of the United States, a former commissioner of the INS, and the six presidents who have served since 1965. Because almost every immigration reform involves the enactment of legislation, members of Congress play important roles in the process. In one sense, all 535 members of the two chambers are "actors" in the immigration arena. Space permits only biographical sketches for some of the more important senators and members of the House of Representatives in the section that follows.

Dick Armey (1940–)

Rep. Dick Armey (R.–Tex.) received his B.A. from Jamestown College in 1963. He took his M.A. in economics from the University of Notre Dame in 1964 and his Ph.D. from the University of Oklahoma in 1969. He was a professor at Western Texas State University from 1967 to 1968, Austin College from 1968 to 1972, and then at the University of Texas from 1972 to 1977, where he also served as chairman of the Department of Economics from 1977 to 1983. He was elected to the U.S. House of Representatives in 1984.

In 1992, he was elected chairman of the Republican Conference in the House and then majority leader in 1994, a post he still holds. His most notable immigration-related activity is as House sponsor of and leading advocate for the bill to establish the Department of Homeland Security. He favored moving the functions of the INS to the new department, including the provisions to move the Border Patrol functions there and to keep the immigration services and naturalization functions in a separate division within the newly formed department.

John Ashcroft (1942–)

John Ashcroft was appointed attorney general by President George W. Bush in 2000. He graduated with honors from Yale University in 1964 and received his J.D. from the University of Chicago in 1967. He began in public service as Missouri auditor in 1973, was later elected to two terms as the state's attorney general, and served a term as the chairman of the National Association of Attorneys General. He served as governor of Missouri from 1984 until 1993. In 1991, the National Governors Association elected him chairman. He was elected to the U.S. Senate in 1994 and served there until 2000. In the Senate, he cosponsored the reauthorization of the Violence against Women Act and served on the Foreign Relations Committee and the Senate Judiciary Committee, which held hearings on all immigration bills. In the current administration, he is at the forefront of efforts to implement immigration law, especially regarding expedited removal and the more rapid adjudication of asylum cases. As attorney general, he has primary oversight responsibility for the INS. He was a leading proponent for the creation of the Department of Homeland Security, which dramatically restructured the INS.

Roy Beck (1948–)

Roy Beck is the executive director of NumbersUSA. He took his degree in journalism from the University of Missouri. In the late 1970s, he wrote on business news for the *Cincinnati Enquirer* and later covered religion and politics, including covering Congress as chief Washington correspondent for the Booth chain of daily newspapers. He has authored two books on immigration, one on its impact on the environment and the other on its impact on the U.S. labor market and on local communities. He has published on the topic in the *Atlantic Monthly,* the *New York Times,* the *National Review,* the *Washington Post,* and the *Christian Science Monitor.* He has studied immigration policy as an area of special concern while covering Congress. He is a frequent speaker on immigration matters before a wide variety of groups and organizations. This career in print media coverage of immigration policymaking finally led him to develop the NumbersUSA Website.

Howard L. Berman (1941–)

Rep. Howard L. Berman (D.–Calif.) received his B.A. from UCLA in 1962 and took his LL.B. there in 1965. He practiced law from 1967 to 1972. In 1973, he was elected to the California Assembly, where he served until 1982, including as majority leader from 1974 to 1979. He was elected to the U.S. House of Representatives in 1982 and has served there since. Being from California, he became active in immigration matters from the start. His most important committee assignments, in terms of immigration matters, are International Relations: East Asian and Pacific Affairs; Judiciary: Courts and Intellectual Property, Immigration and Claims; and Standards of Official Conduct, where he is the ranking minority member. His notable impact concerned key compromises making it possible to pass IRCA in 1986 and IMMACT in 1990.

Sanford D. Bishop (1947–)

Rep. Sanford D. Bishop (D.–Ga.) graduated with his B.A. from Morehouse College in 1968. He took his J.D. from Emory University in 1971. He served in the U.S. Army from 1971 to 1972 and was a practicing attorney from 1971 to 1992. His political career began with his election to and service in the Georgia House of Representatives (1976–1990); he then served in the Georgia Senate (1990–1992). He was elected to the U.S. House of Representatives in 1992. He serves on the Agriculture Committee and on the Permanent Select Committee on Intelligence, on whose subcommittee for Technical and Tactical Intelligence he is the ranking minority member. His most notable effort on the immigration issue was sponsoring the 1998 Guest-Worker Program bill in the House.

George Walker Bush (1946–)

George W. Bush enrolled at Phillips Academy in Andover, Massachusetts, in 1961. He worked for his father's Senate bid in 1964.

He graduated from Yale University in 1968 and enlisted in the Texas Air National Guard. In 1973, he entered Harvard Business School, taking his M.B.A. in 1975. He founded an oil and gas–exploration company that year. In 1978, he lost a bid to the U.S. House, and in the same year, he helped his father's campaign for the presidency. He joined a group of investors buying the Texas Rangers baseball team in 1989. He was elected governor of Texas in 1994 and reelected in 1998. In 2000, he won the presidency: He lost the popular vote, but, being certified as the winner in Florida by a U.S. Supreme Court case that prevented recounts of disputed votes in Florida, he won the electoral college vote. He was inaugurated in 2001. On September 11, 2001, terrorists struck the Pentagon and the World Trade Center Twin Towers in New York City. He launched a "war on terrorism," and his administration authored and pushed through Congress a bill to create a Department of Homeland Security, which restructured the INS by moving most of its activities to the new department. The administration is noted for its crackdown on illegal immigrants and for its efforts to enforce expedited removal, but Bush has also discussed with President Vicente Fox of Mexico plans for bilateral efforts that may include some sort of guest-worker program or an amnesty program.

Jimmy Carter Jr. (1924–)

Jimmy Carter entered the Georgia Institute of Technology in 1941. In 1943, he entered Annapolis Naval Academy, from which he graduated in 1946. In 1962, he was elected to the Georgia Senate. In 1966, he lost a race for governor of Georgia, but he was elected to that office in 1970. He was elected president in 1976. In 1978, he deregulated the oil industry, pushed the Panama Canal Treaty through the Senate, and signed the Camp David Accords. His significant contribution to immigration policy was the establishment, with Congress, of SCIRP, which has formed the basis for much of the debate over illegal immigration reform since then and whose recommendations led to the IRCA. In 1980, the hostage crisis in Iran, and in part the notorious failure of the INS to even track Iranian students in the United States, led to his failed reelection bid in 1980. As a former president, his humanitarian work has involved him in negotiations regarding the Haitian crisis, and he has worked with the United Nations on refugee problems.

Saxby Chambliss (1943–)

Rep. Saxby Chambliss (R.–Ga.) received a B.A. degree from the University of Georgia in 1966 and his J.D. from the University of Tennessee in 1968. He was a practicing attorney from 1968 to 1994. He was elected to the U.S. House of Representatives in 1994. He serves on the Agriculture Committee, the Budget Committee, and the Armed Services Committee. To date, his most significant involvement in the immigration issue has been his cosponsorship of the 1998 Guest-Worker Program bill.

William Jefferson Clinton (1946–)

William Jefferson Clinton entered Georgetown University in 1964, and in 1966, he clerked for Senator J. William Fulbright of Arkansas. He graduated from Georgetown in 1968 and went on to Oxford University as a Rhodes Scholar. In 1970, he entered Yale Law School, from which he received his law degree in 1973. He began teaching at the University of Arkansas Law School in 1973. In 1974, he lost an electoral bid for the U.S. House of Representatives. He was elected Arkansas attorney general in 1976. He lost his first bid for governor of the state in 1980, but he was elected to the office in 1982 and was reelected in 1984. In 1986, he chaired the National Governors Association. In 1988, he was reelected governor. He was elected president in 1992 and was reelected in 1996. His most significant role in immigration policy was in seeing through the Congress and signing into law the Welfare Reform Act of 1996, with its numerous and important immigration provisions, and the IIRIRA of 1996. A scandal over a sexual affair led to his impeachment in 1998. He was acquitted by the U.S. Senate in 1999 and served out his term as president.

Ralston H. Deffenbaugh Jr. (1952–)

Ralston H. Deffenbaugh Jr. is president of the Lutheran Immigration and Refugee Service (LIRS). He took the helm of LIRS in 1991. He received his B.A. in economics from the University of Colorado in 1973 and his law degree from Harvard in 1977. He joined the Lutheran World Federation (LWF) in Geneva in 1981 and in 1985 became director of the Lutheran Office for World Community in New York, representing the LWF to the United Nations. In 1989, he acted as legal counsel to the Namibian Lutheran Bishops in Windhoek, assisting them in their transition to independence, representing the Council of Churches in Namibia in relations with the United Nations and with South Africa, and advising on the implementation of the independence plan. He served as a consultant to the committee drafting Namibia's constitution. In 1991, he became chief executive officer of the LIRS, where he emphasized strategic planning and oversaw significant increases in their budget. In 1999, he moved to the national headquarters of LIRS, serving as chair of the Refugee Council USA. In late 1998, he led a delegation of representatives of refugee rights groups investigating the denial to Bosnian refugees of admission to the United States. He has also been an observer of political trials for Amnesty International, the Lutheran World Federation, and the Lawyers' Committee for Civil Rights under Law. He has written extensively on the legal, moral, and political aspects of resettlement. Awards he has earned include the Sylvester C. Michelfelder Award for Christian Service (1995), the Henry and Helen Graven Award for Faith in Action (1994), and the Arnold E. Carlson Award, Gustavus Adolphus College (1991).

Tom Delay (1947–)

Rep. Tom Delay (R.–Tex.) received a B.S. degree from the University of Texas in 1970. From 1973 to 1984, he owned and operated the Albo Pest Control business in Laredo, Texas. He served in the Texas House of Representatives from 1978 to 1984 and was elected to the U.S. House of Representatives in 1984. He serves as the highly controversial majority whip and also is a member of the powerful Appropriations Committee. He was a House leader in the effort to impeach President Clinton. On immigration matters, he is outspokenly in favor of very restricted immigration and was a leading proponent of the move to form the Department of Homeland Security.

Joshua Eilberg (1921–)

Rep. Joshua Eilberg (D.–Pa.) took a B.S. degree from the University of Pennsylvania in 1941 and a J.D. from Temple University in 1948. He practiced as a private attorney from 1948 to 1952 and then served as the assistant district attorney of Philadelphia from 1952 to 1954. He was elected to the Pennsylvania legislature in 1954 and served there until 1966, including as majority leader from 1965 to 1966. He was elected to Congress in 1966 and served until 1978. His major committee related to immigration was the Judiciary Committee. He introduced the employer-sanctions idea in 1982 and cosponsored IRCA. Notably, he led the House effort to establish the SCIRP.

Dianne Feinstein (1933–)

Sen. Dianne Feinstein (D.–Calif.) is California's senior senator. She was elected in 1992 and reelected in 2000. She received a B.A. from Stanford University in 1955. Prior to serving in the Senate, she served on California's Women's Parole Board (1960–1966), on the San Francisco Board of Supervisors (1970–1978). and as mayor of San Francisco (1978–1988). Senator Feinstein serves on several committees important to immigration: Appropriations; Agriculture and Rural Development; Interior; Labor and Health and Human Services; Judiciary; Immigration; and Technology, Terrorism, and Government Information. A tough critic of the INS, she has been notably involved in bills to strengthen the Border Patrol and to sponsor increased fees to fund the "fencing-in" pilot program in the San Diego area.

Hamilton Fish Jr. (1926–)

Rep. Hamilton Fish Jr. (R.–N.Y.) was born to the distinguished Fish family, long active in Republican and New York politics. He took his B.A. degree from Harvard in 1949 and an LL.B. from New York University in 1957. He served in the naval reserves during World War II and then as vice consul in the U.S. foreign service in Ireland. He practiced law from 1957 to 1968 and served as counsel to the New York Assembly's Judiciary Committee in 1961 and as Dutchess County's civil defense director from 1967 to 1968. In 1968, he was elected to the U.S. House of Representatives, where he served with distinction until he retired in 1994. His committee assignments of note were the Judiciary, where he was the ranking minority member, and Intellectual Property and Judicial Administration. He made his most notable impact on immigration law during the debates over IRCA from 1982 to 1986. A moderate Republican, he played a pivotal role in reaching compromises enabling passage of IRCA, the Fair Housing Act of 1988, the Americans with Disabilities Act of 1990, and the 1991 Civil Rights Act.

Barney Frank (1940–)

Rep. Barney Frank (D.–Mass.) took his B.A. from Harvard in 1962 and took a J.D. there in 1977. He served in the Massachusetts House from 1972 to 1980, at which time he was elected to the U.S. House of Representatives. He serves on Banking and Financial Services, Domestic and International Monetary Policy, Housing and Community Opportunity (where he is ranking minority member), and Judiciary: Immigration and Claims. He is an important advocate of civil rights, civil liberties, and antidiscrimination measures on all immigration bills, and he was instrumental in reaching key compromises on IRCA in 1986 and IMMACT in 1990.

Richard Gephardt (1941–)

Rep. Richard Gephardt (D.–Mo.) received his B.S. degree from Northwestern University in 1962. In 1965, he received his J.D. from the University of Michigan. He served in the Air National Guard from 1965 to 1971 and was a practicing attorney from 1965 to 1977. His political career began with his service as a St. Louis City alderman from 1971 to 1976. He was elected to the U.S. House of Representatives in 1976. In 1988, he was briefly a candidate for the Democratic Party's presidential nomination. He has served on the powerful Ways and Means Committee and is one of the founders of the Democratic Leadership Council. In 1984, he was elected as chair of the Democratic Caucus. He was the majority leader in the House from 1989 to 1994, and from 1994 to 2002 as minority leader. As such, he played a leading role in the 1990 IMMACT. As majority leader, he helped establish the House Democratic Policy Committee. He was a leading opponent of NAFTA. In 2002, he sponsored a bill to enact a new legalization (amnesty) program.

Leonard S. Glickman (1962–)

Leonard S. Glickman is president and chief executive officer of the Hebrew Immigrant Aid Society (HIAS). He took a B.A. degree from the University of Pittsburgh and holds an M.A. degree in international affairs from American University. Before joining HIAS in 1998, he served as executive assistant at the U.S. Office of Refugee Resettlement in the Department of Health and Human Services for five years. Prior to that, he was press secretary for Governor Tom Ridge, currently director of Homeland Security, and had previously served as minority staff director and legislative assistant for Sen. John Heinz (R.–Penn.). He is currently also chair of Refugee Council USA, a coalition of agencies concerned about refugee protection. In 1997, he received the secretary of health and human services' Award for Distinguished Service, and he is a five-time recipient of the Administration for Children and Families' Special Act and Service Award. In 1998, he was honored by the Kurdish Human Rights Watch with the Friends of Kurds Award for his efforts in the rescue and resettlement of nearly 7,000 Kurdish refugees from northern Iraq.

Bob Graham (1936–)

Sen. Bob Graham (D.–Fla.) took his B.A. degree from the University of Florida in 1959 and a J.D. from Harvard University in 1962. After working for the Sangra Development Corporation from 1962 to 1966, he was elected to the Florida House of Representatives, where he served until 1970. He then served in the Florida Senate from 1970 to 1978. He served as governor of Florida from 1978 to 1986, at which time he was elected to the U.S. Senate, where he has served since then. His main committees have been Energy and Natural Resources, Environment and Public Works, Finance, Intelligence, and Veterans' Affairs. His most important immigration-related activity was as the principal Senate sponsor of the 1998 bill to amend the Guest-Worker Program.

Philip A. Hart (1912–)

Sen. Philip A. Hart (D.–Mich.) took his B.A. from Georgetown University in 1934 and his J.D. from the University of Michigan in 1937. He served in the U.S. Army during World War II. He served on Michigan's Corporation and Securities Commission, was the director of its Office of Price Stabilization in 1951, and was U.S. attorney for eastern Michigan in 1952. From 1953 to 1954, he was a legal adviser to the governor and was lieutenant governor from 1955 to 1958. He was elected to the U.S. Senate in 1958, serving as assistant majority whip from 1966 to 1967. He served on numerous committees, but most notably for immigration issues, on the Judiciary Committee and on Immigration and Naturalization. His most important contribution to immigration-policy reform was sponsoring and successfully seeing through Congress the Immigration and Naturalization Act of 1965. He retired from the Senate in 1976.

Jesse Helms (1921–)

Sen. Jesse Helms (R.–N.C.) served in the U.S. Navy during World War II. He was city editor of the *Raleigh Times,* administrative assistant to two U.S. senators, and executive director of the North Carolina Bankers Association from 1953 to 1960. From 1960 to 1972, he was the executive vice president of WRAL-TV and the Tobacco Radio Network. He was elected to the U.S. Senate in 1972. He serves on numerous committees of interest to immigration and migration issues, for example, Foreign Relations (of which he is the chair): East Asian and Pacific Affairs; International Operations; Western Hemisphere: Peace Corps, and Narcotics, and Terrorism. He is notable for opposing amnesty and legalization and was an important advocate of the bill to establish the Homeland Security Department. He was instrumental in the expedited removal effort as well.

Lyndon Baines Johnson (1908–1973)

Lyndon Johnson graduated from the Southwest Texas State Teachers College in 1927. He began teaching at Pearsall High School and Sam Houston High School in Houston in 1930. He was named director of the National Youth Administration in Texas in 1935 and was elected to Congress in 1938. In 1941, he lost a U.S. senate bid and then served in the U.S. Navy. He was sent to the Pacific by President Franklin D. Roosevelt to observe fighting conditions. He was elected to the U.S. Senate in 1948, served as Democratic whip in 1951, and became Senate minority leader in 1953. In 1954 he was reelected and became Senate majority leader that year. He directed passage of the 1957 Civil Rights Act. He was elected John F. Kennedy's vice president in 1960. He became president upon Kennedy's assassination in 1963 and was elected president in 1964. His significant immigration-policy action was successfully advocating and then signing into law the Immigration and Naturalization Act of 1965. He chose not to run for reelection in 1968 and retired to his ranch.

Edward Kennedy (1932–)

Sen. Edward Kennedy (D.–Mass.) received his B.A. degree from Harvard in 1956, attended the Hague International Law School in 1958, and took his LL.B. from the University of Virginia Law School in 1959. He worked on John F. Kennedy's presidential bid in 1960 and then served as assistant district attorney for Suffolk County from 1961 to 1962. He was elected to the U.S. Senate in 1962. He is without doubt the single most influential member of Congress on immigration matters. From 1965 until today, every major bill dealing with immigration has borne the Kennedy stamp. His critical committee assignments regarding immigration are the Judiciary Committee, Immigration, and the Joint Economic Committee.

John Fitzgerald Kennedy (1917–1963)

John F. Kennedy graduated from the Choate School Studies at the London School of Economics and also attended Princeton. He graduated from Harvard University in 1940, when he also authored the award-winning *Why England Slept.* He served in the Pacific in World War II and became a war hero when his PT 109 was sunk by the Japanese. He was elected to the U.S. House of Representatives in 1946 and served there until his election to the U.S. Senate in 1952. In 1956, his book *Profiles in Courage* was published; it won a Pulitzer Prize in 1957. Reelected to the Senate in 1958, he also wrote *A Nation of Immigrants.* He was elected president in 1960 and was inaugurated in 1961. In July 1963, he sent to Congress the bill that became the Immigration and Naturalization Act of 1965. He was assassinated in Dallas, Texas, on November 22, 1963. Congress passed his legislation, in part to honor the "martyred" president, in October 1965.

Mark Krikorian (1961–)

Mark Krikorian is executive director of the Center for Immigration Studies. He has a B.A. degree from Georgetown University and took an M.A. from the Fletcher School of Law and Diplomacy. He also studied two years at Yerevian State University in the then Soviet Armenia. He has held various editorial and writing positions, and in 1995, he joined the Center for Immigration Studies in Washington, D.C. He frequently testifies before Congress and has published numerous articles in such periodicals as the *Washington Post,* the *New York Times, Commentary,* and the *National Review.* He has appeared on *60 Minutes, Nightline,* the *News Hour with Jim Lehrer,* and similar television and radio programs on CNN and National Public Radio.

Joseph I. Lieberman (1942–)

Sen. Joseph I. Lieberman (D.–Conn.) took his B.A. from Yale University in 1964 and an LL.B. from Yale in 1967. He was a practicing attorney from 1964 to 1980. In his political career, he served in the Connecticut Senate from 1970 to 1980, including serving as its majority leader from 1974 to 1980. He was attorney general of Connecticut from 1983 to 1988, at which time he was elected to the U.S. Senate. He notably rebuked President Clinton during the scandal over Clinton's affair with Monica Lewinsky, but he supported the president during the impeachment process and the Senate vote to acquit. Lieberman ran as the Democratic nominee for vice president with Al Gore in 2000 and also for reelection to the U.S. Senate. He lost the former election but won the latter. In the Senate, he serves on the Armed Services Committee, including as ranking minority member of its Air and Land Forces subcommittee; on Environment and Public Works; on Small Business; and on Governmental Affairs (again as ranking minority member). He serves as the chairman of the Democratic Leadership Council. In terms of immigration policy, he was a leading spokesman for and the Senate sponsor of the Democratic alternative bill for the establishment of the Department of Homeland Security, with its broad implications for restructuring the INS.

Romano Mazzoli (1932–)

Rep. Romano Mazzoli (D.–Ky.) received a B.S. degree from Notre Dame in 1954 and his J.D. from the University of Louisville in 1960. He served in the U.S. Army from 1954 to 1956 and then worked in the law department of the L&N Railroad from 1960 to 1962. He practiced law from 1962 to 1970 and was also a lecturer at Bellarmine College from 1964 to 1968. He served in the Kentucky Senate from 1968 to 1970, at which time he was elected to the U.S. House of Representatives. He served on the Judiciary Committee; Crime and Criminal Justice, Intellectual Property, and Judicial Administration; International Law, Immigration, and Refugees (of which he was the chair); and Small Business: SBA Legislation and the General Economy. A consistent liberal advocate, in 1992 he led the effort to give Haitian refugees protected status. From 1981 to 1986, he led the effort at immigration reform but lost the lead to the chair of the Judiciary Committee, Peter Rodino (D.–N.J.), in 1985. He was chair of the Immigration Subcommittee until he lost the position to Bruce Morrison (D.–Conn.)

in 1989. Mazzoli returned as chair in 1991 when Morrison retired. He served until retiring in 1994.

Bill McCollum (1944–)

Rep. Bill McCollum (R.–Fla.) took a B.A. from the University of Florida in 1965 and took his J.D. there in 1968. He served in the U.S. Navy from 1969 to 1972 and in the naval reserves from 1972 to 1992. He practiced law from 1973 to 1981 and served as chair of the Seminole County Republican Committee in 1976. Elected to the U.S. House of Representatives in 1980, he serves on the Banking and Financial Services Committee (where he is vice chair) and on the Judiciary Committee and its subcommittee on immigration. He played a prominent role in the impeachment of President Clinton. His most important impact on immigration concerns was his thirteen-year campaign for expedited exclusion, which was enacted in the expedited removal provision of the 1996 act. He played a leading role in the 1996 Antiterrorism and Effective Death Penalty Act as well.

Doris Meissner (1941–)

Doris Meissner was sworn in as INS commissioner in October 1993 following the Senate's unanimous confirmation of her appointment by President Clinton. She had earlier served as acting commissioner in 1981 and as executive associate commissioner until 1986. In 1986, she moved to the private sector, working as a senior associate and director of the Immigration Policy Project of the Carnegie Endowment for International Peace in Washington, D.C., to which she returned upon leaving the INS in November 2000. She wrote or contributed to numerous reports and articles, testified on policy matters before many congressional committee hearings, and addressed professional meetings and academic forums on a wide variety of immigration issues. Her career began as a White House fellow, as a special assistant to the attorney general in 1973–1974. She remained at the Justice Department, becoming assistant director of the Office of Policy and Planning (1975), executive director of the Cabinet Committee on Illegal Aliens (1976), and deputy associate attorney general (1977–1980). Her professional credentials include membership on several distinguished boards and panels, such as the Council on Foreign Relations (1990 to present), the Twenty-First Century Trust Workshop on International Migration in Cambridge, England (1991), the board of trustees for both the Refugee Policy Group (1987–1993) and the Washington Office on Latin America (1989–1993), and the advisory board for the Program for Research on Immigration Policy of the Rand Corporation/Urban Institute (1981–1986). In addition to the White House Fellowship, she received a Department of Justice Special Commendation Award and is listed in *Who's Who in America*. She is a native of Milwaukee, Wisconsin, and received her B.A. and M.A. degrees from the University of Wisconsin.

Joe Moakley (1927–)

Rep. Joe Moakley (D.–Mass.) attended the University of Miami and Suffolk University, from which he took his LL.B. in 1956. He served in the U.S. Navy during World War II from 1943 to 1946. He practiced law from 1952 to 1962. He was elected to the Massachusetts House of Representatives in 1952 and served there until 1962, including as majority whip in 1957. He served in the state senate from 1964 to 1970 and then on the Boston City Council from 1971 to 1972. He was elected to the U.S. House of Representatives in 1972. His most important committee assignment is the Rules Committee (where he is ranking minority member). On immigration matters, he proposed amendments to the 1986 IRCA and 1990 IMMACT acts and continues to work for rights for Salvadorans and Guatemalans.

Bruce Morrison (1944–)

Rep. Bruce Morrison (D.–Conn.) took a B.S. degree from the Institute of Technology and an M.S. degree from the University of Illinois. He received his J.D. from Yale in 1973. He served as a New Haven Legal Assistance Association staff attorney in 1973 and then as its managing attorney (1974–1976) and as its executive director (1976–1981). Elected to the U.S. House of Representatives in 1982, he serves on the Banking, Finance, and Urban Affairs Committee and, notably for immigration matters, on the Judiciary Committee and on its subcommittees on Administrative Law and Government Relations and as chair of its Immigration, Refugees, and International Law subcommittee. His most notable contribution on immigration reform was serving as the House author of the Immigration Act of 1990.

Daniel Patrick Moynihan (1927–2003)

Sen. Daniel Patrick Moynihan (D.–N.Y.) took a B.A. degree in 1948, an M.A. degree in 1949, and a Ph.D. in 1961, all from Tufts University. He served as aide to Governor Averell Harriman of New York (1955–1958), U.S. assistant secretary of labor (1966–1969), assistant for urban affairs to President Richard Nixon (1969–1971), professor at Harvard University (1971–1973), U.S. ambassador to India (1973–1975), and U.S. ambassador to the United Nations (1975–1976). He was elected to the U.S. Senate from New York in 1976 and retired from the Senate in 2000. He had an important impact on virtually every bill on immigration passed while he served in the Senate. His committee assignments were many, but those most related to immigration policy issues were Immigration (where he was ranking minority member), Social Security and Family Policy, and Rules and Administration.

Leon Panetta (1938–)

Rep. Leon Panetta (D.–Calif.) took a B.A. from the University of California at Santa Barbara in 1960 and a J.D. there in 1963. He served in the U.S. Army from 1963 to 1965 and then as legislative assistant to U.S. Sen. Thomas Kuchel (D.–Calif.) from 1966 to 1969. He was director of the U.S. Office of Civil Rights in the Department of Health, Education and Welfare from 1969 to 1970. He was executive assistant to the mayor of New York City from 1970 to 1971. He practiced law from 1971 to 1976 and was elected to the U.S. House of Representatives in 1976, where he remained until he moved to join President Clinton's administration as White House chief of staff. He had numerous committee assignments, several of which shaped his role on immigration matters: the Agriculture Subcommittee on Department Operations, Research, and Foreign Agriculture; the Budget Committee (which he chaired); the House Administrative Committee; and the Select Committee on Hunger and on a domestic task force (of which he was chair). He was very involved in key compromises regarding IRCA and the IMMACT of 1990.

Demetrios Papademetriou (1946–)

Demetrios Papademetriou is senior associate and codirector of the International Migration Policy Program of the Carnegie Endowment for Peace. He has published extensively both in the

United States and abroad on immigration and refugee policies, with particular emphasis on immigrants' repercussions on the labor market and development. He has taught at American University, the University of Maryland, and at Duke University and on the graduate faculty of the New School for Social Research. He has served as director of immigration policy and research at the U.S. Department of Labor and chaired the secretary of labor's Immigration Policy Task Force. He also served as the U.S. representative to the Migration Committee of the Organization for Economic Cooperation and Development. Before his service in the government, he was executive editor of the *International Migration Review* and directed the research activities of the Center for Migration Studies in New York. In addition to serving as codirector of the International Migration Policy Program, he now also serves as chair of the OECD Migration Committee. He concentrates on U.S. immigration policies and practices, the migration politics and practices of advanced industrial societies, and the role of multilateral institutions in developing and coordinating collective responses to voluntary and involuntary international population movements.

Richard Pombo (1961–)

Rep. Richard Pombo (R.–Calif.) attended the California Polytechnic Institute from 1979 to 1982. He is a cattle rancher, and in 1986 he cofounded the Citizens Land Alliance. In politics, he served on the Tracy City Council from 1990 to 1992 and was elected to the U.S. House of Representatives in 1992. He serves on the Agriculture Committee and on the Resources Committee. His most notable effort concerning immigration issues was his cosponsorship of the 1998 Guest-Worker Program bill.

Ronald Reagan (1911–)

Ronald Reagan graduated from Eureka College in 1932 and began a career as a sports announcer before signing a movie contract with Warner Brothers Studio in 1939. In 1947, he was elected president of the Screen Actors Guild. In 1954, he hosted the *General Electric Theater* television show. In 1960, he campaigned for Richard Nixon for president. In 1963, he hosted the popular TV show *Death Valley Days*. In 1966, he was elected governor of California and was reelected in 1970. In 1976, he lost a bid for the Republican presidential nomination, but he was elected president in 1980. His contributions to immigration policy center on his establishment of a Task Force on Immigration in his administration, which helped shape the debate over IRCA in 1986. Reelected president in 1984, he signed the IRCA into law, establishing the employer-sanctions approach. He retired from the presidency in 1989. In 1994, he announced that he suffers from Alzheimer's disease.

Janet Reno (1938–)

Janet Reno was the first female attorney general. She was nominated by President Clinton in 1993, reappointed in 1997, and served until 2000. A controversial attorney general, by her own stated goals she strove to ensure that the Department of Justice reflects a diverse government, making integrity, excellence, and professionalism hallmarks of the department. She is the daughter of Henry Reno, an immigrant from Denmark and for forty-three years a police reporter for the *Miami Herald*. She attended public school in Dade County, Florida, where she was her high school debating champion. She graduated from Cornell University, where she was president of the Women's Self-Government Association. In 1960, she enrolled in Harvard Law School, one of sixteen women in a class of more than 500, and received her LL.B. from Harvard in 1963. In 1971, she was named staff director of the Judiciary Committee of the Florida House of Representatives, where she helped revise the state's court system. In 1973, she accepted a position in the Office of the State Attorney of Dade County. She left that position to become a partner in a private law firm. In 1978, she was appointed state attorney general for Dade County, and in the same year, she was elected to the Office of State Attorney, where she served for four terms. She helped reform the juvenile justice system and pursued delinquent fathers for child-support payments. She established the Miami Drug Court. Her most notable roles and impacts in immigration policy involved helping draft the Clinton administration's 1996 immigration reform package and her handling of the controversial Elian Gonzalez case in 1999–2000.

Peter W. Rodino Jr. (1909–)

Rep. Peter W. Rodino (D.–N.J.) took his LL.B. from the New Jersey Law School (now Rutgers) in 1937. He served in the U.S. Army in World War II. He practiced law in 1938, was a senior member of the New Jersey Congressional Delegation in 1971, and was assistant majority whip. He served on the Judiciary Committee, including as chair of the Immigration Subcommittee. His most notable role in immigration issues was during the 1982–1986 efforts to pass what became IRCA.

Edward R. Roybal (1916–)

Rep. Edward R. Roybal (D.–Calif.) attended UCLA and Southwestern University. He served in the U.S. Army during World War II. He was director of health education for the Los Angeles County Tuberculosis and Health Association from 1945 to 1949. He was elected to the Los Angeles City Council in 1949 and served until 1962, including as its president pro tempore from 1961 to 1963. He was elected to the U.S. House of Representatives in 1962 and served there until 1992, when he retired. His major committee service included: member of the Appropriations Committee and its Subcommittee on Labor, Health, Human Services, and Education; chair of the Committee of General Government; member of the Committee on Treasury and the Committee on Postal Services; and chair of the Select Committee on Aging and its Subcommittee on Health and Long-Term Care. He was a leading member of the Hispanic Caucus in the House of Representatives for many years. He led the opposition to employer-sanctions provisions from 1982 to 1984 and was critical to stopping their enactment during those years. In 1986, however, he played a critical role when the caucus split, as he supported passage of IRCA.

Charles E. Schumer (1950–)

Sen. Charles E. Schumer (D.–N.Y.), now the senior senator from New York, took his B.A. degree from Harvard in 1971 and his J.D. from there in 1974. He served in the New York Assembly from 1974 to 1980 and then in the U.S. House of Representatives from 1980 to 1998. He was elected to the U.S. Senate in 1998. He was critically important in crafting compromises enabling the passage of the IRCA, and he has continued to play a critical role in all immigration related bills since then. In the Senate, he serves on several committees of importance to the issue, including Banking, Housing, and Urban Affairs; International Trade and Finance; Judiciary and its Administrative Oversight and Courts Subcommittees; Criminal Justice Oversight; Immigration (of which he is ranking minority member); and Rules and Administration.

Paul Simon (1928–)

Sen. Paul Simon (D.–Ill.) attended the University of Oregon from 1945 to 1946 and Dana College from 1946 to 1948. He served in the U.S. Army from 1951 to 1953. He was editor-publisher of the *Troy Tribune* from 1948 to 1966. Elected to the Illinois House of Representatives in 1954, he served until 1962, when he was elected to the state senate, where he served until 1968. He served as lieutenant governor of Illinois from 1968 to 1972. He was a professor at Sangamon State University from 1972 to 1973. He was elected to the U.S. House of Representatives in 1974 and served there until his election to the U.S. Senate in 1984. His Senate committee service most related to immigration issues were: member of the Budget Committee; member of the Judiciary Committee, chair of its Subcommittee on Immigration and ranking minority member of the Subcommittee on Constitution, Federalism, and Property Rights; member of the Labor and Human Resources Committee and its Subcommittees on Aging, Disability Policy, and Education, Arts, and the Humanities; and member of the Indian Affairs Committee. He was notable for his coauthorship and sponsorship of the Kennedy-Simpson-Simon bill that eventually passed as IMMACT (1990). He retired from the Senate in 1996 but had an impact on the 1996 Welfare and Immigration Reform Acts as well.

Alan Simpson (1931–)

Next to Sen. Edward Kennedy (D.–Mass.), Sen. Alan Simpson (R.–Wyo.) was the most influential member of Congress on immigration matters for much of his career. He took a B.S. degree from the University of Wyoming in 1954 and a J.D. from there in 1958. He served in the U.S. Army from 1954 to 1956. He practiced law from 1959 to 1978, serving also as the city attorney for Cody from 1959 to 1969 and in the Wyoming House of Representatives from 1964 to 1977, including as majority floor leader from 1975 to 1976 and speaker pro tempore in 1977. Elected to the U.S. Senate in 1978, he served on the SCIRP Commission, from which his interest in immigration emerged. In the Senate, he coauthored the bills that became IRCA and played a major role in the IMMACT of 1990. He served on numerous committees, several of which were important to the issue: member of the Finance Committee and its Subcommittees on Long-Term Growth, Debt, and Deficit Reduction along with Medicare, Long-Term Care, and Health Insurance;

member of the Judiciary Committee and its Subcommittees on Antitrust, Business Rights, Compensation, Immigration (of which he served as chair), and Youth Violence; chair of the Veterans Affairs Committee; and member of the Special Committee on Aging.

Christopher H. Smith (1953–)

Rep. Christopher H. Smith (R.–N.J.) received a B.S. degree from Trenton State College in 1975. He was a sales executive in a family-owned sporting goods business from 1975 to 1980. He served as executive director of New Jersey Right to Life from 1976 to 1978. He was elected to the U.S. House of Representatives in 1980. He serves on the International Relations Committee and on two of its subcommittees, International Operations and Human Rights, of which he is chair, and Western Hemisphere; and as vice chair of both the Veterans Affairs Committee and its Subcommittee on Health. His most notable immigration-reform activity was his sponsorship of the Trafficking Victims Protection Act.

Gordon H. Smith (1952–)

Sen. Gordon H. Smith (R.–Ore.) took his B.A. from Brigham Young University in 1976. He received his J.D. from Southwestern University in 1979. He then served as a law clerk to the New Mexico Supreme Court until 1980. He practiced law from 1980 to 1981 and was president of Smith Frozen Foods from 1980 to 1996. He was elected to the U.S. Senate in 1996. His principal committee assignments are Budget, Energy and Natural Resources, and Foreign Relations. On the last, his subcommittees are East Asian and Pacific Affairs, European Affairs (of which he is chair), and Near Eastern and South Asian Affairs. His most notable immigration-related activity was his cosponsorship, in 1998, of the Guest-Worker Program bill.

Lamar S. Smith (1947–)

Rep. Lamar S. Smith (R.–Tex.) took a B.A. degree from Yale in 1969 and a J.D. from Southern Methodist University in 1975. He worked for the U.S. Small Business Administration from 1969 to 1970 and was a business writer for the *Christian Science Monitor* from 1970 to 1972. He practiced law from 1975 to 1976. He was elected to the Texas House of Representatives in 1981 and served to 1982. He served as a Bexar County commissioner from 1982 to

1985, and was then elected to the U.S. House of Representatives in 1986. He serves on the Judiciary Committee, including as chair of its Immigration and Claims Subcommittee; on the Science Committee; and on the Standards of Official Conduct Committee, which he also chairs. Since his arrival in the House, he has been an outspoken critic of immigration policy and one of the House's strongest advocates for restricted immigration, reform of legislation on illegal immigration, and strengthening of the Border Patrol, and he has opposed amnesty proposals.

Georges Vernez (1939–)

Georges Vernez is director of the Center for Research on Immigration Policy of the Rand Corporation. He took his Ph.D. in urban and regional development from the University of California, Berkeley. He has directed and conducted studies on a broad range of immigration issues, including most notably a comprehensive assessment of the implementation of IRCA, with particular focus on its effects on undocumented immigration, supply of labor, and U.S.-Mexican bilateral relations. He has analyzed issues related to the effects of immigration on the demand for state and local services and on labor markets, and issues related to the social and economic adjustments of immigrants in the United States. He has also done comparative studies of immigration and refugee policy regimes and their outcomes in western nations and has recently completed a comprehensive assessment of the demographic, economic, institutional, and distributional effects of thirty years of immigration in California. He is currently conducting a study of the performance of immigrant women in the U.S. labor market and a study of the social benefits from increasing the educational attainments of Hispanics. In 1991, he founded and now directs the Rand Institute on Education and Training, which examines all forms of education and training that people may get throughout their lives.

Ron Wyden (1949–)

Sen. Ron Wyden (D.–Ore.) took his B.A. degree from Stanford University in 1971 and his J.D. from the University of Oregon in 1974. He was cofounder and served as codirector of the Oregon Gray Panthers from 1974 to 1980 and then served as director of Oregon's Legal Services for the Elderly from 1977 to 1979. He was also professor of gerontology at the University of Oregon (1976) and at Portland State University of Oregon (1980). He served in the U.S. House of Representatives from 1980 to 1996, at which time he was elected to the U.S. Senate. His Senate committees of note are Aging; Budget; Commerce, Science, and Transportation; Energy and Natural Resources; and Environment and Public Works. His most notable activity in relation to the immigration issue was his cosponsorship, with Sen. Gordon Smith (R.–Ore.), of the 1998 Guest-Worker Program bill.

References and Further Reading

Barone, Michael, Grant Ujifusa, and Eleanor Evans, eds. 1972, 1976, 1978, 1986, 1990, 1994, 1996, 2000. *The Almanac of American Politics.* Washington, DC: National Journal.

Diller, Daniel C., and Stephen L. Robertson. 2001. *The Presidents, First Ladies, and Vice Presidents: White House Biographies, 1789–2001.* Washington, DC: Congressional Quarterly Press.

Graff, Henry A., ed. 1997. *The Presidents: A Reference History.* New York: Charles Scribner's Sons.

Hamilton, Neil A. 2001. *Presidents: A Biographical Dictionary.* New York: Facts on File.

Immigration and Naturalization Service (INS) Website. Available: http://www.immigration.gov; accessed February 20, 2003.

Jacobson, Doranne. 1995. *Presidents and First Ladies of the United States.* New York: Smithmack.

U.S. Department of Justice (DOJ) Website. Available: http://www.us-doj.gov; accessed Febraury 20, 2003.

6

Key Laws and Court Cases

Public policy is usefully understood as an ongoing process, "a purposive course of action followed by an actor or set of actors in dealing with a problem or matter of concern" (Anderson 1979, 3). Chapter 5 presented biographical sketches of the major actors involved in immigration issues in the United States today. This chapter presents summaries of the "actions"—key legislation and judicial decisions—that collectively provide the "course" directing immigration policy and its frequent reform. It presents all the major laws and cases pertinent to immigration reform since 1965. Since most of the laws and decisions range from dozens to hundreds of pages long, only key points and provisions are reprinted here.

The Immigration and Naturalization Act of 1965 (79 Stat. 911)

On October 3, 1965, the Immigration and Naturalization Act of 1965 was signed into law. It profoundly amended the immigration provisions of the McCarran-Walter Act of 1952. The law dramatically influenced the immigration flow, not only markedly increasing the number of immigrants entering the United States but also altering the origin of the influx from northwestern Europe to Latin America and Asia. Of equal significance, the new law imposed the first ceiling on immigration from the Western Hemisphere, with the preference system extended to that migration eleven years later.

Keeping with the spirit of the Civil Rights Act of 1964, the Kennedy administration's proposal, which became the Immigration and

Naturalization Act of 1965, reasserted the nation's liberal tradition in immigration. It set up individual rather than group criteria for granting immigration visas. The bill was resubmitted by President Johnson in January 1965 and was introduced into the House by Representative Emmanuel Celler, chairman of the House Judiciary Committee, and into the Senate by Senator Hart and by Senators Edward Kennedy and Robert Kennedy. It was cosponsored by thirty-two senators. It sought to balance a number of goals: (1) to preserve family unity and reunite separated families; (2) to meet the need for some highly skilled workers; (3) to ease problems created by emergencies, such as political upheavals, Communist aggression, and natural disasters; (4) to assist cross-national exchange programs; (5) to bar from the United States aliens who were likely to present problems of adjustment due to their physical or mental health, past criminal history, or dependency or for national security reasons; (6) to standardize admission procedures; and (7) to establish immigration limits for the Americas. It replaced the national-origins quota system with a seven-category system of preferences. Thus, the new law not only abolished the national-origins system but also emphasized other terms than quota and nonquota immigrants. Prospective immigrants either were nonpreference, met one of the preferences, or were not subject to new per-country limits because they were immediate relatives of U.S. citizens or were special immigrants. The last group included persons born in the Western Hemisphere, former U.S. citizens seeking to resume their citizenship, ministers, and former (or current) employees of the U.S. government abroad. Those seeking admission under the third or sixth employment preferences would now have to meet more stringent labor-certification rules.

Be it enacted by the Senate and House of Representatives of the United States of America in Congress assembled, That section 201 of the Immigration and Nationality Act . . . be amended to read as follows:

Sec. 201. (a) Exclusive of special immigrants defined in section 101 (a) (27), and of the immediate relatives of United States citizens specified in subsection (b) of this section, the number of aliens who may be issued immigrant visas. . . . shall not in any fiscal year exceed a total of 170,000.

(b) The "immediate relatives" referred to in subsection (a) of this section will mean the children, spouses, and parents of a citizen of the United States . . . Provided, That in the case of parents, such citizen must be at least twenty-one years of age. . . .

(c) During the period from July 1, 1965, through June 30, 1968, the annual quota of any quota area shall be the same as that which existed for that area on June 30, 1965. . . .

(e) The immigration pool and the quota areas shall terminate June 30, 1968. Thereafter immigrants admitted under the provisions of this Act who are subject to the numerical limitations of subsection (a) of this Act will be admitted in accordance with the percentage limitations and in the order of priority specified in section 203.

Sec. 2. Section 202 of the Immigration and Nationality Act . . . is amended to read as follows:

(a) No person shall receive any preference or priority or be discriminated against in the issuance of an immigrant visa because of his race, sex, nationality, place of birth, or place of residence, except as specifically provided in section 101 (a) (27), section 201 (b), and section 203: Provided, That the total number of immigrant visas and the number of conditional entries made available to natives of any single foreign state . . . shall not exceed 20,000 in any fiscal year. . . .

(b) Each independent country, self-governing dominion, mandated territory, and territory under the international trusteeship of the United Nations, other than the United States and its outlying possessions, shall be treated as a separate foreign state for the purposes of the numerical limitation set forth in the proviso to subsection (a) of this section . . .

Sec. 203. (a) Aliens who are subject to the numerical limitations . . . shall be allotted visas or their conditional entry authorized, as the case may be, as follows:

(1) Visas shall be first made available, in a number not to exceed 20 per centum of the number specified in section 201 (a) (ii), to qualified immigrants who are the unmarried sons or daughters of citizens of the United States.

(2) Visas shall next be made available, in a number not to exceed 20 per centum of the number specified in section 201 (a) (ii). . . . to qualified immigrants who are spouses, unmarried sons or unmarried daughters of an alien admitted for permanent residence.

(3) Visas shall next be made available, in a number not to exceed 10 per centum . . . to qualified immigrants who are members of the professions, or who because of their exceptional ability in the sciences or arts will substantially benefit prospectively the national economy, cultural interests, or welfare of the United States.

(4) Visas shall next be made available, in a number not to exceed 10 per centum. . . . to qualified immigrants who are the married sons or married daughters of citizens of the United States.

(5) Visas shall next be made available, in a number not to exceed 24 per centum . . . to qualified immigrants who are the brothers or sisters of citizens of the United States.

(6) Visas shall next be made available, in a number not to exceed 10 per centum of the number specified . . . to qualified immigrants who are capable of performing specified skilled or unskilled labor, not of a temporary or seasonal nature, for which a shortage of employable and willing persons exists in the United States.

(7) Conditional entries shall next be made available by the Attorney General, pursuant to such regulations as he may prescribe and in a number not to exceed 6 per centum . . . to aliens who satisfy an Immigration and Naturalization Service officer. . . . (A) that (i) because of persecution or fear of persecution on account of race, religion, or political opinion they have fled [their country of origin]. . . . and (ii) are unable or unwilling to return to such country or area on account of race, religion, or political opinion, and (iii) are not nationals of the countries or areas in which their application for conditional entry is made; or (B) that they are persons uprooted by catastrophic natural calamity as defined by the President who are unable to return to their usual place of abode.

(8) Visas authorized in any fiscal year, . . . shall be made available to other qualified immigrants strictly in the chronological order in which they qualify. Waiting lists of applicants shall be maintained in accordance with regulations prescribed by the Secretary of State. No immigrant visa shall be issued to a non-preference immigrant under this paragraph, or to an immigrant with a preference under paragraph (3) or (6) of this subsection, until the consular officer is in receipt of a determination made by the Secretary of Labor in pursuant to the provisions of section 212 (a) (14). . . .

(d) Every immigrant shall be presumed to be a nonpreference immigrant until he establishes to the satisfaction of the consular officer and the immigration officer that he is entitled to a preference status. . . .

Sec. 10. Section 212 (a) of the Immigration and Nationality Act . . . is amended as follows:

(a) Paragraph (14) is amended to read as follows: "Aliens seeking to enter the United States, for the purpose of performing skilled or unskilled labor, unless the Secretary of Labor has determined and certified to the Secretary of State and to the Attorney General that (A) there are not sufficient workers in the

United States who are able, willing, qualified, and available at the time of the application for a visa and admission to the United States and at the place to which the alien is destined to perform such skilled or unskilled labor, and (B) the employment of such aliens will not adversely affect the wages and working conditions of the workers in the United States similarly employed. . . .

Sec. 21. (a) There is hereby established a Select Commission of Western Hemisphere Immigration (hereinafter referred to as the "Commission"). . . .

(b) The Commission shall study the following matters:

(1) Prevailing and projected demographic, technological, and economic trends as they pertain to the Western Hemisphere;

(2) Present and projected unemployment in the United States, by occupations, industries, geographic areas, and other factors in relation to immigration from the Western Hemisphere;

(3) The interrelationships between immigration, present and future, and existing and contemplated national and international programs and projects of Western Hemisphere nations, including programs and projects for economic and social development;

(4) The operation of immigration laws of the United States as they pertain to Western Hemisphere nations, including adjustment of status for Cuban refugees. . . .

(5) The implications of the foregoing with respect to the security and international relations of Western Hemisphere nations; and

(6) Any other matters which the Commission believes to be germane to the purposes for which it was established.

Immigration Act of November 2, 1966, to Adjust the Status of Cuban Refugees (80 Stat. 1161)

Congress also recognized and responded to the plight of the Cuban refugees. In November 1966, Congress passed a special act to adjust the status of Cuban refugees to that of lawful permanent residence.

Be it enacted by the Senate and House of Representatives of the United States of America in Congress assembled, That, notwithstanding the provisions of section 245 (c) of the

Immigration and Nationality Act, the status of any alien who is a native or citizen of Cuba and who has been inspected and admitted or paroled into the United States subsequent to January 1, 1959 and has been physically present in the United States for at least two years may be adjusted by the Attorney General, in his discretion and under such regulations as he may prescribe, to that of an alien lawfully admitted for permanent residence if the alien makes application for such adjustment, and the alien is eligible to receive an immigrant visa and is admissible to the United States for permanent residence. Upon approval of such application for adjustment of status, the Attorney General shall create a record of the alien's admission for permanent residence as of the date thirty months prior to the filing of such an application or the date of his last arrival into the United States, whichever date is later. The provisions of this Act shall be applicable to the spouse and child of any alien described in this subsection, regardless of their citizenship and place of birth, who are residing with such alien in the United States.

Afroyim v. Rusk (387 U.S. 253 [May 29, 1967])

The question of how one may lose citizenship was at issue again in 1967 in an important U.S. Supreme Court case on the matter, Afroyim v. Rusk. *The Court decided that a citizen who held dual citizenship with Israel did not lose his citizenship merely by voting in an election of the country in which he held his other citizenship. The case is particularly significant in the strong language used by the justices in stipulating how limited the government is in taking away citizenship once it has been granted by birthright or by naturalization.*

Mr. Justice Black delivered the opinion of the Court.
Petitioner, born in Poland in 1893, immigrated to this country in 1912 and became a naturalized American citizen in 1926. He went to Israel in 1950, and in 1951 he voluntarily voted in an election for the Israeli Knesset, the legislative body of Israel. In 1960, when he applied for renewal of his United States passport, the Department of State refused to grant it on the sole ground that he had lost his American citizenship by virtue of 401(e) of the Nationality Act of 1940, which provides that a United States

citizen shall "lose" his citizenship if he votes "in a political election in a foreign state." . . .

Because neither the Fourteenth Amendment nor any other provision of the Constitution expressly grants Congress the power to take away that citizenship once it has been acquired, petitioner contended that the only way he could lose his citizenship was by his own voluntary renunciation of it. Since the Government took the position that 401(e) empowers it to terminate citizenship without the citizen's voluntary renunciation, petitioner argued that this section is prohibited by the Constitution. . . .

The fundamental issue before this Court here, as it was in Perez, is whether Congress can consistently with the Fourteenth Amendment enact a law stripping an American of his citizenship which he has never voluntarily renounced or given up. The majority in Perez held that Congress could do this because withdrawal of citizenship is "reasonably calculated to effect the end that is within the power of Congress to achieve." That conclusion was reached by this chain of reasoning: Congress has an implied power to deal with foreign affairs as an indispensable attribute of sovereignty. This implied power, plus the Necessary and Proper Clause, empowers Congress to regulate voting by American citizens in foreign elections; involuntary expatriation is within the "ample scope" of "appropriate modes" Congress can adopt to effectuate its general regulatory power. Then, upon summarily concluding that "there is nothing in the . . . Fourteenth Amendment to warrant drawing from it a restriction upon the power otherwise possessed by Congress to withdraw citizenship," the majority specifically rejected the "notion that the power of Congress to terminate citizenship depends upon the citizen's assent."

First we reject the idea expressed in Perez that, aside from the Fourteenth Amendment, Congress has any general power, express or implied, to take away an American's citizenship without his assent. This power cannot, as Perez indicated, be sustained as an implied attribute of sovereignty possessed by all nations. Other nations are governed by their own constitutions, if any, and we can draw no support from theirs. In our country the people are sovereign and the Government cannot sever its relationship to the people by taking away their citizenship. Our Constitution governs us and we must never forget that our Constitution limits the Government to those powers specifically granted or those that are necessary and proper to carry out the specifically granted ones. The Constitution, of course, grants Congress no express power to strip people of their citizenship, whether in the exercise of the implied power to regulate foreign affairs or in the exercise of any specifically granted power. . . .

. . . [A]ny doubt as to whether prior to the passage of the Fourteenth Amendment Congress had the power to deprive a person against his will of citizenship once obtained should have been removed by the unequivocal terms of the Amendment itself. It provides its own constitutional rule in language calculated completely to control the status of citizenship: "All persons born or naturalized in the United States . . . are citizens of the United States. . . . " There is no indication in these words of a fleeting citizenship, good at the moment it is acquired but subject to destruction by the Government at any time. Rather the Amendment can most reasonably be read as defining a citizenship which a citizen keeps unless he voluntarily relinquishes it. Once acquired, this Fourteenth Amendment citizenship was not to be shifted, canceled, or diluted at the will of the Federal Government, the States, or any other governmental unit. . . .

[The] undeniable purpose of the Fourteenth Amendment to make citizenship of Negroes permanent and secure would be frustrated by holding that the Government can rob a citizen of his citizenship without his consent by simply proceeding to act under an implied power to regulate foreign affairs or some other power generally granted. . . .

To uphold Congress' power to take away a man's citizenship because he voted in a foreign election in violation of 401(e) would be equivalent to holding that Congress has the power to "abridge," "affect," "restrict the effect of," and "take . . . away" citizenship. Because the Fourteenth Amendment prevents Congress from doing any of these things, we agree with THE CHIEF JUSTICE's dissent in the Perez case that the Government is without power to rob a citizen of his citizenship under 402(e). . . .

Our holding is the only one that can stand in view of the language and the purpose of the Fourteenth Amendment, and our construction of that Amendment, we believe, comports more nearly than Perez with the principles of liberty and equal justice to all that the entire Fourteenth Amendment was adopted to guarantee. Citizenship is no light trifle to be jeopardized any moment Congress decides to do so under the name of one of its general or implied grants of power. In some instances, loss of citizenship can mean that a man is left without the protection of citizenship in any country in the world—as a man without a country. Citizenship in this Nation is part of a cooperative affair. Its citizenry is the country and the country is its citizenry. The very nature of our free government makes it completely incongruous to have a rule of law under which a group of citizens temporarily in office can deprive another group of citizens of their citizenship. We hold that the Fourteenth Amendment was designed to, and does, protect every citizen of this Nation against a congressional forcible destruction of his citizenship, whatever his creed, color, or race. Our holding does no more than to give to this citizen that which is his own, a constitutional right to remain a citizen in a free country unless he voluntarily relinquishes that citizenship.

Perez v. Brownell is overruled. The judgment is Reversed.

Proclamation of the President of the United States of America, November 6, 1968, Multilateral Protocol Relating to the Status of Refugees

The continuing problem of mass movements involving tens of thousands of refugees generated by war or natural disasters influenced the United Nations to revise its protocols relating to the status of refugees. The United States, as a nation that was a state party to the agreement and the protocols, in essence agreed to changes in its law dealing with the status of refugees as well. This was accomplished by President Lyndon Johnson's issuance of a presidential proclamation regarding the UN protocols. The proclamation runs thirty-five pages, but since most of the protocols were not changed from those originally agreed to in 1951, I here present excerpts of only some major provisions of the protocols as amended in 1967 and contained in the presidential proclamation of 1968.

The States Parties to the present Protocol
Considering that the Convention relating to the Status of Refugees done at Geneva on 28 July 1951 (hereinafter referred to as the Convention) . . . [and]
Considering that it is desirable that equal status should be enjoyed by all refugees covered by the definition in the Convention irrespective of the dateline 1 January 1951,

Have agreed as follows: Article I—General Provisions

1. The States Parties to the present Protocol undertake to apply articles 2 to 34 inclusive of the Convention to refugees as hereinafter defined.

2. For the purpose of the present Protocol, the term "refugee" shall, except as regards the application of paragraph 3 of this article, mean any person within the definition of Article I of the Convention. . . .

3. The present Protocol shall be applied by the States Parties hereto without any geographic limitation. . . .

Article II—Co-operation of the National Authorities with the United Nations

1. The States Parties to the present Protocol undertake to co-operate with the Office of the United Nations High Commissioner for Refugees, or any other agency of the United Nations which may succeed it, in the exercise of its functions, and shall in particular facilitate its duty of supervising the application of the provisions of the present Protocol. . . .

Article III—Non-discrimination

The Contracting States shall apply the provisions of this Convention to refugees without discrimination as to race, religion, or country of origin. . . .

Chapter III, Gainful Employment—Article XVII

1. The Contracting States shall accord to refugees lawfully staying in their territory the most favorable treatment accorded to nationals of a foreign country in the same circumstances, as regards to engage in wage-earning employment. . . .

Article XXXII—Expulsion

1. The Contracting State shall not expel a refugee lawfully in their territory save on grounds of national security or public order.

2. The expulsion of such a refugee shall only be in pursuance of a decision in accordance with due process of law. . . .

3. The Contracting States shall allow such a refugee a reasonable period within which to seek legal admission into another country. The Contracting States reserve the right to apply during that period such internal measures as they may deem necessary.

Article XXXIII—Prohibition of Expulsion or Return ("Refoulement")

1. No Contracting State shall expel or return ("refouler") a refugee in any manner whatsoever to the frontiers of territories where his life or freedom would be threatened on account of his

race, religion, nationality, membership of a particular social group or political opinion.

2. The benefit of the present provision may not, however, be claimed by a refugee for whom there are reasonable grounds for regarding as a danger to the security of the country in which he is, or who, having been convicted by a final judgement of a particularly serious crime, constitutes a danger to the community of that country.

Article XXXIV—Naturalization

The Contracting States shall as far as possible facilitate the assimilation and naturalization of refugees. They shall in particular make every effort to expedite naturalization proceedings and to reduce as far as possible the charges and costs of such proceedings.

Source: (I-70) Orders, Proclamations, and Treaties 1208.233–1208.263

Mathews v. Santiago Diaz et al. (426 U.S. 67 [1976])

Resident aliens who were cut off from Medicare supplemental benefits of the Social Security Act sued the federal government in a class-action case heard in Florida. The U.S. Supreme Court heard the case on appeal, upholding the constitutionality of the congressional act amending the Social Security law.

Certain resident aliens instituted a class action in the United States District Court for Southern District of Florida, challenging the constitutionality of the provisions of the Social Security Act (42 USCS 1395 sec. (2)) which grant eligibility for the Medicare supplemental medical insurance program to resident citizens who are 65 or older, but which deny eligibility to aliens, 65 or older, unless they have been admitted for permanent residence and have resided in the county for at least five years. The three-judge District Court entered judgment for the plaintiffs, holding that the residency requirement violated the due process clause of the Fifth Amendment, and that since it could not be severed from the requirement of admission for permanent residence, the alien eligibility provisions were entirely unenforceable (361 F. Supp. 1).

On direct appeal, the United States Supreme Court reversed. In an opinion by Stevens, J., expressing the unanimous view of the court, it was held that (1) Congress had no constitutional duty to provide all aliens with benefits provided to citizens, and (2) the alien eligibility provisions of 1395 (2) did not deprive aliens who did not meet the eligibility requirements of liberty or property without due process of law under the Fifth Amendment, since (a) it was reasonable for Congress to make an alien's eligibility depend on both the character and duration of his residence, (b) the statutory classification drew a line qualifying those aliens who might reasonably be presumed to have a greater affinity to the United States, and (c) the court would not substitute its judgment for that of Congress.

Source: Briefs of Counsel, p. 964, see infra., U.S. Supreme Court Reports, 48 L Ed 2nd: 478.

Amendment to the Immigration and Naturalization Act of 1965 (1976)

During the final weeks of the congressional session of 1976, Congress passed a law to amend the Immigration Act of 1965 to deal with a perceived problem created by that law. The result of the 1965 law was that all would-be immigrants from the Western Hemisphere were required to apply for visas on a first-come, first-served basis, including those who were skilled foreign workers or close relatives of U.S. citizens, groups that received preferences in the system as it was in effect for the Eastern Hemisphere. By the mid-1970s, the waiting period for immigrant visas in the Western Hemisphere was more than two years. This waiting period caused hardships for those who would otherwise have qualified for a preferred status and gained much faster entry into the United States. To rectify these problems, the 1976 amendment law extended the preference system to the Western Hemisphere nations. It was expected that the amendment would cut the waiting period for immigrants from Mexico, for example, in half. This excerpt presents a Congressional Quarterly Almanac summary of the law's key provisions.

As signed into law, HR 14535:

1. Retained the annual hemispheric immigration ceilings of 170,000 for the Eastern Hemisphere and 120,000 for the Western Hemisphere.

2. Extended the seven-point immigration preference system to visa applicants from the Western Hemisphere as follows: first preference, unmarried sons and daughters under 21 years of age

of U.S. citizens, 20 per cent of the hemispheric limitation; second preference, spouses and unmarried sons and daughters of aliens with permanent resident status, 20 per cent plus any visas not required for the first preference; third preference, professionals whose services are sought by U.S. employers, 10 per cent of the limitation; fourth preference, married children of U.S. citizens, 10 per cent of the limitation plus any visas not required for the first three categories; fifth preference, brothers and sisters of U.S. citizens, 21 years or older, 24 per cent of the limitation plus any visas not required for the previous categories; sixth preference, skilled and unskilled workers in short supply, 10 per cent of the limitation; seventh preference, refugees, 6 per cent of the limitation; nonpreference, others, any numbers not used by the seven preference categories. . . .

6. Set up a country-by-country triggering mechanism whereby the hemispheric visa percentage allotments for the various preference categories would become applicable within a given country whenever immigration from that country reaches its 20,000 limit in a preceding year, in order to assure that visas in lower preference categories would be available.

7. Retained the labor certification requirement for all third, sixth and nonpreference immigrants who intended to work in the United States. . . .

8. Required the Secretary of Labor to certify that equally qualified American professionals are available before denying labor certification for teachers or other immigrants with exceptional skills in the arts and sciences.

9. Recommended the establishment of a special advisory group of experts to advise the Secretary of Labor in difficult cases involving visa applicants with exceptional professional skills.

10. Provided that Cuban refugees present in the U.S. prior to the enactment of the bill who change their status to permanent resident will not be charged to the annual ceiling for Western Hemisphere visas. . . .

11. Allowed natives of the Western Hemisphere to adjust their status from nonimmigrant to permanent resident without first returning to their home countries. This provision had formerly applied only to the Eastern Hemisphere.

12. Prohibited aliens who are not immediate relatives of either U.S. citizens or permanent residents from receiving an adjustment in status to permanent resident after accepting unauthorized employment in the U.S.

13. Prohibited aliens who were admitted to the U.S. in transit without visas from receiving an adjustment in status to permanent resident.

Source: 1976 Congressional Quarterly Almanac (Washington, DC: Congressional Quarterly, 1977), 413–414.

The Refugee Act of 1980 (94 Stat. 102)

In 1980, Congress dealt most specifically with the problem of refugee admissions. Older refugee laws tended to deal with the refugee as a single individual "escaping" communism, for example. But the 1960s and 1970s saw refugee flows in which persons seeking asylum arrived en masse, in tens or even hundreds of thousands. The Refugee Act of 1980, in an effort to systematize refugee policy, incorporated the UN definition of a refugee; initially allowed for the entrance as refugees of 50,000 persons annually who had a "well-founded fear of persecution" on account of race, religion, nationality, membership in a social group or political movement; and stipulated that the president could notify Congress if he determined that it was warranted to increase the number and that, after fiscal year 1982, he would have the responsibility of presenting Congress with a recommended total annual figure.

Be it enacted by the Senate and House of Representatives of the United States of America in Congress assembled, That this Act may be cited as the "Refugee Act of 1980."

Sec. 101. (a) The Congress declares that it is the historic policy of the United States to respond to the urgent needs of persons subject to persecution in their homelands, including, where appropriate, humanitarian assistance for their care and maintenance in asylum areas, efforts to promote opportunities for resettlement or voluntary repatriation, aid for necessary transportation and processing, admission to this country of refugees for special humanitarian concern to the United States, and transitional assistance to refugees in the United States. The Congress further declares that it is the policy of the United States to encourage all nations to provide assistance and resettlement opportunities to refugees to the fullest extent possible.

(b) The objectives of this Act are to provide permanent and systematic procedure for the admission to this country of refugees of special humanitarian concern to the United States, and to provide comprehensive and uniform provisions for the effective resettlement and absorption of those refugees who are admitted.

Sec. 201 (a) Section 101 (a) of the Immigration and Nationality Act . . . is amended by adding after paragraph (41) the following new paragraph:

(42) The term "refugee" means (A) any person who is outside any country of such person's nationality or, in the case of a person having no nationality, is outside any country in which such person last habitually resided, and who is unable or unwilling to return to, and is unable or unwilling to avail himself or herself of the protection of, that country because of persecution or a well-founded fear of persecution on account of race, religion, nationality, membership in a particular social group, or political opinion, or (B) in such special circumstances as the President after appropriate consultation . . . may specify. . . . The term "refugee" does not include any person who ordered, incited, assisted, or otherwise participated in the persecution of any person on account of race, religion, nationality, membership in a particular social group, or political opinion. . . .

Sec. 207. (a) (1) Except as provided in subsection (b), the number of refugees who may be admitted under this section in fiscal year 1980, 1981, or 1982, may not exceed fifty thousand unless the President determines, before the beginning of the fiscal year and after appropriate consultation . . . that admission of a specific number of refugees in excess of such number is justified by humanitarian concerns or is otherwise in the national interest.

(2) Except as provided in subsection (b), the number of refugees who may be admitted under this section in any fiscal year after fiscal year 1982 shall be such number as the President determines, before the beginning of the fiscal year and after appropriate consultation, is justified by humanitarian concerns or is otherwise in the national interest.

(3) Admissions under this subsection shall be allocated among refugees of special humanitarian concern to the United States in accordance with a determination made by the President after appropriate consultation.

(b) If the President determines, after appropriate consultation, that (1) an unforeseen emergency refugee situation exists, (2) the admission of certain refugees in response to the emergency refugee situation is justified by grave humanitarian concern or is otherwise in the national interest, and (3) the admission to the United States of these refugees cannot be accomplished under subsection (a), the President may fix a number of refugees to be admitted to the United States during the succeeding period (not to exceed twelve months) in response to the emergency refugee situation and such admissions shall be allocated among refugees of special humanitarian concern to the United States in accordance with a determination made by the President after the appropriate consultation provided under this subsection. . . .

(4) The refugee status of any alien (and of the spouse or child of the alien) may be terminated by the Attorney General pursuant to such regulations as the Attorney General may prescribe if the Attorney General determines that alien was not in fact a refugee within the meaning of subsection 101 (a) (42) at the time of the alien's admission.

(d)(1) Before the start of each fiscal year the President shall report to the Committees of the Judiciary of the House of Representatives and of the Senate regarding the foreseeable number of refugees who will be in need of resettlement during the fiscal year and the anticipated allocation of refugee admissions during the fiscal year. . . .

Sec. 208. (a) The Attorney General shall establish a procedure for an alien physically present in the U. S. or at a land border or port of entry . . . to apply for asylum, and the alien may be granted asylum in the discretion of the Attorney General if the Attorney General determines that such alien is a refugee within the meaning of section 101(a)(42)(a). . . .

Sec. 209. (b) Not more than five thousand of the refugee admissions authorized under section 207(a) in any fiscal year may be made available by the Attorney General . . .

Sec. 203. (a) Subsection (a) of section 201 of the Immigration and Nationality Act . . . is amended to read as follows:

(a) Exclusive of special immigrants in section 101(a)(27), immediate relatives specified in subsection (b) of this section, and aliens who are admitted or granted asylum under section 207 or 208, the number of aliens born in any foreign country or dependent area who may be issued immigrant visas or who may otherwise acquire the status of an alien lawfully admitted to the United States for permanent residence, shall not in any of the first three quarters of any fiscal year exceed . . . seventy-two thousand and shall not in any fiscal year exceed two hundred and seventy thousand. . . .

(h)(1) The Attorney General shall not deport or return any alien (other than an alien described in section 241(a)(19) to a country if the Attorney General determines that such alien's life or freedom would be threatened in such country on account of race, religion, nationality, membership in a particular social group, or political opinion. . . .

Sec. 204 (2) The Attorney General shall establish the asylum procedure referred to in section 208(a) of the Immigration and Nationality Act (as added by section 201(b) of this title) not later than June 1, 1980. . . .

Sec. 301(a) The President shall appoint, by and with the advice and consent of the Senate, a United States Coordinator for Refugee Affairs (hereinafter referred to as the "Coordinator").

The Coordinator shall have the rank of Ambassador-at-Large.

Executive Summary Recommendations of the Select Commission on Immigration and Refugee Policy, 1981

Of great importance to the reform of immigration policy was the report of the Select Commission on Immigration and Refugee Policy (SCIRP). Begun in the final days of the Carter administration, the commission was a joint presidential and congressionally appointed commission that began its work in 1979. It thoroughly studied immigration law and, more particularly, the problem of illegal immigration. It issued its Final Report *in 1981, and its recommendations formed the basis of subsequent legislative action by the Congress throughout the 1980s and even into the 1990s. I here present some of the major recommendations of the SCIRP's* Final Report.

The Select Commission recommends that:

1. The United States work with other nations and principal international organizations to collect information and research on migratory flows and treatment of international migration.

2. The United States expand bilateral consultation with other governments, especially Mexico and other regional neighbors regarding migration.

3. Border patrol funding levels be raised to provide for a substantial increase in the number and training of personnel, replacement sensor systems . . . and other needed equipment.

4. That regional border enforcement posts be established to

coordinate work with the INS, the U.S. Customs Service, the DEA, and the U.S. Coast Guard in the interdiction of both undocumented/illegal migrants and illicit goods, specifically narcotics.

5. That high priority be given to the training of INS officers to familiarize them with the rights of aliens and U.S. citizens and to help them deal with persons of other cultural backgrounds.

6. That legislation be passed making it illegal for employers to hire undocumented workers.

7. That a program to legalize illegal/undocumented aliens now in the U.S. be adopted.

8. That eligibility for legalization be determined by interrelated measurements of residence—date of entry and length of continuous residence—and by specified groups of excludability that are appropriate to the legalization program.

9. That voluntary agencies and community organizations be given a significant role in the legalization program.

10. An annual ceiling of 350,000 numerically limited immigrant visas with an additional 100,000 visas available for the first five years to . . . allow backlogs to be cleared.

11. That a substantial number of visas be set aside for reunifying spouses and unmarried sons and daughters and it should be given top priority in the numerically limited family reunification. . . .

12. That country ceilings apply to all numerically limited family reunification preferences. . . .

13. That "special" immigrants remain a numerically exempt group but be placed within the independent category.

14. Creating a small, numerically limited subcategory within the independent category to provide for the immigration of certain investors.

15. That specific labor market criteria should be established by the selection of independent immigrants. . . .

16. A fixed-percentage limit to the independent immigration from any one country.

17. That U.S. allocation of refugee numbers include both geographic considerations and specific refugee characteristics. . . .

18. That state and local governments be involved in planning for initial refugee resettlement and that . . . a federal program of impact aid [be established] to minimize the financial. . . .

19. That refugee achievement of self-sufficiency and adjustment to living in the U.S. be reaffirmed as the goal of resettlement.

Source: Select Commission on Immigration and Refugee Policy, *Final Report* (Washington, DC: U.S. Government Printing Office, March 1, 1981), xv–xxxii.

INS v. Chadha et al.
(462 U.S. 919 [1983])

In 1983, the U.S. Supreme Court rendered a decision in an immigration case that had importance beyond the immediate issue of immigration law: INS v. Chadha et al. *In this case, a class-action suit was filed against the INS over its deportation proceedings. The Court ruled that a use by the House of Representative of the "legislative veto" of executive branch (that is, INS) rules and regulations was unconstitutional. The following is a summary of that decision.*

Decision: One-house congressional veto provision in 244(c)(2) of Immigration and Nationality Act held unconstitutional.

Summary:

An immigration judge suspended an alien's deportation pursuant to 244(c)(1) of the Immigration and Nationality Act (8 U.S.C.S. 1254(c)(1)). The United States House of Representatives passed a resolution vetoing the suspension pursuant to 244(c)(2) of the Act (8 USC 1254(c)(2)), which authorizes one House of Congress to invalidate the decision of the executive branch to allow a particular deportable alien to remain in the United States. The immigration judge reopened the deportation proceedings to implement the House order, and the alien was ordered deported. The Board of Immigration Appeals dismissed the alien's appeal, holding that it had no power to declare unconstitutional an Act of Congress. The United States Court of Appeals for the Ninth Circuit held that the House was without constitutional authority to order the alien's deportation and that 244(c)(2) violated the constitutional doctrine of separation of powers (634 F2nd 408).

On appeal, the United States Supreme Court affirmed. In an opinion by Chief Justice Burger, joined by Justices Brennan, Marshall, Blackmun, Stevens, and O'Connor, it was held that the legislative veto provision in 244(c)(2) was unconstitutional since the one-house veto was legislative in purpose and effect and subject to the procedures set out in Article I of the Constitution requiring passage by a majority of both Houses and present-ment to the President.

Justice Powell, concurring in the judgment, expressed the view that the case should be decided on a narrower ground and declared that when Congress finds that a particular person does not satisfy the statutory criteria for permanent residence it has assumed a judicial function in violation of the principle of sepa-ration of powers.

Justice White dissented, expressing the view that the leg-islative veto is an important if not indispensable political inven-tion and that neither Article I nor the doctrine of separation of powers is violated by this mechanism.

Justice Rehnquist joined by Justice White, dissenting, ex-pressed the view that 244(c)(2) was not severable from the rest of the statute.

Source: Briefs of Counsel, p. 1516, see *infra.*, *U.S. Supreme Court Reports*, 77 L Ed 2nd: 317–318.

Jean et al. v. Nelson
(472 U.S. 846 [1985])

In 1985, another class-action suit against the INS reached the U.S. Supreme Court. This case, Jean et al. v. Nelson, *concerned the INS's denial of parole to undocumented Haitian aliens, who had been ruled to be "economic refugees" and therefore excluded from parole status. A fed-eral district court ruled in favor of the Haitians on the basis that the INS's decision to detain the aliens without parole had been made on the basis of race and national origin and was thus in violation of the equal protection clause of the Fifth Amendment to the Constitution. The Supreme Court affirmed the judgment of the appeals court, which, al-though rejecting the constitutional claim, accorded relief on the basis of INS regulation, remanding the case to the district court to ensure that the INS exercised its discretion in parole decisions in a nondiscrimina-tory manner. The following extract presents a summary of the case and decision of the Supreme Court.*

Decision: Court of Appeals held to have improperly reached constitutional issue in deciding case challenging INS' denial of parole to undocumented Haitian aliens.

Summary:

The named representatives of a class of undocumented and

unadmitted aliens from Haiti brought suit against the Commissioner of the Immigration and Naturalization Service (INS) in a Federal District Court, alleging in part that they had been detained without parole by INS officials on the basis of race and national origin, in violation of the equal protection guarantee of the Fifth Amendment to the United States Constitution. The District Court rejected the constitutional claim (544 F Supp 973), but a panel of the United States Court of Appeals for the Eleventh Circuit held that the Fifth Amendment's equal protection guarantee applied to the parole of unadmitted aliens (711 F2nd 1455). After a rehearing en banc, the Court of Appeals held that the Fifth Amendment did not apply to the consideration of unadmitted aliens for parole. Although rejecting the constitutional claim, the Court of Appeals accorded relief based on the applicable INS regulation (8 CFR 212.5), remanding to the District Court to ensure that the INS exercised its discretion in making parole decisions in an individualized and nondiscriminatory manner (727 F2d 957).

On certiorari, the United States Supreme Court affirmed the judgment remanding the case to the District Court. In the opinion of Justice Rehnquist, and joined by Justices White, Blackmun, Powell, Stevens, and O'Connor, it was held that the Court of Appeals should not have reached and decided the parole question on constitutional grounds, since the applicable statute and regulations were facially neutral and since the INS' parole discretion thereunder did not extend to considerations of race or national origin.

Justice Marshall, joined by Justice Brennan, dissented, expressing the view that there was no principled way to avoid reaching the constitutional issue and that aliens have a Fifth Amendment right to parole decisions free from invidious discrimination based on race or national origin.

Source: Briefs of Counsel, p. 826, see *infra., U.S. Supreme Court Reports,* 86 L Ed 2nd: 664–665.

The Immigration Reform and Control Act of 1986 (100 Stat. 3360)

The Immigration Reform and Control Act of 1986, commonly known as IRCA, had a lengthy and tangled history, as has already been discussed. Finally, in 1986, a joint Conference Committee agreed on a package that could be enacted into law. This extract offers portions of the major provisions of IRCA.

Title I—Control of Illegal Immigration
Sec. 101. Control of Unlawful Employment of Aliens
(a) In General
(1) In General—It is unlawful for a person or other entity to hire, or to recruit or refer for a fee, for employment in the United States—

(A) an alien knowing the alien is an unauthorized alien (as defined in subsection (h)(3). . . .

(B) an individual without complying with the requirements of subsection (b).

(2) Continuing employment—It is unlawful for a person or other entity, after hiring an alien for employment in accordance with paragraph (1), to continue to employ the alien in the United States knowing the alien is (or has become) an unauthorized alien with respect to such employment.

(3) Defense—A person or entity that establishes that it has complied in good faith with the requirements of subsection (b) with respect to the hiring, recruiting, or referral for employment of an alien in the United States has established an affirmative defense that the person or entity has not violated paragraph (1)(A) with respect to such hiring, recruiting, or referral.

(4) Use of Labor Through Contract—For the purposes of this section, a person or other entity who uses a contract, subcontract, or exchange, entered into, renegotiated, or extended after the date of the enactment of this section, to obtain the labor of an alien in the United States knowing that the alien is an unauthorized alien . . . with respect to performing such labor, shall be considered to have hired the alien for employment in the United States in violation of paragraph (1)(A).

(5) Use of State Employment Agency Documentation— For the purposes of paragraph (1)(B) and (3), a person or entity shall be deemed to have complied with the requirements of subsection (b) with respect to the hiring of an individual who was referred for such employment by a State employment agency. . . .

(b) Employment Verification System—The requirements referred to in paragraphs (1)(B) and (3) are, in the case of a person or other entity hiring, recruiting, or referring an individual for employment in the United States, the requirements specified in the following three paragraphs:

(1) Attestation After Examination of Documentation—

(A) In General—The person or entity must attest, under penalty of perjury and on a form designated or established by the Attorney General by regulation, that it has verified that the individual is not an unauthorized alien by examining—

(i) a document described in subparagraph (B), or

(ii) a document described in subparagraph (C) and (D).

(B) Documents Establishing Both Employment Authorization and Identity—A document described in this subparagraph is an individual's—

(i) United States passport;

(ii) certificate of United States Citizenship;

(iii) certificate of naturalization;

(iv) unexpired foreign passport, if the passport has an appropriate, unexpired endorsement of the Attorney General authorizing the individual's employment in the United States; or

(v) resident alien card or other alien registration, if the card—

(I) contains a photograph of the individual. . . .

(II) is evidence of authorization of employment in the United States

(C) Documents Evidencing Employment Authorization—A document described . . . is an

(i) social security account number card. . . .

(ii) certificate of birth in the United States or establishing United States nationality at birth;

(iii) other documents evidencing authorization of employment in the United States which the Attorney General finds, by regulation, to be acceptable for the purposes of this section.

(D) Documents establishing identity of an individual—A document described in this subparagraph is an individual's

(i) driver's license or similar document issued for the purpose of identification by a State, if it contains a photograph of the individual. . . .

(ii) in the case of individuals under 16 years of age or in a State which does not provide for issuance of an identification document . . . referred to in clause (ii), documentation of personal identity of such type as the Attorney General finds, by regulation, provides a reliable means of identification. . . .

(3) Definition of Unauthorized Alien—As used in this section, the term "unauthorized alien" means, with respect to the employment of an alien at a particular time, that the alien is not at that time either (A) an alien lawfully admitted for permanent residence, or (B) authorized to be so employed by this Act or by the Attorney General. . . .

Deferral of Enforcement with Respect to Seasonal Agricultural Services—

(A) In General—Except as provided in subparagraph (B), before the end of the application period, it is unlawful for a person or entity (including a farm labor contractor) or an agent of such a person or entity, to recruit an unauthorized alien (other than an alien described in clause (ii) who is outside the United States to enter the United States to perform seasonal agricultural services.

(ii) Exception—Clause (i) shall not apply to an alien who the person or entity reasonably believes to meet the requirements of section 210(a)(2) of this Act (relating to the performance of seasonal agricultural services).

(j) General Accounting Office Reports—

(1) In General—Beginning one year after the date of enactment of this Act, and at intervals of one year thereafter for a period of three years after such date, the Comptroller General of the United States shall prepare and transmit to the Congress and to the task force established under subsection (k) a report describing the results of a review of the implementation and enforcement of this section during the preceding twelve-month period, for the purpose of determining if—

(A) such provisions have been carried out satisfactorily;

(B) a pattern of discrimination has resulted against citizens or nationals of the United States or against eligible workers seeking employment; and

(C) an unnecessary regulatory burden has been created for employers hiring such workers.

(k) Review by Task force—

(1) Establishment of Task force—The Attorney General, jointly with the Chairman of the Commission on Civil Rights and the Chairman of the Equal Employment Opportunity Commission, shall establish a task force to review each report of the Comptroller General.

(2) Recommendations to Congress—If the report transmitted includes a determination that the implementation of this section has resulted in a pattern of discrimination in employment (against other than unauthorized aliens) on the basis of national origin, the task force shall, taking into consideration any recommendations in the report, report to Congress recommendations for such legislation as may be appropriate to deter or remedy such discrimination. . . .

(l) Termination Date for Employer Sanctions—

(1) If Report of Widespread Discrimination and Congressional Approval.—The provisions of this section shall terminate 30 days after receipt of the last report required to be transmitted under subsection (j), if—

(A) the Comptroller General determines, and so reports . . . that a widespread pattern of discrimination has resulted against citizens or nationals of the United States or against eligible workers seeking employment solely from the implementation of this section; and

(B) there is enacted, within such period of 30 calendar days, a joint resolution stating in substance that the Congress approves the findings of the Comptroller General contained in such report.

(2) Senate Procedures for Consideration—Any joint resolution referred to in clause (B) of paragraph (1) shall be considered in the Senate in accordance with subsection (n). . . .

Sec. 111.(b) Increased Authorization of Appropriations for INS and EOIR—In addition to any other amounts authorized to be appropriated, in order to carry out this Act, there are authorized to be appropriated to the Department of Justice—

(1) for the [INS], for FY 1987, $12,000,000, and for FY 1988, $15,000,000 . . . to provide for an increase in the border patrol personnel . . . so that the average level of such personnel in each fiscal year 1987 and 1988 is at least 50 per cent higher than such level for fiscal year 1986. . . .

Title II—Legalization

Sec. 201. Legalization of Status . . .

Sec. 245A. (a) Temporary Resident Status—The Attorney General shall adjust the status of an alien to that of an alien lawfully admitted for temporary residence if the alien meets the following requirements:

(1) Timely Application—

(A) During Application Period—Except as provided in subparagraph (B), the alien must apply for such adjustment during the 12-month period beginning on a date (not later than 180 days after the date of enactment of this section) designated by the Attorney General. . . .

(2) Continuous Lawful Residence Since 1982—

(A) In General—The alien must establish that he entered the United States before January 1, 1982, and that he has resided continuously in the United States in an unlawful status since such date and through the date the application is filed under this subsection.

(B) Nonimmigrants—In the case of an alien who entered the United States as a nonimmigrant before January 1, 1982, the alien must establish that the alien's period of authorized stay as a nonimmigrant expired before such date through the passage of time or the alien's unlawful status was known to the Government as of such date. . . .

(b) Subsequent Adjustment to Permanent Residence and Nature of Temporary Resident Status—

(1) Adjustment to Permanent Residence—The Attorney General shall adjust the status of any alien provided lawful temporary resident status under subsection (a) to that of an alien lawfully admitted for permanent residence if the alien meets the following requirements:

(A) Timely Application After One Year's Residence—The alien must apply for such adjustment during the one-year period beginning with the nineteenth month that begins after the date the alien was granted such temporary status.

(B) Continuous Residence—the alien must establish that he has continuously resided in the United States since the date the alien was granted such temporary resident status.

(C) Admissible as Immigrant—The alien must establish that he—

(i) is admissible to the United States as an immigrant . . . and

(ii) has not been convicted of any felony or three or more misdemeanors committed in the United States.

(D) Basic Citizenship Skills—The alien must demonstrate that he either—

(I) meets the requirements of section 312 (relating to minimal understanding of ordinary English and a knowledge and understanding of the history and government of the United States), or

(II) is satisfactorily pursuing a course of study (recognized by the Attorney General) to achieve an understanding of English and such knowledge and understanding of the history and government of the United States . . .

(h) Temporary Disqualification of Newly Legalized Aliens from Receiving Certain Public Welfare Assistance—

(1) In General—During the five year period beginning on the date an alien was granted lawful temporary resident status under subsection (a). . . . (A) except as provided in paragraphs (2) and (3), the alien is not eligible for—

(i) any program of financial assistance furnished under Federal law . . .

(ii) medical assistance under a State plan approved under Title XIX of the Social Security Act, and

(iii) assistance under the Food Stamp Act of 1977; and

(B) a State or political subdivision therein may, to the extent consistent with paragraph (A) and paragraphs (2) and (3), provide that an alien is not eligible for the programs of financial assistance or for medical assistance described in subparagraph (A) (ii) furnished under the law of that State or political subdivision. . . .

Title III—Reform of Legal Immigration, Part A—Temporary Agricultural Workers

Sec. 301. H-2A Agricultural Workers

(a) Providing New "H-2A" Nonimmigrant Classification for Temporary Agricultural Labor—

Paragraph (15) (H) of section 101 (a) (8 U.S.C. 1101(a)) is amended by striking out "to perform temporary services or labor," in clause (ii) and inserting in lieu thereof, "(a) to perform agricultural labor or services, as defined by the Secretary of Labor in regulations and including agricultural labor defined in section 3121(g) of the Internal Revenue Code of 1954 and agriculture as defined in section 3(f) of the Fair Labor Standards Act of 1938 . . . or a temporary or seasonal nature, or (b) to perform other temporary service or labor."

(b) Involvement of Departments of Labor and Agriculture in H-2A Program—Section 214(c) (8 U.S.C. 1184(c)) is amended by adding to the end the following: "For purposes of this subsection with respect to nonimmigrants described in section 101(a)(15)(H)(ii)(a), the term 'appropriate agencies of Government' means the Department of Labor and includes the Department of Agriculture. The provisions of section 216 shall apply to the question of importing any alien as nonimmigrant under section 101(a)(15)(H)(ii)(a)."

The Immigration Act of 1990 (104 Stat. 4981)

In 1990, Congress moved to enact reform of the laws and processes affecting legal immigration. In doing so, it also modified or clarified certain provisions within IRCA. It set new ceilings for a worldwide level of immigration, especially as related to the reunification of immediate family members, redefined the preference system with respect to family

reunification and to employment, and created a new category of prefer-
ence called "diversity immigrants." It also established a Commission on
Immigration Reform and provided for a temporary stay of deportation
for certain aliens for family unity and temporary protected status. Some
of the key provisions of this rather lengthy act are presented here.

Sec. 201. (a) In General—Exclusive of aliens described in
subsection (b), aliens born in a foreign state or dependent area
who may be issued immigrant visas or who may otherwise acquire the status of an alien lawfully admitted to the United
States for permanent residence are limited to
(1) family-sponsored immigrants described in section
203(a) . . . in a number not to exceed in any fiscal year the number specified in subsection (c) for that year, and not to exceed in
any of the first three quarters of any fiscal year 27 percent of the
worldwide level under such subsection for all such fiscal year;
(2) employment-based immigrants described in subsection
203(b) . . . in a number not to exceed. . . . in any of the first 3 quarters of any fiscal year 27 percent of the worldwide level, . . . and
(3) for fiscal years beginning with fiscal year 1995, diversity
immigrants described in section 203(c) . . . in a number not to exceed in any fiscal year the number specified in subsection (e) for
that year, and not to exceed in any of the first three quarters of
any fiscal year 27 percent of the worldwide level under such
subsection for all such fiscal year.
(2)(A)(i) Immediate Relatives—For purposes of this subsection, the term "immediate relatives" means the children, spouses,
and parents of a citizen of the United States, except that, in the
case of parents, such citizens be at least 21 years of age. In the
case of an alien who was the spouse of a citizen of the United
States for at least 2 years at the time of the citizen's death and
was not legally separated from the citizen at the time of the citizens death, the alien shall be considered, for the purpose of this
subsection, to remain an immediate relative after the date of the
citizen's death. . . . and only until the date the spouse remarries.
(c) Worldwide Level of Family-Sponsored Immigrants— . . .
(i) 480,000 minus
(ii) the number computed under paragraph (2), plus
(iii) the number (if any) computed under paragraph (3).
(B)(i) For each of fiscal years 1992, 1993, and 1994, 465,000
shall be substituted for 480,000 in subparagraph (A)(i).
(ii) In no case shall the number computed under subparagraph (A) be less than 226,000 . . .

(d) Worldwide Level of Employment-Based Immigrants—
(1) The worldwide level of employment-based immigrants under this subsection for a fiscal year is equal to—

(A) 140,000 plus

(B) the number computed under paragraph (2). . . .

(e) Worldwide Level of Diversity Immigrants—The worldwide level of diversity immigrants is equal to 55,000 for each fiscal year.

Sec. 102. Per Country Levels.

Sec. 202 (8 U.S.C. 1152) is amended—(1) by amending subsection (a) to read as follows:

(a) Per Country Level—

(1) Nondiscrimination—Except as specifically provided in paragraph (2) and in sections 101(a)(27), 201(b)(2)(A)(i), and 203, no person shall receive any preference or priority or be discriminated against in the issuance of an immigrant visa because of a person's race, sex, nationality, place of birth, or place of residence.

(2) Per Country Levels for Family-Sponsored and Employment-Based Immigrants—

Subject to paragraphs (3) and (4), the total number of immigrant visas made available to natives of any single foreign state or dependent area under subsections (a) and (b) of section 203 in any fiscal year may not exceed 7 percent (in the case of a single foreign state) or 2 percent (in the case of a dependent area) of the total number of such visas made available under such subsection in that fiscal year.

Subtitle B—Preference System

Part I—Family-Sponsored Immigrants

Sec. 111. Family-Sponsored Immigrants

Sec. 203 (8 U.S.C. 1153) is amended—

(1) by redesignating subsections (b) and (e) as subsections (d) through (g), respectively, and

(2) by striking subsection (a) and inserting the following:

(a) Preference Allocation for Family-Sponsored Immigrants.—Aliens subject to the worldwide level specified . . . for family-sponsored immigrants shall be allotted visas as follows:

(1) Unmarried sons and daughters of citizens . . . in a number not to exceed 23,400 plus any visas required for the class specified in paragraph (4).

(2) Spouses and unmarried sons and unmarried daughters of permanent resident aliens . . . shall be allocated visas in a number not to exceed 114,200 plus the number (if any) by which

such worldwide level exceeds 226,000 plus any visas not required for the class specified in paragraph (1); except that not less than 77 percent of such visa numbers shall be allocated to aliens described in subparagraph (A).

(3) Married sons and married daughters of immigrants— . . .in a number not to exceed 23,400, plus any visas not required for the classes specified in paragraphs (1) and (2).

(4) Brothers and sisters of citizens— . . .in a number not to exceed 65,000, plus any visas not required for the classes specified in paragraphs (1) through (3). . . .

(c) Legalized Alien Defined—In this section, the term "legalized alien" means an alien lawfully admitted for temporary or permanent residence who was provided—

(1) temporary or permanent residence status under section 210 of the Immigration and Nationality Act,

(2) temporary or permanent residence status under section 245A of the Immigration and Nationality Act, or

(3) permanent residence status under section 202 of the Immigration Reform and Control Act of 1986.

Part 2—Employment-Based Immigrants

Sec. 121. Employment-Based Immigrants.

(a) In General—Section 203 (8 U.S.C. 1153) is amended by inserting after subsection (a), as inserted by section 111, the following new subsection:

(b) Preference Allocation for Employment-Based Immigrants.—Aliens subject to the worldwide level specified in section 201(d) for employment-based immigrants in a fiscal year shall be allocated visas as follows:

(1) Priority Workers.—Visas shall first be made available in a number not to exceed 40,000, plus any visas not required for the classes specified in paragraphs (4) and (5), to qualified immigrants who are aliens described in any of the following subparagraphs (A) through (C):

(A) Aliens with extraordinary ability—in sciences, arts, education, business, or athletics which has been demonstrated by sustained national or international acclaim and whose achievements have been recognized in the field through extensive documentation.

(B) Outstanding Professors and Researchers . . .

(C) Certain Multinational Executives and Managers . . .

(2) Alien members of Professions holding advanced degrees or aliens of exceptional ability . . .

(3) Skilled workers, professionals, and other workers . . .

(4) Certain special immigrants—Visas shall be made available, in a number not to exceed 10,000 to qualified special immigrants described in section 101(a)(27) . . . of which not more than 5,000 may be made available in any fiscal year to special immigrants described in subclause (II) or (III) of section 101(a)(27)(C)(ii).

(5) Employment Creation—

(A) In General—Visas shall be made available, in a number not to exceed 10,000, to qualified immigrants seeking to enter the U. S. for the purpose of engaging in a new commercial enterprise—

(i) which the alien has established,

(ii) in which such alien has invested . . . or is actively in the process of investing, capital in an amount not less than the amount specified in subparagraph (C), and

(iii) which will benefit the United States economy and create full-time employment for not fewer than 10 United States citizens or aliens lawfully admitted for permanent residence or other immigrants lawfully authorized to be employed in the United States (other than the immigrant and the immigrant's spouse, sons, or daughters).

Part 3—Diversity Immigrants

Sec. 131. Diversity Immigrants

Sec. 203, as amended by sections 111 and 121 of this Act, is further amended by inserting after subsection (b) the following new subsection:

(c) Diversity Immigrants—

(1) In General.—Except as provided in paragraph (2), aliens subject to the worldwide level specified in section 201(e) for diversity immigrants shall be allotted visas each fiscal year as follows:

(A) Determination of Preference Immigration—The Attorney General shall determine for the most recent previous 5-year period for which data are available, the total number of aliens who are natives of each foreign state and who (i) were admitted or otherwise provided lawful permanent resident status . . . and (ii) were subject to the numerical limitations of section 201(a) . . . or who were admitted or otherwise provided lawful permanent resident status as an immediate relative or other alien described in section 201(b)(2). . . .

(iv) Redistribution of Unused Visa Numbers—If the Secretary of State estimates that the number of immigrant visas to be issued to natives in any region for the fiscal year under this paragraph is less than the number of immigrant visas made available to such natives under this paragraph for the fiscal year, subject to clause (v), the excess visa numbers shall be made available to natives (other than the natives of a high-admission state) of the other regions in proportion to the percentages otherwise specified in clauses (ii) and (iii).

Subtitle C—Commission and Information

Sec. 141. Commission of Legal Immigration Reform.

(a) Establishment and Composition of Commission.—(1) Effective October 1, 1991, there is established a Commission on Legal Immigration Reform . . . which shall be composed of 9 members to be appointed as follows:

(A) One member who shall serve as Chairman, to be appointed by the President.

(B) Two members to be appointed by the Speaker of the House of Representatives. . . .

(C) Two members to be appointed by the Minority Leader of the House . . .

(D) Two members to be appointed by the Majority Leader of the Senate. . . .

(E) Two members appointed by the Minority Leader of the Senate. . . .

Title III—Family Unity and Temporary Protected Status

Sec. 301. Family Unity.

(a) Temporary Stay of Deportation and Work Authorization for Certain Eligible Immigrants.

The Attorney General shall provide that in the case of an alien who is an eligible immigrant . . . who has entered the United States before [May 5, 1988], who has resided in the United States on such date, and who is not lawfully admitted for permanent residence, the alien—

(1) may not be deported . . . and . . . shall be granted authorization to engage in employment

(2) The term "legalized alien" means an alien lawfully admitted for temporary or permanent residence who was provided—

(A) such under section 210 of the Immigration and Nationality Act;

(B) temporary or permanent residence status under section 245A of the Immigration and Nationality Act, or

(C) permanent residence status under section 202 of the Immigration Reform and Control Act of 1986. . . .

California's Proposition 187 (1994)

Despite the national legislation intended to curb illegal immigration, the size of that flow seemed unabated, and the political pressure to do more to address the problem increased during the 1990s. States that received the largest number of legal and illegal immigrants—California, Florida, and Texas—sued the federal government in their respective federal district courts for the billions of dollars that they estimated they were having to pay in extra costs for education, health care, and law enforcement for illegal immigrants and their children. In 1994, California also attempted to legislatively reduce the draw of its economy and services and to "send a message to Congress" by passing an anti-immigration initiative commonly referred to as Proposition 187. It is presented below in full.

Section 1. Findings and Declaration

The People of California find and declare as follows:

That they have suffered and are suffering economic hardship by the presence of illegal aliens in the state. That they have suffered and are suffering personal injury and damage by the criminal conduct of illegal aliens in the state. That they have a right to the protection of their government from any person or persons entering this country unlawfully.

Therefore, the People of California declare their intention to provide for cooperation between their agencies of state and local government with the federal government, and to establish a system of required notification by and between such agencies to prevent illegal aliens in the United States from receiving benefits or public services in the State of California.

Section 2. Manufacture, Distribution or Sale of False Citizenship or Resident Alien Documents: Crime and Punishment.

Section 113. Is added to the Penal Code, to read:

Section 113. Any person who manufactures, distributes or sells false documents to conceal the true citizenship or resident alien status of another is guilty of a felony and shall be punished by imprisonment in the state prison for five years or by a fine of seventy-five thousand dollars.

Section 3. Use of False Citizenship or Resident Alien Documents: Crime and Punishment.

Section 114. Is added to the Penal Code, to read:

Section 114. Any person who uses false documents to conceal his or her true citizenship or resident alien status is guilty of a felony, and shall be punished by imprisonment in a state prison for five years or by a fine of twenty-five thousand dollars.

Section 4. Law Enforcement Cooperation with INS.

Section 834b is added to the Penal Code, to read:

Section 834b. (a) Every law enforcement agency in California shall fully cooperate with the United States Immigration and Naturalization Service regarding any person who is arrested if he or she is suspected of being present in the United States in violation of federal immigration laws.

(b) With respect to any such person who is arrested, and suspected of being present in the United States in violation of federal immigration laws, every law enforcement agency shall do the following:

(1). Attempt to verify the legal status of such person as a citizen of the United States, an alien lawfully admitted as a permanent resident, an alien lawfully admitted for a temporary period of time or as an alien who is present in the United States in violation of immigration laws. The verification process may include, but shall not be limited to, questioning the person regarding his or her date and place of birth and entry into the United States, and demanding documentation to indicate his or her legal status.

(2). Notify the person of his or her apparent status as an alien who is present in the United States in violation of federal immigration laws and inform him or her that, apart from any criminal justice precedings [sic], he or she must obtain legal status or leave the United States.

(3). Notify the Attorney General of California and the United States Immigration and Naturalization Service of the apparent illegal status and provide any additional information that may be requested by any other public entity.

(c) Any legislative, administrative, or other action by a city, county, or other legally authorized local governmental entity with jurisdictional boundaries, or by a law enforcement agency, to prevent or limit the cooperation required by subdivision (a) is expressly prohibited.

Section 5. Exclusion of Illegal Aliens from Public Social Services.

Section 10001.5. is added to the Welfare and Institutions Code, to read:

Section 10001.5. (a) In order to carry out the intention of the People of California that only citizens of the United States and aliens lawfully admitted to the United States may receive the benefits of public social services and to ensure that all persons employed in the providing of those services shall diligently protect public funds from misuse, the provisions of this section are adopted.

(b) A person shall not receive any public social services to which he or she may not otherwise be entitled until the legal status of that person has been verified as one of the following:

(1) A citizen of the United States.

(2) An alien lawfully admitted as a permanent resident.

(3) An alien lawfully admitted for a temporary period of time.

(c) If any public entity in this state to whom a person has applied for public social services determines or reasonably suspects, based upon the information provided to it, that the person is an alien in the United States in violation of federal law, the following procedures shall be followed by the public entity:

(1). The entity shall not provide the person with benefits or services.

(2). The entity shall, in writing, notify the person of his or her apparent illegal immigration status, and that the person must either obtain legal status or leave the United States.

(3). The entity shall also notify the State Director of Social Services, the Attorney General of California and the United States Immigration and Naturalization Service of the apparent illegal status, and shall provide any additional information that may be requested by any other public entity.

Section 6. Exclusion of Illegal Aliens from Publicly Funded Health Care.

Chapter 1.3 (commencing with Section 130) is added to Part 1 of Division 1 of the Health and Safety Code to read:

Chapter 1.3. Publicly-Funded Health Care Services.

Section 130. (a) In order to carry out the intention of the People of California that, excepting emergency medical care as required by federal law, only citizens of the United States and aliens lawfully admitted to the United States may receive the benefits of publicly-funded health care, and to ensure that all persons employed in the providing of those services shall diligently protect public funds from misuse, the provisions of this section are adopted.

(b) A person shall not receive any health care service from a publicly-funded health care facility to which he or she is otherwise entitled until the legal status of that person has been verified as one of the following:

(1). A citizen of the United States.

(2). An alien lawfully admitted as a permanent resident.

(3). An alien lawfully admitted for a temporary period of time.

(c) If any publicly-funded health care facility in this state from whom a person seeks health care services, other than emergency medical care as required by federal law, determines or reasonably suspects, based on the information provided it, that the person is an alien in the United States in violation of the federal law, the following procedures shall be followed by the facility:

(1). The facility shall not provide the person with services.

(2). The facility shall, in writing, notify the person of his or her apparent illegal immigration status, and that the person must either obtain legal status or leave the United States.

(3). The facility shall also notify the State Director of Social Services, the Attorney General of California and the United States Immigration and Naturalization Service of the apparent illegal status, and shall provide any additional information that may be requested by any other public entity.

(d) For purposes of this section "publicly-funded health care facility" shall be defined as specified in Section 1200 and 1250 of the Health and Safety Code as of January 1, 1993.

Section 7. Exclusion of Illegal Aliens from Public Elementary and Secondary Schools.

Section 48215. Is added to the Education Code to read:

Section 48215. (a) No public elementary or secondary school shall admit, or permit the attendance of, any child who is not a citizen of the United States, an alien lawfully admitted as a permanent resident, or a person who is otherwise authorized under federal law to be present. . . .

(b) Commencing January 1, 1995, each school district shall verify the legal status of each child enrolling in the school district for the first time in order to ensure the enrollment or attendance only of citizens, aliens lawfully admitted as permanent residents, or persons who are otherwise authorized under federal law to be present in the United States.

(d) By January 1, 1996, each school district shall also have verified the legal status of each parent or guardian of each child referred to in subdivision (b) and (c) above, to determine whether such parent or guardian is one of the following.

(1). A citizen of the United States.

(2). An alien lawfully admitted as a permanent resident.

(3). An alien admitted lawfully for a temporary period of time.

(e) Each school district shall provide information to the State Superintendent of Public Instruction, the Attorney General of California and the United States Immigration and Naturalization Service regarding any enrollee or pupil, or parent or guardian, attending a public elementary or secondary school in the school district determined or reasonably suspected to be in violation of federal immigration laws within forty-five days after becoming aware of an apparent violation. The notice shall also be provided to the parent or legal guardian of the enrollee or pupil, and shall state that an existing pupil may not continue attending school after ninety calendar days from the date of the notice unless legal status is established.

(f) For each child who cannot establish legal status in the United States, each school district shall continue to provide education for a period of ninety days from the date of the notice. Such ninety day period shall be utilized to accomplish an orderly transition to a school in the child's country of origin. Each school district shall cooperate in this transition effort to ensure that the educational needs of the child are best served for that period of time.

Section 8. Exclusion of Illegal Aliens from Public Postsecondary Educational Institutions.

Section 66010.8. is added to the Education Code to read:

Section 66010.8. (a) No public institution of postsecondary education shall admit, enroll, or permit the attendance of any person who is not a citizen of the United States, an alien lawfully admitted as a permanent resident, in the United States, or a person who is otherwise authorized under federal law to be present in the United States.

(c) Commencing with the first term or semester that begins after January 1, 1996, and at the end of each term or semester thereafter, each public postsecondary educational institution shall verify the status of each person enrolled or in attendance at that institution in order to ensure the enrollment or attendance only of United States citizens, aliens lawfully admitted as permanent residents in the United States, and persons who are otherwise authorized under federal law to be present in the United States.

(c) No later than 45 days after the admission officer of a public postsecondary educational institution becomes aware of the application, enrollment, or attendance of a person determined to be, or who is under reasonable suspicion of being, in the United States in violation of federal immigration laws, that officer shall provide that information to the State Superintendent of Public Instruction, the Attorney General of California and the United States Immigration and Naturalization Service. The information shall be provided to the applicant, enrollee, or person admitted.

Section 9. Attorney General Cooperation with the INS.

Section 53609.65. Is added to the Government Code, to read:

Section 53609.65. Whenever the state or a city, or a county, or any other legally authorized local government entity with jurisdictional boundaries reports the presence of a person who is suspected of being present in the United States in violation of federal immigration laws to the Attorney General of California, that report shall be transmitted to the United States Immigration and Naturalization Service. The Attorney General shall be responsible for maintaining on-going and accurate records of such reports, and shall provide any additional information that may be requested by any other government entity.

Section 10. Amendment and Severability.

The statutory provisions contained in this measure may not be amended by the Legislature except to further its purposes by statute passed in each house by a roll call vote entered in the journal, two-thirds of the membership concurring, or by a statute that becomes effective only when approved by the voters. In the event that any portion of this act or the application thereof to any person or circumstances is held invalid, that invalidity shall not affect any other provision or application of the act, which can be given effect without the invalid provision or application, and to that end the provisions of this act are severable.

LULAC et al. v. Pete Wilson et al.
(908 F.Supp. 755; C.D. Cal. [1995])

The last provision of Proposition 187, as presented in the preceding document, anticipated a federal court challenge to the law's constitutionality. The challenge was immediately brought by the League of United Latin American Citizens (LULAC). The federal district court did rule that much of the law was unconstitutional. The following extract presents the summary judgment of the federal court decision on the initia-

tive measure that granted an injunction to bar the state from enforcing Proposition 187.

Public interest groups and individual citizens, in consolidated actions, brought suit for declaratory and injunctive relief to bar California Governor, Attorney General and other state actors from enforcing provisions of voter-approved California initiative measure requiring state personnel to verify immigration status of persons with whom they come into contact, report persons in United States unlawfully to state and federal officials, and deny those persons social services, health care, and education benefits. On plaintiff's motions for summary judgment, the District Court, Pfaelzer, J., held that: (1) classification, notification, cooperation and reporting provisions of the measure had direct and substantial effect on immigration, so as to be preempted by federal immigration law; (2) initiative's denial of public benefits based on federal determinations of immigration status was not impermissible regulation of immigration; (3) provision excluding illegal aliens from public elementary and secondary schools was preempted by federal law as being prohibited by equal protection clause of Fourteenth Amendment; (4) verification components of measure prohibiting public postsecondary education to persons not authorized under federal law to be in the United States were permissible; (5) provisions of measure criminalizing making and using false documents to conceal true citizenship or resident alien status were legitimate exercise of state's police power; (6) provisions denying public social services to illegal immigrants as applied to federally funded programs administered by state that awarded benefits regardless of immigration status conflicted with and was preempted by federal law; (7) provisions of measure prohibiting public postsecondary educational institutions from admitting, enrolling or permitting attendance of persons not authorized under federal law to be present in the United States were not preempted by federal law; and (8) criminal penalties contemplated by provision criminalizing manufacture, distribution, sale or use of false documents to conceal immigration status were not preempted by federal law.

Source: LULAC et al. v. Pete Wilson et al. (908 F.Supp. 755; C.D. Cal., [1995]): 787–791.

Immigration Provisions of the Welfare Reform Act of 1996

The highly favorable voter response to Proposition 187 and Governor Pete Wilson's easy margin of victory in his reelection bid did not pass unheeded by the U.S. Congress. Even though much of Proposition 187 was overturned by the federal district court decision, Congress moved to enact national legislation that essentially enforced those portions of the proposition that had been ruled unconstitutional as state infringements on the national government's sole authority to enact immigration law or as state actions preempted by existing federal law. In 1996, Congress passed and President Clinton signed into law two measures that essentially enacted the provisions of Proposition 187. Congress enacted a welfare reform act that contained several provisions related to immigrants (both legal and illegal), provisions similar in some aspects to those of Proposition 187. These immigrant-related provisions are shown in the following document.

Regarding Illegal Aliens

1. *RESTRICTIONS:* RESTRICTED FEDERAL BENEFITS FOR WHICH ILLEGAL ALIENS AND LEGAL NONIMMIGRANTS, SUCH AS TRAVELERS AND STUDENTS, COULD QUALIFY. THE BENEFITS DENIED ARE THOSE PROVIDED BY A FEDERAL AGENCY OR FEDERAL FUNDS FOR

  • Grants, contracts, loans, professional or commercial licenses
  • Retirement, welfare, health, disability, food assistance, or unemployment benefits

2. *Exceptions:* Allowed
  • Some emergency medical services under Medicaid
  • Short-term, noncash emergency disaster relief
  • Immunizations and testing for treatment for the symptoms of communicable diseases
  • Some noncash programs identified by the attorney general such as soup kitchens, counseling, and short-term shelter
  • Certain housing benefits (for existing recipients only)
  • Licenses and benefits directly related to work for which a nonimmigrant has been authorized to enter the United States
  • Certain Social Security retirement benefits protected by treaty or statute

Regarding Legal Immigrants

3. MADE MOST LEGAL IMMIGRANTS, INCLUDING THOSE ALREADY IN THE UNITED STATES, INELIGIBLE FOR SUPPLEMENTAL SECURITY INCOME (SSI) AND FOOD STAMPS UNTIL THEY BECOME CITIZENS; EXCEPT FOR:

- Refugees, those granted asylum, and aliens whose deportation was being withheld
- Those who had worked in the United States for ten years.
- Veterans and those on active military duty, as well as their spouses, and unmarried children

4. *Future immigrants:* Legal immigrants who arrived in the United States after August 22, 1996 were barred from receiving most low-income federal benefits for five years after their arrival; except:

- Refugees and those granted asylum and aliens whose deportation has been withheld, as well as Cuban and Haitian entrants
- Veterans and those on active military duty, their spouses, and minor children

A few specific programs were exempt from this ban:

- Emergency medical service under Medicaid
- Short-term, noncash emergency disaster relief
- Child nutrition, including school lunch programs, Women, Infants, Children (WIC), and the like.
- Immunization and testing for treatment of symptoms of communicable diseases
- Foster care and adoption assistance
- Noncash programs identified by the attorney general (soup kitchens, short-term shelter, and the like)
- Loans and grants for higher education
- Elementary and secondary education
- Head Start programs for pre-school children
- Assistance from the Job Training Partnership Act

5. *State options:* Allowed states to deny benefits from the welfare block grant and Medicaid and social service block grants to most legal immigrants; exemptions were the same as for SSI and food stamps. Future immigrants subject to the five-year ban noted above.

6. *Sponsors:* Expanded circumstances under which an immigrant's sponsor would be financially responsible for that individual.

7. *Reporting and verifying:* Required agencies that administer SSI, housing assistance, or the welfare block grant to report quarterly to the Immigration and Naturalization Service (INS) the names and addresses of people they knew were unlawfully in the United States.

Source: Summary by author: HR 3734—PL104–193

Immigration-Related Provisions of the Illegal Immigration Reform and Immigrant Responsibility Act of 1996

Regarding Illegal Aliens

1. *RESTRICTIONS:* RESTRICTED FEDERAL BENEFITS FOR WHICH ILLEGAL ALIENS AND LEGAL NONIMMIGRANTS, SUCH AS TRAVELERS AND STUDENTS, COULD QUALIFY. THE BENEFITS DENIED ARE THOSE PROVIDED BY A FEDERAL AGENCY OR FEDERAL FUNDS FOR

- Grants, contracts, loans, professional or commercial licenses
- Retirement, welfare, health, disability, food assistance, or unemployment benefits

2. *Exceptions:* Allowed

- Some emergency medical services under Medicaid
- Short-term, noncash emergency disaster relief
- Immunizations and testing for treatment for the symptoms of communicable diseases
- Some noncash programs identified by the attorney general such as soup kitchens, counseling, and short-term shelter
- Certain housing benefits (for existing recipients only)
- Licenses and benefits directly related to work for which a nonimmigrant has been authorized to enter the United States
- Certain Social Security retirement benefits protected by treaty or statute

Regarding Legal Immigrants

3. MADE MOST LEGAL IMMIGRANTS, INCLUDING THOSE

ALREADY IN THE UNITED STATES, INELIGIBLE FOR SUP-
PLEMENTAL SECURITY INCOME (SSI) AND FOOD STAMPS
UNTIL THEY BECOME CITIZENS; EXCEPT FOR:
- Refugees, those granted asylum, and aliens whose deportation was being withheld
- Those who had worked in the United States for ten years.
- Veterans and those on active military duty, as well as their spouses, and unmarried children

4. *Future immigrants:* Legal immigrants who arrived in the United States after August 22, 1996 were barred from receiving most low-income federal benefits for five years after their arrival; except:
- Refugees and those granted asylum and aliens whose deportation has been withheld, as well as Cuban and Haitian entrants
- Veterans and those on active military duty, their spouses, and minor children

A few specific programs were exempt from this ban:
- Emergency medical service under Medicaid
- Short-term, noncash emergency disaster relief
- Child nutrition, including school lunch programs, Women, Infants, Children (WIC), and the like.
- Immunization and testing for treatment of symptoms of communicable diseases
- Foster care and adoption assistance
- Noncash programs identified by the attorney general (soup kitchens, short-term shelter, and the like)
- Loans and grants for higher education
- Elementary and secondary education
- Head Start programs for pre-school children
- Assistance from the Job Training Partnership Act

5. *State options:* Allowed states to deny benefits from the welfare block grant and Medicaid and social service block grants to most legal immigrants; exemptions were the same as for SSI and food stamps. Future immigrants subject to the five-year ban noted above.

6. *Sponsors:* Expanded circumstances under which an immigrant's sponsor would be financially responsible for that individual.

7. *Reporting and verifying:* Required agencies that administer SSI, housing assistance, or the welfare block grant to report quarterly to the Immigration and Naturalization Service (INS)

the names and addresses of people they knew were unlawfully in the United States.

Source: Summary by author: HR 3734—PL104–193

Immigration Provisions of the Omnibus Spending Bill, 1996

From 1994 through 1996, Congress grappled with bills that would have reformed immigration law more generally rather than dealing just with problems of illegal immigration. Sufficient consensus to enact broadscale reform of the laws and processes affecting legal immigration could not be reached. Congress cleared a measure to restrict illegal immigration only after folding its provisions into the fiscal 1997 Omnibus Spending Bill (HR 3610—PL 104-208) that President Clinton signed into law on September 30, 1996. The full measure is more than 200 pages long, so only the immigration section of the Omnibus Spending Bill is summarized here.

Omnibus Spending Act of September 30, 1996—The Immigration-Related Provisions

1. Border Controls. Authorized funding to increase the number of Border Patrol agents by 1,000 annually through fiscal year 2001, doubling the total force from 5,000 to 10,000. The INS was to relocate as many agents as possible to border areas with the largest number of illegal aliens, to coordinate relocation plans with local law enforcement agencies, and to report to Congress on such activities within six months of enactment.

2. Authorized $1.2 million for the second and third tiers of a triple fence along a 14-mile strip at the U.S.-Mexico border south of San Diego and for roads surrounding the fence.

3. Required the INS to develop alien identification cards with biometric identifiers, such as a fingerprint, that could be machine-read, and future cards that could use devices like retina scanners.

4. Ordered the Attorney General, by 1998, to create a data base of information from the documents people filled out as they legally entered and left that would allow the INS to match entry and exit records to identify people who overstayed their visas.

5. Required the INS to establish "pre-inspection" stations at five of the 10 foreign airports serving as departure points for the largest number of inadmissible immigrants to screen people who did not have proper documents.

Document Fraud and Alien Smuggling Provisions such as:

6. Granted wiretap authority to the Department of Justice for investigating immigration document fraud.

7. Created felonies for alien smuggling from up to 10 years in prison for the first and second offenses, and 15 years for subsequent offenses.

8. Created 25 positions for Assistant United States Attorneys to prosecute cases of alien smuggling and fraud.

9. Granted sweeping authority to the INS to conduct undercover operations aimed at smuggling rings, including allowing the INS to establish or acquire companies, deposit funds in banks without regard to federal regulations, and use profits from such front companies to offset expenses.

10. Increased the penalty for document fraud from 5 years to 10 to 15 years in most cases; and if fraud was used in facilitating a drug trafficking crime, a new penalty of 20 years in prison, and if involving terrorism, the penalty was 25 years.

11. Created a criminal penalty for up to one year in prison for unlawfully voting in a federal election.

12. Allowed courts in imposing sentences against immigration law violaters to seize vehicles, boats, airplanes, and real estate if used in the commission of the crime or profit from the proceeds of a crime.

Detention and Deportation Provisions such as:

13. Barred any alien deported from re-entry for five years, and up to 10 years if the alien left while deportation proceedings were in progress or attempted to re-enter unlawfully, and barred repeat offenders for two years, as would people convicted of aggravated felonies.

14. Denied legal status to anyone who resided in the United States unlawfully for at least 180 days, and persons so convicted could not gain legal status for three years.

15. Allowed people who arrived in the United States without legal documents to be detained and deported without hearing unless they could demonstrate a credible fear of persecution back home.

16. Required detention of most illegal aliens serving criminal sentences after their prison terms were completed.

17. Streamlined deportation by replacing multiple proceed-

ings with one, allowing proceedings by telephone or teleconference, and after 10-day notice a hearing.

18. Required aliens to be deported within 90 days of a deportation order, with mandatory detention during that time.

19. Limited judicial review of deportation orders.

20. Authorized $5 million for a criminal alien tracking center using criminal alien data base to be used to assist local governments in identifying criminals who might be deportable

Employee Verification provisions such as:

21. Ordered the attorney general to create three pilot programs to test the effectiveness of workplace verification systems, in which participation would be voluntary for employers and all federal departments and agencies within selected states were required to participate.

Public Benefit restrictions such as:

22. Allowed any consular agent to deny an immigrant a visa on the basis that the person was likely to become a public charge.

23. Required sponsors of legal immigrants to earn at least 25 percent more than the federal poverty level and to sign an affidavit that they would be financially responsible for the people they sponsored.

24. Allowed states to create pilot programs to explore the feasibility of denying driver's licenses to illegal immigrants; the attorney general to report to Congress on these programs after three years.

25. Required the GAO to report to Congress within 180 days on the unlawful use of means-tested benefits—such as food stamps and cash welfare—by illegal immigrants.

26. Required the INS to report by the end of 1996 whether or not the United States had an adequate number of temporary agricultural workers.

Source: Summary by author: HR 3610—PL 104–208

Legal Immigration and Family Equity Act (LIFE) of 2000

As economic conditions improved and the anti-immigrant fervor eased, a few adjustments to the restrictiveness of the 1996 enactments were passed. In December 2000, Congress passed two such laws, described briefly in this document and the next.

It temporarily reinstated Section 245(i) of the Immigration and Nationality Act of 1952 (Public Law 82–414), allowing undocumented immigrants to apply for visas without first leaving the U.S. [Such] visa allows an illegal alien to stay in the country and wait for adjustment to lawful permanent resident status. Prior to this, illegal aliens were required to leave the United States and to apply for a visa at a U.S. consulate abroad. Illegal aliens who were in the United States for at least six months could be barred from re-entry for up to 10 years. [Section 245(i) had been added to the 1952 Act in 1994, but it expired in 1998.]

About 640,000 undocumented aliens were covered by this section. The alien had to be sponsored by a lawfully resident relative or by an employer. Naturalized U.S. citizens could apply on behalf of their spouses, children, parents, or siblings. Lawful permanent residents could apply on behalf of their spouses and unmarried children. The application had to be filed prior to April 30, 2001. When the visa became available, the applicant was required to pay a $1,000 penalty fee and other filing fees.

Source: Information Plus, *Immigration and Illegal Aliens: Burden or Blessing?* (Wylie, TX: Information Plus, 2001), 28.

Child Citizenship Act of 2000 (PL 106-395)

This Act enabled automatic U.S. citizenship to foreign-born children of Americans, including adopted children. About 150,000 persons became U.S. citizens on February 27, 2001 when the Act officially took effect.

To be eligible, the child had to satisfy the definition of "child" for naturalization purposes under the Immigration and Nationality Act (INA) of 1952, and to meet the following requirements:

1) The child has at least one U.S. citizen parent (by birth or by naturalization).

2) The child is under 18 years of age.

3) The child is currently residing permanently in the United States and in the legal and physical custody of the U.S. citizen parent.

4) The child is a lawful permanent resident.

5) The child, if adopted, must meet the requirements of the INA as it applies to an adoptive child.

This new law, however, is NOT retroactive. Persons age 18 or older on February 27, 2001, do not qualify for automatic citizenship under the law. If they subsequently seek naturalization, they have to fulfill the same eligibility requirements that currently exist for any adult lawful permanent resident.

Source: Information Plus, *Immigration and Illegal Aliens: Burden or Blessing?* (Wylie, TX: Information Plus, 2001), 28.

USA Patriot Act of 2001 (HR 3162)

In response to the terrorist attacks on the World Trade Center in New York City and on the Pentagon in Washington, D.C., Congress passed the USA Patriot Act. It was a lengthy bill, 288 pages. Its key immigration-related provisions broadened the definition of terrorism, expanded grounds for inadmissibility to include aliens who were suspected of terrorist activity or who publicly endorsed such, and required the attorney general to detain aliens whom he certified as threats to national security.

Sec. 102. Sense of Congress Condemning Discrimination against Arab and Muslim Americans.

(a) Findings, Congress makes the following findings:

(1) Arab Americans, Muslim Americans, and Americans from South Asia play a vital role . . . and are entitled to nothing less than the full rights of every American.

(2) The acts of violence . . . taken against [them] since September 11, 2001 . . . should be condemned by all Americans who value freedom. . . .

(b) Sense of Congress. It is the sense of Congress that—

(1) the civil rights and civil liberties of all Americans, including Arab Americans, Muslim Americans, and Americans from South Asia, must be protected, and every effort made to preserve their safety.

(2) any acts of violence or discrimination against any Americans be condemned;

(3) the Nation is called upon to recognize the patriotism of fellow citizens of all ethnic, racial, and religious backgrounds.

Title IV—Protecting the Border goes on to the following sections:

Subtitle A—Protecting the Northern Border

Sec. 401—Ensures adequate personnel on the northern border.

Sec. 403—Grants access by the Department of State and the INS to certain identifying records of visa applicants and applicants for admission to the United States.

Sec. 405—Establishes an integrated automated fingerprint identification system for ports of entry and overseas consular posts.

Subtitle B—Enhanced Immigration Provisions

Sec. 411—Defines definitions relating to terrorism.

Sec. 412—Mandates detention of suspected terrorists; suspends habeas corpus under certain conditions; and limits judicial review.

Sec. 413—Ensures multilateral cooperation against terrorists.

Sec. 414—Provides for increased integrity and security of visas.

Sec. 415—Mandates the participation of the Office of Homeland Security on the Entry-Exit Task Force.

Sec. 416—Establishes a foreign student monitoring program.

Sec. 417—Calls for machine-readable passports.

Subtitle C—Preservation of Immigration Benefits for Victims of Terrorism

Sec. 421—Grants special immigrant status to victims of the 9/11 attacks.

Sec. 423—Grants humanitarian relief for certain surviving spouses and children.

Sec. 427—Denies such benefits to terrorists or family members of terrorists

Title X—Miscellaneous

Sec. 1006—Provides for the inadmissibility of aliens engaged in money laundering.

Source: Electronic Privacy Information Center (EPIC) Website. Available: http://www.epic.org/privacy/terrorism/hr3162.html; accessed April 20, 2003.

Homeland Security Act of 2002 (HR 5005)

About a year later, on November 19, 2002, Congress enacted the Homeland Security Act of 2002, which established a new Department of Homeland Security. It is a massive law, more than 400 printed pages long, that merges twenty-two federal agencies and results in the most extensive reorganization of the federal bureaucracy since creation of the Department of Defense after World War II. It creates within the new department two bureaus, each headed by an undersecretary: The Directorate of Border and Transportation Security is headed by an undersecretary for border and transportation security; and a Bureau of Citizenship and Immigration Services is headed by the undersecretary for citizenship and immigration services. These key provisions from Title IV of the Act are highlighted in the following document.

Title IV—Border and Transportation Security.
Subtitle A—General Provisions
Sec. 401. Creates the Under Secretary for Border and Transportation Security.
Sec. 402—Responsibilities—Transfers functions of the INS to the DHS.
The Secretary, acting through the Under Secretary for Border and Transportation Security, shall be responsible for the following:
(1) Preventing the entry of terrorists and the instruments of terrorism into the U.S.
(2) Securing the borders, territorial waters, ports, terminals, waterways, and air, land and sea transportation systems of the United States, including managing and coordinating those functions transferred to the Department at ports of entry.
(3) Carrying out the immigration enforcement functions vested by statute in, or performed by, the Commissioner of Immigration and Naturalization (or any officer, employee, or component of the Immigration and Naturalization Service) immediately before the date on which the transfer of functions specified under section 441 takes effect [March 1, 2003].
(4) Establishing and administering rules, in accordance with section 428, governing the granting of visas or other forms of permissions, including parole, to enter the United States to individuals who are not a citizen or an alien lawfully admitted for permanent residence in the United States.
(5) Establishing national immigration enforcement policies and priorities.
Subtitle B—Immigration and Nationality Functions
Chapter 1—Immigration Enforcement
Sec. 411—Details the transfer of functions of the Border Patrol, INS to the Under Secretary for Border and Transportation Security in the DHS.

Sec. 412—Establishes a Bureau of Border Security headed by a Director.

Sec. 415—Calls for a report to Congress on improving enforcement functions.

Chapter 2—Citizenship and Immigration Services
Subchapter A—Transfer of Functions

Sec. 421—Establishes a Bureau of Citizenship and Immigration Services headed by a Director.

Sec. 422—Establishes a Citizenship and Immigration Services Ombudsman office.

Sec. 425—Establishes an Office of Immigration Statistics within Bureau of Justice Statistics.

Sec. 426—Concerns preservation of the Attorney General's authority.

Subchapter B—Other Provisions

Sec. 431—Concerns funding for citizenship and immigration services.

Sec. 432—Calls for elimination of backlogs

Sec. 433—Requires a report to Congress on efforts at improving immigration services.

Sec. 435—Calls for the application of Internet-based technologies.

Chapter 3—General Provisions

Sec. 41—Abolishes the INS as of March 1, 2003.

Sec. 45—Requires reports and implementation plans to Congress.

Sec. 46—Details immigration functions.

References and Further Reading

Anderson, James. 1979. *Public Policymaking.* New York: Holt, Rinehart, and Winston.

Information Plus. 2001. *Immigration and Illegal Aliens: Burden or Blessing?* Wylie, TX: Information Plus.

LeMay, Michael, and Elliott Robert Barkan. 1999. *U.S. Immigration and Naturalization Law and Issues: A Documentary History.* Westport, CT: Greenwood Press, 1999.

7

Directory of Agencies and Organizations

This chapter lists and briefly discusses the major agencies and organizations involved in the immigration-policy arena and concerned with immigration-policy reforms. It discusses national domestic government agencies first.

The domestic government section is followed by a list of some of the more important international organizations active on the global scene, with particular emphasis on those involved in migration and especially in refugee issues and concerns. It briefly lists a few examples of the organizations found in several of the most significant immigrant- and refugee-receiving nations.

In addition to governmental agencies and organizations, there are numerous important NGOs. This chapter discusses those most active in advocacy for or against immigration and discusses their stands on immigration reform. Finally, the chapter lists and discusses scholarly organizations involved in the policy arena of immigration reform—exemplary, so-called immigration-related think tanks or centers for study of immigration and immigration policy.

There are many federal agencies involved in the administration and implementation of U.S. immigration policy. They are thereby all involved in immigration-policy reform affairs as well.

U.S. Government Agencies and Organizations

U.S. Census Bureau
1100 Vermont Avenue NW
Washington, DC 20005
Phone: (202) 728-6829
Fax: (301) 457-3620
Website: http://www.census.gov

The bureau collects and analyzes statistical data on the population, including immigrants. Its numerous statistical studies and reports enable the tracking of immigrants and provides demographic data as to their gradual incorporation into the major institutions of society.

U.S. Commission on Civil Rights
1121 Vermont Avenue NW
Washington, DC 20425
Phone: (202) 376-8177
E-mail: publications@usccr.gov
Website: http://www.admin@usccr.gov

The commission is an independent, bipartisan, fact-finding agency of the executive branch established under the Civil Rights Act of 1957. It investigates complaints as to discrimination; appraises federal laws and policies with respect to discrimination because of race, color, religion, sex, age, disability, or national origin; studies and collects information relating to such discrimination; serves as a clearinghouse for such information; and submits reports, findings, and recommendations, many of which concern rights of immigrants and refugees, to the president and Congress.

U.S. Commission on Immigration Reform
2430 E Street
South Building
Washington, DC 20037
Phone: (202) 776-8400
Fax: (202) 776-8635

The bipartisan U.S. Commission on Immigration Reform was authorized by IMMACT (1990) and given the mandate to review and evaluate the implementation and impact of U.S. immigration policy and to transmit reports of its findings and recommendations to Congress. It issued its first interim report on September 30, 1994, its second interim report in 1995, and, in 1997, two final reports: *U.S. Refugee Policy: Taking Leadership;* and *Becoming an American: Immigration and Immigration Policy.*

U.S. Department of Agriculture
1400 Independence Avenue SW
Washington, DC 20250-7600
Phone: (202) 720-2777
Fax: (202) 690-2064
E-mail: IraHobbs@usda.gov
Website: http://www.ocio.usda.gov

The immigration role of the Department of Agriculture is largely supportive of that of other departments and agencies, such as supplying information and data on the need for temporary agricultural workers. It assists immigrants through programs such as its Food and Nutrition Service.

U.S. Department of Education
400 Maryland Avenue SW
Washington, DC 20202-5130
Phone: (800) USA-LEARN or (202) 401-2000
Fax: 202-401-0689
E-mail: customerservice@inet.ed.gov

The Department of Education is the agency of the federal government that establishes policy for, administers, and coordinates most federal assistance to education. The department's role in immigration issues is to assist, supplement, and complement the efforts of states, local school systems and other state agencies, the private sector, public and private educational institutions, public and private nonprofit educational research institutions, and community-based organizations to serve the educational needs of immigrants, particularly in the educational aspects of the naturalization process.

U.S. Department of Health and Human Services
Office of Refugee Resettlement
370 L'Enfant Promenade SW
Washington, DC 20447
Phone: (202) 401-9246

Fax: (202) 401-5487

Website: http://www.acf.dhhs.gov/programs/orr

The Department of Health and Human Services affects immigration and refugee policy through its administration of such programs as the Administration for Children and Families, the Health Care Financial Administration, the Division of State Legalization Assistance, the Financial Support Administration, the U.S. Public Health Service Office of Refugee Health, and the Office of Planning, Research, and Evaluation.

U.S. Department of Homeland Security
425 I Street NW
Washington, DC 20536
Phone: (202) 514-1900
Fax: (202) 514-3296
Website: http://www.usdhs.gov

Just established in 2002 and in the process of merging the functions of many federal agencies into this newest cabinet-level department of the federal bureaucracy, the new Department of Homeland Security, as of March 1, 2003, is the principal agency responsible for administering immigration-related policy. Its immigration-related functions are implemented by two bureaus headed by an undersecretary: a Bureau of Border and Transportation Security and a Bureau of Citizenship and Immigration Services. The department deals with all visa, passport, and citizenship matters; monitors all U.S. borders; ensures mass transit security; and provides airport security.

U.S. Department of Housing and Urban Development
451 Seventh Street SW
Washington, DC 20410
Phone: (202) 708-1112
Fax: (202) 708-1455
E-mail: CA_Webmanager@hud.gov
Website: http://www.hud.gov

The mission of the Department of Housing and Urban Development is to promote a decent, safe, sanitary, and suitable home environment for every American. Its impact on immigration matters is primarily through its programs designed to assist low-income persons; to create, rehabilitate, and maintain the nation's affordable housing; to enforce fair housing laws; to help the homeless;

to spur economic growth in distressed neighborhoods; and to help local communities meet their development needs.

U.S. Department of Labor
Bureau of International Labor Affairs
200 Constitution Avenue NW
Room S-2235
Washington, DC 20210
Phone: (202) 693-4770
Website: http://www.dol.gov/dol/ilab

The Department of Labor oversees all labor-related policy and law, including matters related to temporary labor. Agencies within the department that have immigration-related policy roles are its Office of Federal Contract Compliance Program and its Wage and Hour Division.

U.S. Department of State
Bureau of Population, Refugees, and Migration
2401 E Street NW
Suite L-505, SA-1
Washington, DC 20522-0105
Phone: (202) 647-8472
E-mail: askpublicaffairs@state.gov
Website: http://www.state.gov/prm

See also Bureau of Migration and Refugee Affairs and their Bureau of Consular Affairs. The Bureau of Consular Affairs administers laws, formulates regulations, and implements policies relating to the broad range of consular services provided to U.S. citizens abroad.

U.S. Equal Employment Opportunity Commission
1801 L Street NW
Washington, DC 20507
Phone: (202) 663-4900
Fax: (202) 663-4494
Website: http://www.eeoc.gov

Housed within the Department of Health and Human Services, the Equal Employment Opportunity Commission administers three basic programs: an affirmative employment program; the special emphasis/diversity programs; and the discrimination-complaint program. The commission attempts to promote and ensure equal opportunity for all employees and to foster a culture and environment free from discrimination.

U.S. General Accounting Office
441 G Street NW
Washington, DC 20548
Phone: (202) 512-5400
Fax: (202) 512-6000
E-mail: webmaster@gao.gov
Website: http://www.gao.gov

The General Accounting Office is an agency that works for the U.S. Congress and the American people. Congress asks the GAO to study the programs and expenditures of the federal government. The GAO is commonly called the investigative arm of Congress, or the congressional watchdog. It is independent and nonpartisan. It studies how the federal government spends taxpayer dollars and advises Congress and the heads of executive departments about ways to make government more effective and responsive. It evaluates federal programs, audits federal expenditures, and issues legal opinions, many of which in recent years have focused on the INS and the Department of Justice's efforts and programs related to immigration law and policy.

U.S. House Committee on the Judiciary
Subcommittee on Immigration and Claims
B370B Rayburn House Office Building
Washington, DC 20515
Phone: (202) 225-5727
Website: http://www.house.gov/judiciary

This standing committee of the U.S. House of Representatives deals with all bills introduced to Congress that concern immigration law and policy matters.

U.S. Senate Committee on the Judiciary
Subcommittee on Immigration
Room SD-323, Dirksen Senate Office Building
Washington, DC 20510
Phone: (202) 224-6098
Website: http://www.senate.gov/~judiciary

This standing committee of the U.S. Senate deals with all legislative matters concerning immigration policy and law.

U.S. Social Security Administration
Office of Public Inquiries
Windsor Park Building
6401 Security Boulevard
Baltimore, MD 21235
Phone: (800) 772-1213
Fax: (800) 325-0778
E-mail: webmaster@ssa.gov
Website: http://www.ssa.gov/reach.htm

The Social Security Administration's role in immigration policy is supportive of other agencies' immigration policies and programs. Its data bank is used to verify a person's identity and to guard against fraud, waste, abuse, and mismanagement in the administration of the benefit programs. These programs are based upon contributory financing of social insurance programs, and protection is a matter of right for those persons, whether natural-born citizens, naturalized citizens, or legal resident aliens, who have worked and contributed to the system. This is in contrast to public-assistance programs, in which only those persons in need are eligible for benefits.

International Agencies and Organizations

Human Rights Watch
350 Fifth Avenue
Thirty-Fourth Floor
New York, NY 10118-3299
Phone: (212) 290-4700
Fax: (212) 736-1300
E-mail: hrwnyc@hrw.org
Website: http://www.hrw.org

Human Rights Watch is an organization dedicated to protecting the human rights of people around the world. It stands with victims and activists to prevent discrimination, to uphold political freedom, to protect people from inhumane conduct in wartime, and to bring offenders to justice. It investigates and exposes human rights violations and holds abusers accountable, challenging governments to respect international human rights laws. It is an independent NGO supported by private individuals and foundations worldwide.

International Committee of the Red Cross
801 Second Avenue
Eighteenth Floor
New York, NY 10017
Phone: (212) 599-6021
Fax: (212) 599-6009
2100 Pennsylvania Avenue NW
Suite 545
Washington, DC 20037
Phone: (202) 239-9340
E-mail: washington.was@icrc.com
Website: http://www.icrc.org

Established in 1863, the International Committee of the Red Cross is an impartial, neutral, and independent organization whose exclusively humanitarian mission is to protect the lives and dignity of victims of war and internal violence and to provide them with assistance. It also directs and coordinates the international relief activities of the Red Crescent Movement in situations of conflict. It endeavors to prevent suffering by promoting and strengthening humanitarian law and universal humanitarian principles.

International Immigrants Foundation
1435 Broadway
Second Floor
New York, NY 10018-1909
Phone: (212) 302-2222
Fax: (212) 221-7206
E-mail: info@10.org
Website: http://www.10.org

Founded in 1973, the International Immigrants Foundation has consultative status with the UN Economic and Social Affairs Council and is associated with the Department of Public Information as a charitable, nongovernmental, nonpolitical, nonprofit, tax-exempt organization whose stated mission is to help immigrant families and children to achieve their aspirations for a better life in the United States. The organization addresses its mission by providing support to promote positive intercultural relations.

UN Department of Humanitarian Affairs
UN Headquarters
New York, NY 10017

Phone: (212) 963-4832
Fax: (202) 963-1388
Website: www.un.org/depts/dha

The UN Department of Humanitarian Affairs, established with the General Assembly, was created to "mobilize and coordinate the collective efforts of the international community, in particular those of the UN system, to meet in a coherent and timely manner the needs of those exposed to human suffering and material destruction in disasters and emergencies. This involves reducing vulnerability, promoting solutions to root causes and facilitating the smooth transition from relief to rehabilitation and development."

UN High Commissioner for Refugees
1775 K Street NW
No. 300
Washington, DC 20006-1502
Phone: (202) 296-5191
Fax: (202) 296-5660
E-mail: usawa@unhcr.ch
Website: http://www.unhcr.ch

The UN High Commissioner for Refugees is the UN agency responsible for all matters relating to refugees. It leads and coordinates international action for the worldwide protection of refugees and the resolution of refugee problems. Its primary purpose is to safeguard the rights and well-being of refugees, the right to asylum and safe refuge in another state, and the right to return home voluntarily. It was established by the 1951 UN Convention Relating to the Status of Refugees and its 1967 protocol. It seeks to reduce situations of forced displacement by encouraging states and other institutions to create conditions that are conducive to the protection of human rights and the peaceful resolution of disputes, assists the reintegration of returning refugees into their country of origin, and offers protection and assistance to refugees and others on the basis of their need and irrespective of their race, religion, political opinion, or gender. It pays particular attention to the needs of children and seeks to promote the equal rights of women and girls.

U.S. Advocacy Organizations

American Bar Association
750 North Lake Shore Drive
Chicago, IL 60611
Phone: (312) 988-5000
740 Fifteenth Street NW
Washington, DC 20005-1019
Phone: (202) 662-1000
E-mail: askaba@abanet.org
Website: http://www.abanet.org/about/home.html

With more than 400,000 members, the American Bar Association claims to be the largest voluntary professional association in the world. It accredits law schools, promotes education and information about the law, provides programs to assist lawyers and judges in their work, and sponsors initiatives to improve the legal system for the public.

American Civil Liberties Union
125 Broad Street
Eighteenth Floor
New York, NY 10004
Phone: (212) 549-2500
E-mail: aclu@aclu.org
Website: http://www.aclu.org

The American Civil Liberties Union (ACLU) works nationally and with local chapters to protect the civil rights of citizens as guaranteed in the U.S. Constitution. It annually publishes many policy statements, pamphlets, studies, and reports on civil rights issues. Its newsletter, *Civil Liberties Alert,* is published semiannually.

American Immigration Control Foundation
P.O. Box 525
Monterey, VA 24465
Phone: (540) 468-2022
Fax: (540) 468-2024
E-Mail: aicfndn@cfw.com
Website: http://www.aicfoundation.com/index.htm

The American Immigration Control Foundation is a nonprofit research and educational organization whose stated primary goal is to inform Americans about the need for a reasonable immigration policy based on the nation's interest and needs. It is a large publisher and distributor of publications on the U.S. immigration crisis. Founded in 1983, it is a prominent national voice for immigration control and is committed to educating citizens on the disastrous effects of uncontrolled immigration.

American Immigration Law Foundation

918 F Street NW
Washington, DC 20004
Phone: (202) 742-5600
Fax: (202) 742-5619
E-mail: info@ailf.org
Website: http://www.ailf.org/about.htm

The American Immigration Law Foundation was founded in 1987 as a tax-exempt, not-for-profit educational and service organization. Its stated mission is to promote understanding among the general public of immigration law and policy through education, policy analysis, and support to litigators. It has three core program areas: the Legal Action Center, the Public Education Program, and an Exchange Visitor Program.

American Immigration Lawyers Association

1400 I Street NW
No. 1200
Washington, DC 2005
Phone: (202) 371-9377
Fax: (202) 371-9449
E-mail: webmaster@aila.org
Website: http://www.aila.org

The American Immigration Lawyers Association is the national association of immigration lawyers established to promote justice, advocate for fair and reasonable immigration law and policy, advance the quality of immigration and nationality law and practice, and enhance the professional development of its members.

American Refugee Committee International Headquarters USA

430 Oak Grove Street
Suite 204
Minneapolis, MN 55404
Phone: (612) 872-7060
Fax: (612) 872-4309

E-mail: archq@archq.org
Website: http://www.archq.org/

Begun in 1978, the American Refugee Committee's stated mission is to work for the survival, health, and well-being of refugees, displaced persons, and those at risk. It seeks to enable them to rebuild productive lives of dignity and purpose, striving always to respect the values of those served. It is an international, nonprofit, and nonsectarian organization that has provided multisectoral humanitarian assistance and training to millions of beneficiaries for more than twenty years.

Business Roundtable
1615 L Street NW
Suite 1100
Washington, DC 20036
Phone: (202) 872-1260
Website: http://www.brtable.org/newsroom_about.htm

The Business Roundtable is an association of chief executive officers of leading U.S. corporations; the corporations have a combined workforce of more than 10 million employees in the United States. It is committed to advocating public policies that foster vigorous economic growth, a dynamic global economy, and a well-trained and productive U.S. workforce essential for future competitiveness. The Roundtable is selective in the issues it studies; a principal criterion for selecting an issue for attention is the impact the problem will have on the economic well-being of the nation. Through task forces on specific issues, it directs research, supervises the preparation of position papers, recommends policy, and lobbies Congress and the administration on selected issues.

Catholic Charities USA
1731 King Street
Alexandria, VA 22314
Phone: (703) 549-1390
Fax: (703) 549-1656
Website: http://www.catholiccharitiesusa.org/who/index/htm

Catholic Charities USA is a membership organization based in Alexandria, Virginia. It provides leadership, technical assistance, training, and other resources to enable local agencies to better devote their own resources to serving their communities. It promotes innovative strategies that address human needs and social injustices. It advocates policies that aim to reduce poverty, improve the lives of children and families, and strengthen communities. One of its major service programs involves refugee and immigration assistance.

Center for Human Rights and the Constitution
256 South Occidental Boulevard
Los Angeles, CA 90057
Phone: (213) 388-8693
Fax: (213) 386-9484
Website: http://www.reachout.org/losangeles/children/center.html

The Center for Human Rights and Constitution Homeless Youth Project is an organization that helps homeless twelve-to-seventeen-year-old inner-city youth find an alternative to life on the streets. It provides case management, job assistance, individual counseling, placement assistance, school placement, legal and medical referrals, life-skill training, and aftercare. Of particular importance to immigrants is its assistance in ESL classes; tutoring; clerical, recreation, and outdoor activities; art, gardening, and a variety of other assignments.

Center for the Applied Study of Prejudice and Ethnoviolence
Stephens Hall Annex
Towson State University
Towson, MD 21204-7097
Phone: (410) 243-6987
E-mail: prejinst@aol.com
Website: http://www.prejudiceinstitute.org

The Center for the Applied Study of Prejudice and Ethnoviolence examines responses to violence and intimidation based on prejudice, whether racial, ethnic, or other. It issues a quarterly newsletter, *Forum*, as well as periodic reports and study papers.

Center for the Study of Hate Crimes and Extremism
California State University, San Bernardino
5500 University Parkway
San Bernardino, CA 92407-2397
Phone: (909) 880-7711
Fax: (909) 880-7711
Website: http://csbs.csusb.edu/cjus/Levin.htm

The Center for the Study of Hate Crimes and Extremism is a nonpartisan, domestic research and policy center that serves regionally and nationally to examine the ways that bigotry operates, the methods used to advocate extremism, and the use of terrorism to deny civil or human rights to people on the basis of race, ethnicity, religion, gender, sexual orientation, disability, or other relevant status characteristics. It sponsors public conferences, collaborates with international news media, and maintains an Internet site with information about and in cooperation with government organizations, human relations organizations, nonprofit organizations, and law enforcement.

Central American Refugee Center
1459 Columbia Road NW
Washington, DC 20009
Phone: (202) 328-9799
Fax: (202) 328-0023
Website: http://www.icomm.ca.carecen

The Central American Refugee Center is a nonprofit immigration and human rights organization serving the refugee community on Long Island and throughout southern New York State. Founded in 1983, it works to protect the civil rights of immigrants, increase understanding between the native-born and newcomer communities, and raise awareness of the interaction between human rights disasters and immigration.

Church World Service
28606 Phillips Street
P.O. Box 968
Elkhart, IN 46515
Phone: (800) 297-1516
Fax: (219) 262-0966
E-mail: cws@nccusa.org
Website: http://www.churchworldservice.org

Founded in 1946, the Church World Service is the relief, development, and refugee-assistance ministry of thirty-six Protestant, Orthodox, and Anglican denominations in the United States. Working with indigenous organizations in more than eighty countries, it operates worldwide to meet human needs and to foster self-reliance for all whose way is hard. One of its major programs is its Immigration and Refugee Services.

Episcopal Migration Ministries
Episcopal Church Center
815 Second Avenue
New York, NY 10017
Phone: (212) 867-8400 or (800) 334-7626
E-mail: jbutterfield@episcopalchurch.org
Website: http://www.ecusa.anglican.org/emm

This group serves as the organizational arm of the Episcopal church in all matters related to immigration and migration relief and assistance, and it works in close consultation and coalition with other churches in pursuing humanitarian immigration policy.

Ethiopian Community Development Council
1038 South Highland Street
Arlington, VA 22204
Phone: (703) 685-0510
Fax: (703) 685-0529
E-mail: ecdc@erols.com
Website: http://www.ecdcinternational.org

The stated mission of the Ethiopian Community Development Council is to resettle refugees, to promote cultural, educational, and socioeconomic development in the refugee and immigrant community in the United States, and to conduct humanitarian and development programs in the Horn of Africa. It provides programs and services to assist newcomers to the United States to become productive members of their communities; conducts outreach and educational activities to increase public awareness of refugee and immigrant issues; promotes civic participation by newcomers in the decisionmaking processes at local, state, and national levels; provides cross-cultural training to service providers; and assists in educational development and cultural preservation of the Ethiopian community.

Federation for American Immigration Reform
1666 Connecticut Avenue NW
No. 400
Washington, DC 20009
Phone: (202) 328-7004
Fax: (202) 386-3447
E-mail: info@fairus.org
Website: http://www.fairus.org/

Founded in 1979, the Federation for American Immigration Reform is a national, nonpartisan, nonprofit, public-interest membership organization of concerned citizens who share a common belief that the unforeseen mass immigration that has occurred over the past thirty years should be curtailed. It advocates a moratorium on all immigration except for spouses and minor children of U.S. citizens and a limited number of refugees. In its view, a workable immigration policy is one that allows time to regain control of the U.S. borders and reduce overall levels of immigration to more traditional levels of about 300,000 a year. It believes the United States can and must have an immigration policy that is nondiscriminatory and that is designed to serve U.S. social, economic, and environmental needs.

Hebrew Immigrant Aid Society
337 Seventh Avenue
Seventeenth Floor
New York, NY 10001
Phone: (212) 967-4100
Fax: (212) 967-4483
E-mail: info@hias.org
Website: http://www.hias.org

Founded in 1881, the Hebrew Immigrant Aid Society (HIAS) has assisted more than 4.5 million people in their quest for freedom, including the million Jewish refugees it helped migrate to Israel and the thousands it helped resettle in Canada, Latin America, Australia, New Zealand, and elsewhere. As the oldest international migration and refugee-resettlement agency in the United States, HIAS played a major role in the rescue and relocation of Jewish survivors of the Holocaust and Jews from Morocco, Ethiopia, Egypt, and the Communist countries of eastern Europe. It advocates on behalf of refugees and migrants on the international, national, and community level.

Humane Borders
740 East Speed Boulevard
Tucson, AZ 85719
Phone: (520) 628-7753
E-mail: info@humaneborders.org
Website: http://www.humaneborders.org/

Humane Borders' mission statement describes it as an organization of people motivated by faith and committed to work to create a just and humane border environment. Its members respond with humanitarian assistance to those who are risking their lives and safety crossing the United States border with Mexico. It encourages the creation of public policies toward a humane, non-militarized border with legalized work opportunities for migrants in the United States and legitimate economic opportunities in migrants' countries of origin.

Jesuit Relief Service International
C.P. 6139
I-00195 Roma Prati
Italy
Phone: + 39-066977386
Fax: + 39-066806418
E-mail: international@jrs.net
Website: http://www.jrsref.org/refugee/jrs.htm

Jesuit Relief Service USA
1616 P Street NW
Suite 400
Washington, DC 20036
Phone: (202) 462-5200
Fax: (202) 462-7009

The Jesuit Relief Service is an international Catholic organization working in more than forty countries to accompany, serve, and defend the rights of refugees and forcibly displaced people. It embraces all who are driven from their homes by conflict, humanitarian disaster, or violation of human rights, following Catholic social teaching that applies the expression "de facto refugee" to many categories of people.

League of United Latin American Citizens (LULAC)
201 East Main Drive
Suite 605
El Paso, TX 79901
Phone: (915) 577-0726
Fax: (915) 577-0914
Website: http://www.lulac.org/About/Creeds/html

LULAC is organized to promote the democratic principle of individual political and religious freedom, the right of equality of social and economic opportunity, and the cooperative endeavor toward the development of a U.S. society wherein the cultural resources, integrity, and dignity of every individual and group constitute basic assets of the American way of life. Among its goals are to be a service organization that actively promotes and establishes cooperative relations with civic and governmental institutions and agencies in the field of public service, that upholds the rights guaranteed to every individual by state and national laws, that assures justice and equal treatment under those laws, and that opposes any infringement upon the constitutional political rights of any individual to vote and/or be voted upon at local, state, and national levels.

Lutheran Immigration and Refugee Service
700 Light Street
Baltimore, MD 21230
Phone: (410) 230-2700
Fax: (410) 230-2890
E-mail: lirs@lirs.org
Website: http://www.lirs.org

The Lutheran Immigration and Refugee Service states as its mission to welcome the stranger, bringing new hope and new life, through ministries and justice. It mobilizes action on behalf of uprooted people and sees that they receive fair and equal treatment, regardless of national origin, race, religion, culture, or legal status. It advocates for just and humane solutions to migration crises and their root causes, both national and international; works to turn solutions into reality; and encourages citizens to take part in shaping just and fair public policies, practices, and law.

Mexican American Legal Defense Fund (MALDEF)
926 J Street
No. 408
Sacramento, CA 95814
Phone: (916) 443-7531
Fax: (916) 443-1541
Website: http://www.maldef.org/about/index.htm

Founded in 1968 in San Antonio, Texas, MALDEF is a leading nonprofit Latino litigation, advocacy, and educational outreach institution whose stated mission is to foster sound public policies, laws, and programs to safeguard the civil rights of the 40 million Latinos living in the United States and to empower the Latino community to fully participate in society.

National Council of La Raza
1111 Nineteenth Street NW
No. 1000
Washington, DC 20036
Phone: (202) 785-1670
Fax: (202) 776-1792
E-mail: info@nclr.org
Website: http://www.nclr.org

The National Council of La Raza is a private, nonprofit, nonpartisan, tax-exempt organization established in 1968 to reduce poverty and discrimination and to improve life opportunities for Hispanic Americans. It assists the development of Hispanic, community-based organizations in urban and rural areas nationwide and conducts applied research, policy analysis, and advocacy. It works to provide a Hispanic perspective on issues such as education, immigration, housing, health, employment and training, and civil rights enforcement, to increase policymaker and public understanding of Hispanic needs, and to encourage the adoption of programs and policies that equitably serve Hispanics. Its Policy Analysis Center is a prominent Hispanic think tank serving as a voice for Hispanic Americans in Washington, D.C.

National Federation of Independent Business
53 Century Boulevard
Suite 250
Nashville, TN 37214
Phone: (800) NFIB-NOW
E-mail: web_membership@NFIB.org
Website: http://www.nfib.com/cgi-bin/NFIB.dll

The National Federation of Independent Business, with offices in Washington, D.C., and all fifty state capitols, is the largest advocacy organization representing small and independent businesses. Its Education Foundation promotes the importance of free enterprise and entrepreneurship. Its Research Foundation researches policy-related small-business problems and affects public policy debate by making its findings widely available. Its Legal Foundation fights for small businesses in the courts and seeks to educate small employers on legal issues.

National Immigration Forum
2201 I Street NE
Suite 220

Washington, DC 20002-4362
Phone: (202) 544-0004
Fax: (202) 544-1905
E-mail: info@immigrationforum.org
Website: http://www.immigrationforum.org

The National Immigration Forum states that its mission is "to embrace and uphold America's tradition as a nation of immigrants. The Forum advocates and builds public support for public policies that welcome immigrants and refugees and that are fair and supportive to newcomers in our country."

National Immigration Law Center
3435 Wilshire Boulevard
Suite 2850
Los Angeles, CA 90010
Phone: (213) 639-3900
Fax: (213) 639-3911
E-mail: info@nilc.org
Website: http://www.nilc.org

The National Immigration Law Center is a national support center whose mission is to protect and promote the rights and opportunities of low-income immigrants and their family members. Its staff specializes in immigration law and in the employment of public benefits for the rights of immigrants. It conducts policy analyses and litigation and provides publications, technical services, and training to a broad constituency of legal aid agencies, community groups, and pro bono attorneys. It has offices in Los Angeles and Oakland, California, and in Washington, D.C., and it operates the Sacramento policy office for the California Immigrant Welfare Collaborative.

National Network for Immigrant and Refugee Rights
310 Eighth Street, Suite 303
Oakland, CA 94607
Phone: (510) 465-1984
Fax: (510) 465-1885
E-mail: nnirr@nnirr.org
Website: http://www.nnirr.org

This national organization is composed of local coalitions and immigrant, refugee, community, religious, civil rights, and labor organizations and activists. It serves as a forum to share information and analysis, to educate communities and the general public, and to develop and coordinate plans of action on important immigrant and refugee issues. It works to promote a just immigration and refugee policy in the United States and to defend and expand the rights of all immigrants and refugees, regardless of immigration status. It seeks the enfranchisement of all immigrant and refugee communities in the United States through organizing and advocating for their full labor, environmental, civil, and human rights. It emphasizes the unparalleled change in global, political, and economic structures that has exacerbated regional, national, and international patterns of migration, and it highlights the need to build international support and cooperation to strengthen the rights, welfare, and safety of migrants and refugees.

New York Association for New Americans
17 Battery Place
New York, NY 10004-1102
Phone: (212) 425-2900
Website: http://www.nyana.org

The New York Association for New Americans works to help both those new to the United States and those who have been here for some time to fashion a plan for accomplishing their goals and dreams. It works to assist refugees and immigrants, their families, their sponsors, the companies that employ them, other institutions that serve them, and the communities in which they live.

NumbersUSA
1601 North Kent Street
Suite 1100
Arlington, VA 22209
Phone: (703) 816-8820
E-mail: info@numbersusa.com
Website: http://www.numbersusa.com

NumbersUSA is a nonprofit, nonpartisan, public policy advocacy organization that seeks an environmentally sustainable and economically just society that protects individual liberties. Toward that end, it advocates stopping mass illegal immigration. Its stated goals are to examine numerical levels of annual legal and illegal immigration and to educate the public about the immigration-reduction recommendations from two national commissions of the 1990s: the 1995 bipartisan Commission on Immigration Reform (the Jordan Commission), and the 1996 President's Council on Sustainable Development. It specifically advocates the elimination of chain migration (immigrants bringing family members, friends, etc. to the United States) and the elimination of the visa lottery, viewing the elimination of these two immigration categories as the best way to protect vulnerable U.S. workers and their families. It promotes itself as pro-environment, pro-worker, pro-liberty, and pro-immigrant. It networks with Americans of all races and includes many immigrants and their spouses, children, and parents.

Office of Migration and Refugee Services,
U.S. Conference of Catholic Bishops
3211 Fourth Street NE
Washington, DC 20017-1194
Phone: (202) 541-3000
Website: http://www.nccbuscc.org/mrs

Since the turn of the twentieth century, the Catholic church in the United States has engaged in the resettlement of refugees, advocating on behalf of immigrants and people on the move and providing pastoral care and services to newcomers from all over the world. Since 1970 alone, it has assisted resettlement of more than a million refugees. The Office of Migration and Refugee Services is committed to its resettlement, pastoral care, and advocacy roles on behalf of immigrants, migrants, and refugees. It assists the bishops in the development and advocacy of policy positions at the national and international levels to address the needs and conditions of immigrants, refugees, and other people on the move. It works with the federal government and with local churches in resettling refugees admitted to the United States into caring and supportive communities.

Tolstoy Foundation
104 Lake Road
Valley Cottage, NY 10989
Phone: (845) 268-6722
Fax: (845) 268-6937
E-mail: TFHQ@aol.com
Website: http://www.tolstoyfoundation.org

The Tolstoy Foundation describes itself as an organization that, for more than a half-century, has been committed to its founder, Alexandra Tolstoy, whose empathy for the plight of the peoples of her homeland and abhorrence of all forms of oppression and human suffering remains at the heart of the foundation's charitable activities today. Its stated mission is to promote respect for human dignity, freedom of choice, and the building of self-reliance through education and practical training and to provide assistance and relief to the distressed, the children, the aged, the sick, and the forgotten at home and abroad. It maintains a home for elderly Russian immigrants, which is dedicated to caring for their physical, spiritual, and intellectual needs. It seeks to preserve the cultural traditions, heritage, and resources of the Russian diaspora and has now come full circle, from its beginning, assisting new immigrants in their assimilation process, to the present, helping the peoples of Russia and the former Soviet Union acquire the knowledge and skills necessary to achieve self-reliance in their own homelands.

U.S. Catholic Conference, Migration and Refugee Services
3211 Fourth Street NE
Washington, DC 20017-1194
Phone: (202) 541-3000
Fax: (202) 541-3390
Website: http://www.nccbuscc.org/mrs

The Migration and Rescue Services committee of the U.S. Catholic Conference serves immigrants and other peoples on the move. Its service is rooted in the Gospel mandate that every person is to be welcomed as Christ himself would be. The committee advises bishops on national and international policy on addressing the needs and conditions of immigrants, refugees, and other migrants, works with the federal government and local churches in refugee resettlement, and assists local churches to respond to the pastoral needs of such persons by aiding in the development and nurturing of an ethnically integrated church in the United States.

U.S. Committee for Refugees
1717 Massachusetts Avenue NW
Suite 701
Washington, DC 20036
Phone:(202) 347-3507
Fax: (202) 347-3418
E-mail: uscr@irsa-uscr.org
Website: http://www.refugees.org

The U.S. Committee for Refugees describes its mission as defending the rights of all uprooted people regardless of their nationality, race, religion, ideology, or social group. Its members believe that once the consciences of men and women are aroused, great deeds can be accomplished. They base their work on the following principles: (1) Refugees have basic human rights, and no person with a well-founded fear of persecution should be forcibly returned to his or her homeland. (2) Asylum seekers have the right to a fair and impartial hearing to determine their refugee status. (3) All uprooted victims of human conflict, regardless of whether they cross a border, have the right to humane treatment, adequate protection, and assistance.

U.S. Research Centers and Think Tanks

The American Assembly
475 Riverside Drive
Suite 456
New York, NY 10115
Phone: (212) 870-3500
Fax: (212) 870-3555
Website: http://www.americanassembly.org

The American Assembly's major objectives are to focus attention and stimulate information on a range of critical U.S. policy topics, both domestic and international; to inform government officials, community and civic leadership, and the general public with factual background and the range of policy options on a given issue; and to facilitate communication among decisionmakers and the public and private sectors.

The Brookings Institution, Center on Urban and Metropolitan Policy
1775 Massachusetts Avenue NW
Washington, DC 20036
Phone: (202) 797-6000
Fax: (202) 797-6004
E-mail: webmaster@brookings.edu
Website: http://www.brook.edu/about/aboutbi.htm

The Brookings Institution is an independent, nonpartisan organization devoted to research, analysis, education, and publication focused on public policy issues in the areas of economics, foreign policy, and governance. Its stated goal is to improve the performance of U.S. institutions and the quality of public policy by using social science to analyze emerging issues and to offer practical approaches to those issues in language aimed at the general public. It does so through three research programs, Economic Studies, Foreign Policy Studies, and Governance Studies, as well as through the Center for Public Policy Education and the Brookings Institution Press, which publishes about fifty books a year.

The Cato Institute
1000 Massachusetts Avenue NW
Washington, DC 20001-5403
Phone: (202) 842-0200
Fax: (202) 842-3490
E-mail: cato@cato.org
Website: http://www.cato.org

The Cato Institute, headquartered in Washington, D.C., was founded in 1977 as a public policy research foundation. Named for *Cato's Letters*, a series of libertarian pamphlets that helped lay the philosophical foundation of the U.S. revolution, the institute describes its mission as seeking to broaden the parameters of public policy debate to allow consideration of the traditional U.S. principles of limited government, individual liberty, free markets, and peace. To pursue that goal, the institute strives to achieve greater involvement of the intelligent, concerned lay public in questions of policy and the proper role of government. It is a nonprofit, tax-exempt educational foundation.

Center for Immigration Studies
1522 K Street NW
No. 820
Washington, DC 20005-1202
Phone: (202) 466-8185
Fax: (202) 466-8076
E-mail: center@cis.org
Website: http://www.cis.org

The Center for Immigration Studies is an independent, nonpartisan, nonprofit research organization founded in 1985. It is the nation's only think tank devoted exclusively to research and policy analysis on the economic, social, demographic, fiscal, and other impacts of immigration on the United States. Its stated mission is to expand the base of knowledge and understanding of the need for an immigration policy that gives first concern to the broad national interest. It is animated by a pro-immigrant, low-immigration vision that seeks fewer immigrants but a warmer welcome for those admitted. It publishes the *Immigration Review.*

Center for Migration Studies
209 Flag Place
Staten Island, NY 10004-1122
Phone: (718) 351-8800
Fax: (718) 667-4598
E-mail: imr@cmsny.org
Website: http://www.cmsny.org

The Center for Migration Studies of New York was founded in 1964. It is one of the premier institutes for migration studies in the United States. Its stated mission is to facilitate the study of the sociodemographic, historical, economic, political, legislative, and pastoral aspects of human migration and refugee movements. In 1969, it incorporated as an educational, nonprofit institute. It brings an independent perspective to the interdisciplinary study of international migration and refugees without either the institutional constraints of government analysts and special interest groups or the profit considerations of private research firms. It claims to be the only institute in the United States devoted exclusively to understanding and educating the public on the causes and consequences of human mobility in both origin and destination counties. It generates and facilitates the dissemination of new knowledge and the fostering of effective policies. It publishes the leading scholarly journal in the field, the *International Migration Review.*

Immigration History Research Center
University of Minnesota
College of Liberal Arts
311 Andersen Library
222 Twenty-First Avenue South
Minneapolis, MN 55455-0439
Phone: (612) 625-4800
Fax: (612) 626-0018
Website: http://www1.umn.edu/ihrc

Founded in 1965, the Immigration History Research Center is an international resource on U.S. immigration and ethnic history. It collects, preserves, and makes available archival and published resources documenting immigration and ethnicity on a national scope and is a particularly rich source for information on ethnic groups that originated in eastern, central, and southern Europe and the Near East. It sponsors academic programs and publishes bibliographic and scholarly works.

Migration Policy Institute
1400 Sixteenth Street NW
Suite 300
Washington, DC 20036
Phone: (202) 266-1940
Fax: (202) 266-1900
Website: http://www.migrationpolicy.org/about

The Migration Policy Institute is an independent, nonpartisan, nonprofit think tank in Washington, D.C., dedicated to the study of the movement of people worldwide. It provides analysis, development, and evaluation of migration and refugee policies at the local, national, and international levels. It aims to meet the rising demand for pragmatic and thoughtful responses to the challenges and opportunities that large-scale migration, whether voluntary or forced, presents to communities and institutions in an increasingly integrated world. Founded in 2001 by Kathleen Newland and Demetrios Papademetriou, the institute grew out of the International Migration Policy Program of the Carnegie Endowment for International Peace.

Migrationwatch UK
P.O. Box 765
Guildford
GU2 4XN
United Kingdom
Phone: + 4 (0) 1869-337007
E-mail: info@migrationwatchUK.org
Website: http://www.migrationwatchuk.org/

Established in October 2001, Migrationwatch UK is an independent think tank that has no connections to any political party. Chaired by Sir Andrew Green, a former British ambassador to Saudi Arabia, it monitors developments, conducts research, and provides the public with full and accurate facts placed in their proper context. In the future, it will make policy recommendations. It believes arguments in favor of the current large-scale immigration are unsound—either in fact or in economics or in both—and need to be thoroughly examined.

National Immigration Forum
220 I Street NE
Suite 220
Washington, DC 20002
E-mail: info@immigrationforum.org
Website: http://www.immigrationforum.org/

The purpose of the National Immigration Forum is to embrace and uphold the U.S. tradition as being a nation of immigrants. It advocates and builds public support for public policies that welcome immigrants and refugees and that are fair and supportive to newcomers to the country.

PEW Hispanic Center
USC Annenberg School for Communication
1919 M Street NW
Suite 460
Washington, DC 20036
Phone: (202) 292-3300
Fax: (202) 785-8282
E-mail: info@pewhispanic.org
Website: http://www.pewhispanic.org/

Founded in 2001, the Pew Hispanic Center is a nonpartisan research organization supported by the Pew Charitable Trusts. Its mission is to improve the understanding of the U.S. Hispanic population and to chronicle Latinos' growing impact on the entire nation. Timeliness, relevance, and scientific rigor characterize the center's work. It does not advocate for or take positions on policy issues.

The Prejudice Institute
2743 Maryland Avenue
Baltimore, MD 21218
Phone: (410) 243-6987
E-mail: prejinst@aol.com
Website: http://www.prejudiceinstitute.org/

The Prejudice Institute describes itself as a resource for activists, lawyers, and social scientists. It is devoted to policy research and education on all dimensions of prejudice, discrimination, and ethnoviolence.

Public Policy Institute of California
500 Washington Street
Suite 800

San Francisco, CA 94111
Phone: (415) 291-4400
Fax: (415) 291-4401
Website: http://www.ppic.org/

The Public Policy Institute of California is a private, nonprofit organization dedicated to improving public policy in California through independent, objective, nonpartisan research. It was established in 1994 with an endowment from William R. Hewlett. Its research focuses on three program areas: population, economy, and governance and public finance. Its publications include reports, research briefs, surveys, fact sheets, special papers, and demographic bulletins. It also communicates its research and analysis through conferences, forums, luncheons, and other targeted outreach efforts.

The RAND Corporation
1700 Main Street
P.O. Box 2138
Santa Monica, CA 90407-2138
Phone: (213) 393-0411
Website: http://www.rand/org/about/

The RAND (a contraction of the term "research and development") Corporation was the first organization to be called a think tank. Established in 1946 by the U.S. Air Force, today it is a nonprofit institution that helps improve policy and decisionmaking through research and analysis. Its areas of expertise include child policy, civil and criminal justice, community and U.S. regional studies, drug policy, education, health, immigration, infrastructure, international policy, methodology, national security, population and aging, science and technology, and terrorism. On occasion, its findings are considered so compelling that it advances specific policy recommendations. In all cases, it serves the public interest by widely disseminating its research findings.

The Southern Poverty Law Center
400 Washington Avenue
Montgomery, AL 36104
Phone: (334) 956-8200
Fax: (334) 956-8488
Website: http://www.tolerance.org/

The Southern Poverty Law Center is a national civil rights organization whose stated mission is to create a national community committed to human rights by centralizing e-mail addresses and inviting users to view special features and stories on its Web project, Tolerance.org. It promotes and disseminates scholarship on all aspects of prejudice and discrimination, promoting tolerance, exposing hate groups and hate news, providing assistance on litigation and legal matters, and publishing such anti-hate and pro-tolerance tracts as *Ten Ways to Fight Hate, 101 Tools for Tolerance,* and *Center Information Packet.*

Urban Institute
2100 M Street NW
Washington, DC 20037
Phone: (202) 833-7200
Fax: (202) 223-3043
E-mail: paffairs@ui.urban.org
Website: http://www.urban.org

One of the oldest of the think tanks, the Urban Institute researches policy matters in which it measures effects, compares options, shows which stakeholders get the most and which the least, tests conventional wisdom, reveals trends, and makes cost, benefits, and risks explicit on a broad array of public policy issues by employing the right methodologies and quantitative modeling, survey design, and statistical analyses. It publishes an extensive list of books that follow standard academic peer-review procedures for an audience of program administrators, other researchers and university students, the media, nonprofit organizations, private-sector stakeholders, and that important segment of the public engaged in policy debates through the media.

8

Print and Nonprint Resources

There are literally thousands of books, articles in scholarly journals, government reports and documents, and reports and publications by nongovernmental agencies concerning immigration policy, the immigration processes, and its reform. This chapter presents a briefly annotated bibliography of some leading scholarly journals, major reference and scholarly books, government reports, and videos. Websites of interest were presented along with the organizations hosting the sites in Chapter 7. The print and nonprint outlets below cover major sources in the field so that the reader can quickly identify resources most likely to be useful and hopefully insightful for them. There are innumerable government reports and studies from a variety of agencies that emphasize immigration laws and policies and their impact. This chapter lists some exemplary sources. The chapter is divided into print resources, books and journals, and video sources.

Books and Government Reports

Aleinikoff, T. Alexander, and Douglas Klusmeyer, eds. *Citizenship Policies for an Age of Migration.* Washington, DC: Brookings Institution Press, 2002.

This Carnegie Endowment for International Peace book by two leading immigration lawyers focuses on naturalization policy in a global context.

——. *Citizenship Today: Global Perspectives and Practices.* Washington, DC: Brookings Institution Press, 2001.

This Carnegie Endowment for International Peace book is written by two leading immigration lawyers who are experts in the subject.

———. *From Migrants to Citizens: Membership in a Changing World.* Washington, DC: Brookings Institution Press, 2000.

This scholarly work discusses the incorporation of immigrants and includes a thorough discussion of naturalization law and policy.

Andreas, Peter, and Timothy Snyder, eds. *The Wall around the West: State Borders and Immigration Controls in North America and Europe.* Lanham, MD: Rowman and Littlefield, 2000.

This book offers a balanced but critical examination of the increasing barriers being enacted to control immigration flows into Canada, the United States, and the major immigrant-receiving nations of Europe, particularly the EU countries.

Baker, Susan Gonzales. *The Cautious Welcome: The Legalization Program of the Immigration Reform and Control Act.* Santa Monica, CA: RAND Corporation; Washington, DC: Urban Institute, 1990.

This carefully researched study is one volume among several in the series published on the effects of the IRCA. Baker's study chronicles the design, implementation, and outcomes of the legalization provisions. It shows that change in the U.S. immigration system can be effected as much by reforming the benefits side as by modifying immigration law enforcement.

Barringer, Herbert, Robert Gardner, and Michael Levin. *Asians and Pacific Islanders in the United States.* New York: Russell Sage Foundation, 1995.

This work thoroughly examines the social and economic adaptation of Asians and Pacific Islanders to U.S. culture and economy.

Bean, Frank B., and Stephanie Bell-Rose, eds. *Immigration and Opportunity: Race, Ethnicity, and Employment in the U.S.* New York: Russell Sage Foundation, 1999.

This extensive collection of essays from leading sociologists and demographers provides a systematic account of the sundry ways in which immigration affects the labor market experiences of native-born Americans.

Bean, Frank, Barry Edmonston, and Jeffrey Passell. *Undocumented Migration to the U.S.* Santa Monica, CA: RAND Corporation; Washington, DC: Urban Institute, 1990.

One of several books resulting from the RAND Corporation/Urban Institute massive study of immigration policy, this volume presents thorough coverage of the issue of undocumented immigration and focuses especially on the degree to which IRCA did not have a long-term effect on decreasing illegal immigration.

Bean, Frank, Georges Vernez, and Charles B. Keely. *Opening and Closing the Doors.* Santa Monica, CA: RAND Corporation; Washington, DC: Urban Institute, 1989.

This is one of the more important books in a series of excellent books and monographs that were published as a result of a joint RAND Corporation/Urban Institute major research project examining immigration policy, particularly as to the impact of the IRCA.

Beck, Roy H. *The Case against Immigration.* New York: Norton, 1996.

This book offers a thorough articulation of all the arguments and data that can be marshaled against high levels of immigration.

Boeri, Tito, Gordon H. Hanson, and Barry McCormick, eds. *Immigration Policy and the Welfare State.* New York: Oxford University Press, 2002.

This book draws together and unifies analyses of immigration into the major EU countries and the United States, covering the major trends and dramatic developments of the 1990s. It emphasizes the influence of the welfare state on immigration incentives but also examines other influences on both legal and illegal migration and on their market outcomes on these two continents.

Borjas, George. *Friends and Strangers: The Effects of Immigration on the U.S. Economy.* New York: Basic Books, 1997.

One of the most noted scholars examines and critically evaluates the economic impact of high levels of immigration to the United States.

Briggs, Vernon M. Jr., and Stephen Moore. *Still an Open Door? U.S. Immigration Policy and the American Economy.* Washington, DC: American University Press, 1994.

Noted scholars of the economic impact of immigration stress the negative effects of large-scale immigration.

Brubaker, William Roger, ed. *Immigration and the Politics of Citizenship in Europe and North America.* New York: University Press of America; German Marshall Fund of the United States, 1989.

This is an interesting collection of essays on naturalization, citizenship, and the impact of immigration on the politics of the United States and of the EU nations.

Calavita, Kitty. *Inside the State: The Bracero Program, Immigration, and the INS.* New York: Routledge, 1992.

One of the best examinations of the Bracero Program, this book offers insights into temporary-worker programs and the problems associated with that approach.

Camarota, Steven A. *Immigrants in the United States—1998: A Snapshot of America's Foreign-Born Population.* Washington, DC: Center for Immigration Studies, 1999.

This extensive demographically based book looks at immigrants in the United States and the degree to which they are assimilating into the socioeconomic structures of society.

Chang, Leslie. *Beyond the Narrow Gate: The Journey of Four Chinese Women from the Middle Kingdom to Middle America.* New York: Penguin Putnam, 2002.

This book presents poignant stories of four Chinese immigrants to the United States and their gradual acculturation and assimilation into U.S. life.

Chavez, Leo R. *Shadowed Lives: Undocumented Immigrants in American Society.* New York: Harcourt Brace Jovanovich, 1992.

This sharply focused book examines all the problems and negative impacts and discrimination facing undocumented aliens.

Chiswick, Barry R., ed. *The Gateway: U.S. Immigration Issues and Policies.* Washington, DC: American Enterprise Institute, 1982.

This collection of scholarly essays covers many aspects of immigration policy and the problems and need for reform as a result of the Immigration and Naturalization Act of 1965. It covers the pre-IRCA immigration policy reform debate thoroughly.

Crane, Keith, Beth Asch, Joanna Zorn Heilbrunn, and Danielle Cullinane. *The Effects of Employer Sanctions on the Flow of Undocumented Immigrants to the United States.* Santa Monica, CA: RAND Corporation; Washington, DC: Urban Institute, 1990.

This excellent volume in a series of studies by the RAND Corporation and the Urban Institute studies the impact of IRCA and especially the effects of the employer-sanctions approach to control illegal immigration.

Daniels, Roger. *Coming to America: A History of Immigration and Ethnicity in American Life.* New York: Harper, 1990.

This brief but insightful book by one of the most noted of immigration historians presents the history of the interplay of immigration and ethnicity and how they affect U.S. society.

———. *Not Like Us: Immigrants and Minorities in America, 1890–1924.* Lanham, MD: Ivan R. Dee, 1998.

One of the premier U.S. immigration historians focuses on the wave of "New Immigrants" from the 1890s to the 1920s and on the buildup to demands for the quota-system approach to immigration policy following the largest wave of immigrants coming to the United States, mostly from south, central, and eastern Europe.

Daniels, Roger, and Otis L. Graham. *Debating American Immigration, 1882–Present.* Lanham, MD: Rowman and Littlefield, 2003.

Two noted historians of immigration debate the U.S. immigration experience.

Duleep, Harriot O., and Wunrava Phanindra. *Immigrants and Immigration Policy.* Greenwich, CT: JAI Press, 1996.

This book presents a brief discussion of "all you need to know" for persons considering immigration to the United States.

Faist, Thomas. *The Volume and Dynamics of International Migration and Transnational Social Spaces.* New York: Oxford University Press, 2000.

This volume offers an innovative theoretical account of the causes, nature, and extent of the movement of international migrants between affluent and poorer countries and provides a conceptual framework for migration decisionmaking and the dynamics of the international movement of peoples.

Ferris, Elizabeth G., ed. *Refugees and World Politics.* New York: Praeger Publishers, 1985.

This thorough collection of essays on the refugee crisis up to the early 1980s is an important source for world refugee numbers up to that point in time. Most of the issues and many of the problems remain relevant today.

Fitzgerald, Keith. *The Face of the Nation: Immigration, the State, and the National Identity.* Stanford, CA: Stanford University Press, 1996.

This book is a scholarly examination of how the newest wave of large-scale immigration influences the nature and sense of national identity.

Foner, Nancy, Ruben Rumbant, and Steven J. Gold, eds. *Immigration Research for a New Century: Multidisciplinary Perspectives.* New York: Russell Sage, 2000.

This thorough examination of current research on the post-1965 wave of immigrants presents the work of a new generation of immigration scholars from the various social science disciplines.

General Accounting Office (GAO). *Alien Smuggling: Management and Operational Improvements Needed to Address Growing Problem.* Washington, DC: U.S. Government Printing Office, 2002.

GAO's report on alien smuggling has the latest estimates of its extent and suggestions to curb the trend.

——. *H-1B Foreign Workers: Better Controls Needed to Help Employers and Protect Workers.* Washington, DC: U.S. Government Printing Office, 2000.

In 1998, Congress enacted the American Competitiveness and Workforce Improvement Act, which increased the number of H-1B visas (specialty worker visas) from 65,000 to 115,000. This GAO report studies the complex and often abuse-ridden program and documents the continuing need for highly trained H-1B workers, but underscores the risks of exploitative conditions.

———. *Illegal Aliens: Extent of Welfare Benefits Received on Behalf of U.S. Citizen Children.* Washington, DC: U.S. Government Printing Office, 1997.

This GAO study measures the extent of welfare given to the children of illegal aliens.

———. *Illegal Aliens: National Net Cost Estimates Vary Widely.* Washington, DC: U.S. Government Printing Office, 1995.

This book summarizes all the various studies that found pro and con measures of the net cost effect of immigration on the U.S. economy.

———. *Illegal Aliens: Opportunities Exist to Improve the Expedited Removal Process.* Washington, DC: U.S. Government Printing Office, 2000.

The enactment of the IIRIRA (1996) enhanced the expedited removal (ER) provisions that applied to aliens at ports of entry, along with those interdicted at sea and brought to the Untied States for processing. This report is the third such GAO report on its ongoing study of the ER issue. It focuses on recommendations to cope with inconsistent screening for "credible fear" and with reforms to improve due process procedures.

———. *Illegal Aliens: Significant Obstacles to Reducing Unauthorized Alien Employment Exists.* Washington, DC: U.S. Government Printing Office, 1998.

One in a series of GAO studies of unauthorized employment since the enactment of IRCA in 1986, IMMACT in 1990, and IIRIRA in 1996, this report documents continuing problems with the process resulting from the lack of truly "tamper-proof" documentation to show employers to prove eligibility to work.

———. *Illegal Immigration: Status of Southwest Border Strategy*

Implementation. Washington, DC: U.S. Government Printing Office, 1999.

The GAO examines post-IIRIRA implementation of various strategies to enhance the border patrol operations and to better control for illegal entry along the Mexico/U.S. border. This report finds that many programs result in simply shifting points of entry used when increasing control is implemented in a given area.

————. *Immigration Reform: Employer Sanctions and the Question of Discrimination.* Report to Congress. Washington, DC: U.S. Government Printing Office, 1990.

This study found and measured an increase in discrimination as a result of IRCA.

————. *Welfare Reform: Many States Continued Some Federal or State Benefits for Immigrants.* Washington, DC: U.S. Government Printing Office, 1999.

The enactment of IIRIRA in 1996 mandated that the GAO study how states reacted to its provisions. This GAO study found that many states continued welfare benefits and that several states increased state benefits to compensate for cuts in federal programs.

————. *Welfare Reform: Public Assistance Benefits Provided to Recently Naturalized Citizens.* Washington, DC: U.S. Government Printing Office, 1999.

This GAO report, after IIRIRA, studies extensive data on how states were providing public assistance benefits to the recently naturalized citizens following the post-1996 surge (to more than 1 million) in naturalization rates.

Gerstle, Gary, and John Mollenkopf, eds. *E Pluribus Unum? Contemporary and Historical Perspectives on Immigrant Political Incorporation.* New York: Russell Sage Foundation, 2001.

This path-breaking volume brings together historians and social scientists exploring the dynamics of political incorporation (assimilation) of the twentieth century's two great immigration waves. Covering topics from political machines to education, transnational loyalties, and racial exclusion, these essays provide insights into the way immigration has changed and continues to change the United States—both its civic culture and its political life.

Gjerde, Jon, ed. *Major Problems in American Immigration and Ethnic History.* Boston: Houghton Mifflin, 1998.

This book collects essays from leading scholars about a wide variety of problems emerging from large-scale immigration flows to the United States.

Glazer, Nathan, ed. *Clamor at the Gates: The New American Immigration.* San Francisco: ICS Press, 1985.

One of the most noted scholars of immigration focuses on the "New Wave" of post-1965 immigration and examines its demographics.

Gorman, Robert F. *Historical Dictionary of Refugee and Disaster Relief Organizations.* Metuchen, NJ: Scarecrow Press, 1994.

This book provides a comprehensive listing and brief discussion of the refugee/disaster relief problems and the major international relief organizations coping with it.

Hamermesh, Daniel S., and Frank Bean, eds. *Help or Hindrance? The Economic Implications of Immigration for African Americans.* New York: Russell Sage Foundation, 1998.

The debate over how and how much immigration adversely affects African Americans is thoroughly examined in this collection of essays edited by two leading scholars-demographers of the U.S. immigration process.

Hammamoto, Darrell Y., and Rodolfo Torres, eds. *New American Destinies: A Reader in Contemporary Asian and Latino Immigration.* New York: Routledge, 1997.

This collection of scholarly essays focuses on the changed nature in the flow of immigrants since 1965 and the shift in the origins of that flow from northwestern Europe to Latin America and Asia.

Hayslip, Le Ly, and Jay Wurts. *When Heaven and Earth Changed Places: A Vietnamese Woman's Journey from War to Peace.* New York: Penguin Putnam, 2002.

The author recalls her perilous and courageous life, from her youth in central Vietnam, where she was a war child, through her escape to the United States, to her founding of a charitable relief organization.

Hing, Bill Ong. *Making and Remaking Asian America through Immigration Policy, 1850–1990.* Stanford, CA: Stanford University Press, 1993.

This book is a careful and thorough study of Asian immigrants to the United States and their gradual though still partial assimilation.

Hirschman, Charles, Josh DeWind, and Philip Kasinitz, eds. *The Handbook of International Migration.* New York: Russell Sage Foundation, 1999.

This book is an extensive collection of essays on the basics of international migration flows.

Huddle, Donald. *The Costs of Immigration.* Washington, DC: Carrying Capacity Network, 1993.

Huddle's study was among the first careful scholarly attempts to measure the impact of immigration using an economist's cost-benefit-analysis approach. Its assumptions for measuring especially the cost side of the issue were controversial, and the study spurred a host of other studies of the economic impact of immigration over the remainder of the decade.

Hutchinson, Edward. *Legislative History of American Immigration Policy, 1798–1965.* New Brunswick, NJ: Rutgers University Press, 1981.

This book offers a succinct but thorough study of U.S. immigration law and how it changed and evolved from the end of the colonial era until the 1965 Immigration and Nationality Act.

Immigration and Naturalization Service (INS). 1992. *An Immigrant Nation: United States Regulation of Immigration, 1798–1991.* Washington, DC: U.S. Government Printing Office.

This summary report gives the broad outline of the history of immigration regulation through the 1990 IMMACT.

Information Plus. *Immigration and Illegal Aliens: Burden or Blessing?* Wylie, TX: Information Plus, 2001.

This book is the latest in a series of brief but thorough monographs that examine the issue of illegal aliens from a variety of perspectives. It presents many graphs, figures, and tables of data that touch upon every aspect of the influx of illegal aliens. Pros and cons of all sides of the issue and a solid historical perspective are included in every volume in the series.

Isbister, John. *The Immigration Debate: Remaking America.* 1996. On-line; available: www.kpbooks.com; accessed August 12, 2002.

This comprehensive examination of the past and present arguments for and against immigration, with background information, includes discussion of such topics as U.S. history of immigration, the structure of current immigration policy, and the demographic impact of immigration on population growth.

Jones-Correa, Michael, ed. *Governing American Cities.* New York: Russell Sage Foundation, 2001.

This volume focuses on the impact of the newest wave of immigration on the nation's major metropolitan areas. The volume provides what is clearly among the best analyses of how immigration has reshaped urban politics in the United States. It covers especially New York, Los Angeles, and Miami. It provides valuable insight into the new U.S. urban melting pot by offering sophisticated theoretical perspectives on intergroup coalitions and conflicts. It provides rich detail and analyses of class and generational dynamics as these forces influence the political behavior of diverse immigrant groups.

Kastoryano, Riva. *Negotiating Identities: States and Immigrants in France and Germany.* Princeton: Princeton University Press, 2000.

Immigration is even more hotly debated in Europe than it is in the United States. This pivotal work of action and discourse analysis draws on extensive field interviews with politicians, immigrant leaders, and militants to analyze interactions between state and immigrants in France and Germany.

Kim, Hyung-Chan. *Asian Americans and Congress: A Documentary History.* Westport, CT: Greenwood Press, 1996.

One in a series of library reference volumes that offer basic documents of historical significance for a given topic, this book thoroughly covers immigration law as it affected Asian immigration and naturalization (or the lack thereof for so long) into U.S. society.

Klopp, Brett. *German Multiculturalism: Immigrant Integration and the Transformation of Citizenship.* New York: Praeger Publishers, 2002.

Migration, asylum, and citizenship have become issues of primary focus in EU politics. This volume examines issues of immigration, political incorporation, and multiculturalism as found in Germany, Europe's premier immigrant-receiving nation-state. It examines an emerging multicultural society through the perspectives of the immigrants themselves, as well as through the perspectives of such social institutions as unions, employer associations, schools, and city governments.

Koehn, Peter. *Refugees from Revolution: U.S. Policy and Third World Migration.* Boulder, CO.: Westview Press, 1991.

This book examines the way U.S. policy responds to refugee flows and immigration waves induced by the political turmoil in Third World countries.

Kyle, David, and Rey Koslowski. *Global Human Smuggling: Comparative Perspectives.* Baltimore: Johns Hopkins University Press, 2001.

This careful examination of human smuggling in historical and comparative perspectives examines the emergence of international law and of a global moral order of human rights and at the same time explores the economic and political facets of illegal trafficking in humans. It is a comprehensive examination of illegal immigration and those who profit most from it.

Lamm, R. D., and G. Imhoff. *The Immigration Time Bomb: The Fragmenting of America.* New York: Truman Tally Books, E. P. Dutton, 1985.

Published prior to the enactment of IRCA, this book marshals all the arguments and data to show the cost or detrimental effects of large-scale immigration, particularly those arguments used to promote policy reforms to control the flow of illegal immigrants.

LeMay, Michael. *Anatomy of a Public Policy: The Reform of Contemporary American Immigration Law.* New York: Praeger Publishers, 1994.

This detailed case-study examines the 1986 IRCA and the IM-MACT of 1990. It looks at the political movement to enact these two acts using roll-call analyses and interviews with key political actors to explain why the laws were passed with the key provisions each contained.

————. *From Open Door to Dutch Door: An Analysis of U.S. Immigration Policy since 1820.* New York: Praeger Publishers, 1987.

This historical overview of immigration policymaking since 1820 presents the immigration waves. It distinguishes four phases of immigration policy that dominated historical eras in reaction to preceding waves, employing a "door" analogy to characterize each phase or era of immigration policy.

————, ed. *The Gatekeepers: Comparative Immigration Policies.* New York: Praeger Publishers, 1989.

This book collects six original essays, each examining the immigration policy and the reforms thereof of six leading immigrant-receiving nations.

LeMay, Michael, and Elliott Robert Barkan, eds. *U.S. Immigration and Naturalization Law and Issues: A Documentary History.* Westport, CT: Greenwood Press, 1999.

This unique volume summarizes 150 documents covering all major laws and court cases concerning U.S. immigration and naturalization law from colonial times to 1996.

Levitt, Peggy, and Mary C. Waters, eds. *The Changing Face of Home: The Transnational Lives of the Second Generation.* New York: Russell Sage Foundation, 2002.

A significant debate among immigration scholars concerns the extent to which second-generation immigrant children will participate in transnational practices. This volume is divided into three parts. A rich array of contributors to this volume present evidence of transnationalism among the second generation, but they disagree as to the long-term effects of these activities. The first part explores variations by gender, country of origin, and life-cycle stage. Contributors find that both distance and politics play important roles in determining levels of incorporation activities. In the second part, contributors comment on the findings, offering suggestions for reconceptualizing the issues and bridging analytical differences. The essays in the final set examine how home and host-country value systems shape how second-generation immigrants construct their identities and examine the economic, social, and political communities to which they ultimately align.

Loescher, Gil, and Ann Dull Loescher. *The Global Refugee Crisis.* Santa Barbara, CA: ABC-CLIO, 1994.

Another in its series of volumes on contemporary issues viewed in a global perspective, this volume thoroughly examines the current global refugee crisis in the "research handbook" format of the series.

Lowe, Lisa. *Immigrant Acts: On Asian American Cultural Politics.* Durham, NC: Duke University Press, 1997.

This book examines Asian immigration to the United States as fundamental to understanding the racialized foundation of the United States as a nation and to the development of U.S. capitalism. It focuses on the period from 1850 to World War I.

Lutton, Wayne, and John Tanton. *The Immigration Invasion.* Petosky, MI: Social Contact Press, 1994.

This "indictment" of immigration discusses all the problems it can be viewed as having "caused" and marshals every conceivable argument against it.

Lynch, James P., and Rita J. Simon. *Immigration the World Over: Statutes, Policies, and Practices.* Lanham, MD: Rowman and Littlefield, 2003.

This volume offers a current, thorough, though necessarily somewhat brief discussion, in comparative perspective, of the immigration policies and practices of the major immigrant-receiving countries of the world.

Majaridge, Dale. *The Coming White Minority: California's Eruptions and America's Future.* New York: Random House, 1996.

This book makes a polemical argument for all the ills that can (or, the author believes, will) befall the United States as the rest of the nation experiences California's high level of immigration, both legal and illegal.

Martinez, Oscar J. *Border People: Life and Society in U.S.-Mexico Borderlands.* Tucson: University of Arizona Press, 1994.

The author makes a sociological examination of life in the borderlands and of how the flow of people living near and working across the porous Mexican-U.S. border affects all aspects of their daily lives.

Massey, Douglas, Jorge Durand, and Nolan Malone. *Beyond Smoke and Mirrors: Mexican Immigration in an Era of Economic Integration.* New York: Russell Sage Foundation, 2002.

The authors provide a fresh perspective of Mexican migration history by systematically tracing the predictable consequences of highly unsystematic policy regimes. They provide an incisive analysis of the current policy dilemma by marshaling new and compelling evidence to expose the flagrant contradiction of allowing the free flow of goods and capital but not people, and they argue for much-needed policy reforms.

McCarthy, Kevin F., and George Vernez. *Immigration in a Changing Economy: California's Experience.* Santa Monica, CA: RAND Corporation, 1997.

Another in a series of volumes and studies that emerged from the massive RAND Corporation study of immigration policy post-IRCA, this volume is an authoritative case study of the impact of immigration on California's economy and politics.

McClain, Charles J., ed. *Chinese Immigrants and American Law.* New York: Garland Publishing, 1994.

Seventeen original essays by legal scholars, historians, and other social scientists examine the complex relationship between Chinese immigration flows and U.S. law, including discussion of Chinese immigrants' use of the courts to protect themselves against popular violence or discriminatory state or local laws, federal exclusion laws and their impact, and the impact of laws on Chinese women.

McDowell, Lorraine, and Paul T. Hill. *Newcomers in America's Schools.* Santa Monica, CA: RAND Corporation.

One of the volumes of careful research that the RAND Corporation published on the impact of the new immigration flow, this book focuses on the effect of large-scale legal and illegal immigration on California's schools.

Memodovic, Olga, Arie Kuyvnhoven, and Wilhelm T. M. Molle, eds. *Globalization of Labor Markets, Challenges, Adjustment, and Policy Responses in the European Union and the Less Developed Countries.* Dordrecht: Kluwer Academic Publishers, 1998.

The essays in this extensive collection thoroughly examine the globalization of labor markets and how this trend is affecting both the major receiving nations in the European Union, variations in their respective policies toward the migration of labor, and the effects on the less developed sending nations.

Mendelbaum, Michael, ed. *The New European Diasporas: National Minorities and Conflicts in Eastern Europe.* Washington, DC: Brookings Institution Press, 2002.

This thorough and interesting collection of essays deals with the movements of Europeans, east to west, in the migrations flowing from the ethnic conflicts that resulted with the breakup of the former Soviet Union.

Messina, Anthony, ed. *West European Immigration and Immigration Policy in the New Century.* New York: Praeger Publishers, 2002.

The essays in this interesting collection analyze why the major immigrant-receiving nations of western Europe have historically permitted relatively high levels of migration since World War II. They assess how governments in western Europe are currently attempting to control the flow of immigration and to manage the domestic social, economic, and political effects induced by such large-scale immigration.

Morris, Milton. *Immigration: The Beleaguered Bureaucracy.* Washington, DC: Brookings Institution Press, 1985.

Milton Morris, at the time of this writing a senior fellow at the Brookings Institution, addresses the concerns over contemporary immigration by focusing on the character and performance of the INS and the State Department's Bureau of Consular Affairs. His emphasis is on the problems resulting from serious shortcomings in administration: inadequate funding, unclear objectives, and faulty structures and procedures.

Muller, Thomas, and Thomas Espanshade. *The Fourth Wave.* Washington, DC: Urban Institute, 1985.

This groundbreaking book was among the first and most thoroughly analytical examinations of the post-1965 wave of immigrants to the United States. It contributed significantly to renewing the scholarly debate over the costs and benefits to the United States of large-scale immigration.

National Research Council (NRC). *The New Americans: Economic, Demographic, and Fiscal Effects of Immigration.* Washington, DC: NRC; National Academy Press, 1997.

This book contributes to the now extensive literature examining the post-1965 wave of immigration and the degree to which the new immigrants are incorporating into U.S. society, socially, politically, and economically. In many ways, this book is Muller and Espanshade's *Fourth Wave,* circa 1997.

O'Hanlon, Michael E., Peter R. Orszag, Ivo H. Daalder, I. M. Destler, David L. Gunter, Robert E. Latan, and James B. Steinberg, eds. *Protecting the American Homeland: A Preliminary Analysis.* Washington, DC: Brookings Institution Press, 2002.

This work is a discussion of the four-tier plan to guide and bolster the Bush administration's efforts to convince Congress of the need for homeland security. It includes a rationale and recommendations on spending, an analysis of projected costs to the private sector, and suggestions for the restructuring of federal agencies associated with the establishment of a Department of Homeland Security. Its recommendations include the restructuring of the INS and the Border Patrol as well as visa and naturalization activities into the new department.

Papademetriou, Demetrios, Alexander Aleinikoff, and D. W. Meyers. *Reorganizing the U.S. Immigration Function: Toward a New Framework for Accountability.* Washington, DC: Carnegie Endowment for International Peace, 1999.

This volume presents the Carnegie Endowment plan for restructuring the INS and reforming immigration policy. Many of its ideas and concerns are reflected in the new Department of Homeland Security approach. Its analysis presents a good picture of what was wrong with the INS and with U.S. immigration policy, justifying the concern that the INS was broken and needed a major reorganization to fix it, rather than the incremental tinkering with reform that characterized efforts during the 1990s.

Papademetriou, Demetrios, and Mark J. Miller, eds. *The Unavoidable Issue.* Philadelphia: Institute for the Study of Human Issues, 1984.

This volume is an impressive array of essays discussing all the major issues of U.S. immigration policy and the need for reforms in policy. It is a particularly good review of the topic for the period 1965 to 1980.

Passel, Jeffrey. *Immigrants and Taxes: A Reappraisal of Huddle's "The Cost of Immigration."* Washington, DC: Urban Institute, 1994.

This book, a major and important reappraisal of how to measure the costs of immigration, rebuts Donald Huddle's approach and finds considerable differences from Huddle in such costs, essentially concluding that immigration is a benefit rather than a significant cost to the U.S. economy.

Passel, Jeffrey S., and Rebecca L. Clark. *How Much Do Immigrants Really Cost?* Washington, DC: Urban Institute, 1994.

This book, another extensive rebuttal of Donald Huddle's analysis, helped fuel the academic debate over how to measure the costs and benefits of immigration, both legal and illegal, that raged during the 1990s as a result of the Huddle thesis.

Perea, Juan F. *Immigrants Out! The New Nativism and the Anti-Immigrant Impulses in the United States.* New York: New York University Press, 1997.

A collection of eighteen original and specially commissioned essays by leading immigration scholars, this volume uses interdisciplinary perspectives to examine the current surge in nativism in light of past waves of immigration. It takes an unflinchingly critical look at the realities and the rhetoric of the new nativism and examines the relationship between the races of immigrants and the perception of a national immigration crisis.

Portes, Alejandro, ed. *The Economic Sociology of Immigration.* New York: Russell Sage Foundation, 1998.

This definitive volume presents the new scholarship on the political, social, and economic incorporation of the second-generation immigrants.

———, ed. *The New Second Generation.* New York: Russell Sage Foundation, 1996.

This book details the transformation of the postimmigrant generation during the current age of diversity in the United States.

Portes, Alejandro, and Ruben G. Rumbaut. *Legacies: The Story of the Immigrant Second Generation.* Berkeley and Los Angeles: University of California Press; New York: Russell Sage Foundation, 2001.

This study reports on a series of surveys of immigrant children and their parents conducted between 1992 and 1996 in Miami, Florida, and San Diego, California. It uses interview data and school records to provide an overview of the "New Americans." The book emphasizes segmented assimilation and its determinants, how to measure "making it" in the United States, immigrants' outlooks on the United States, language and ethnic identities, the role of schools and education on the psychology of the second generation, and the causes and consequences of school achievement or failure.

———, eds. *Ethnicities: Children of Immigrants in America.* **2 vols.** New York: Russell Sage Foundation, 2001.

These two volumes present the findings of an extensive examination of the political incorporation of second-generation immigrants. These volumes make clear that, in the editors' view, although assimilation was in the past a relatively homogeneous linear process, now it is a segmented one.

Pozzetta, George, ed. *Contemporary Immigration and American Society.* New York: Garland Publishing, 1991.

The volume is the last in a series of twenty relating to immigration history. It is somewhat spotty and varied in its quality and relevance to contemporary society. It covers many groups one would expect to see: Filipinos, Mexicans, Koreans, Haitians, Hispanics, Cubans, and Vietnamese. Yet some groups one might look for are puzzlingly absent: Cambodians, Laotians, Chinese, Indians, Canadians, and Russians. No attention is paid to the influx during the 1980s from Ireland or eastern Europe. The collection's twenty-three articles, drawn from seventeen journals, provide a useful cross-disciplinary perspective. Because the editor selected only previously published articles rather than original essays, the volume's ability to make a significant contribution to the literature is limited. Devoid of any post-IRCA perspective, it is also limited in its contribution toward new methodologies and interpretations relevant to contemporary U.S. society.

Reimers, David. *Still the Golden Door: The Third World Comes to America.* 2nd ed., New York: Columbia University Press, 1985.

One of the foremost U.S. historians of immigration examines post-1965 and particularly post-1980s immigration, including the impact of IRCA (1986) and IMMACT (1990) and the unforeseen consequences of these laws. Looking at the new "third-world coming to America," the book's assessment of these laws is that they are less restrictive in their impact than their opponents suggested.

Sayer, Lucy E. *Laws Harsh as Tigers: Chinese Immigrants and the Shaping of Modern Immigration Law.* Chapel Hill: University of North Carolina Press, 1995.

This volume presents an impressive examination of the laws—national, state, and local—used to restrict Chinese immigration to the United States and Chinese immigrants' battle to overcome their discriminatory impact.

Select Commission on Immigration and Refugee Policy (SCIRP). *Final Report.* Washington, DC: U.S. Government Printing Office, 1981.

The final report of the SCIRP laid the groundwork for what became the Immigration Reform and Control Act of 1986 (IRCA), with its employer sanctions and amnesty provisions, as well as for expanded provisions for seasonal agricultural workers.

Simcox, David. *Measuring the Fallout: The Cost of the IRCA Amnesty after Ten Years.* Washington, DC: Center for Immigration Studies, 1997.

An extensive examination of all of the costs attributable to the legalization program of the 1986 IRCA, this work fuels the calls by the Center for Immigration Studies for strictly limiting immigration and its opposition to new proposals for another amnesty program.

———. *U.S. Immigration in the 1980s: Reappraisal and Reform.* Boulder, CO: Westview Press; Washington, DC: Center for Immigration Studies, 1985.

This collection of sixteen original essays by outstanding immigration scholars from various fields surveys current literature on immigration and its effects on the United States and on the problems or advantages immigration brings to a rapidly changing society. Its major topics include the effects on U.S. workers, national unity, California as the nation's immigrant laboratory, the demographics of displacement, and approaches to a more rational, enforceable immigration policy.

Singh, Jaswinder, and Kolyani Gopal. *Americanization of New Immigrants.* Lanham, MD: University Press of America, 2002.

This book discusses what new immigrants to the United States need to know to adapt.

Stedman, Stephen J., and Fred Tanner, eds. *Refugee Manipulations: War, Politics, and the Abuse of Human Suffering.* Washington, DC: Brookings Institution Press, 2003.

This volume examines why and how armed groups manipulate refugees and how and why international actors assist in their manipulation.

Tomasi, Lydio, ed. *In Defense of the Alien.* New York: Center for Migration Studies.

These annual volumes collect the essays and papers presented at the annual Center for Migration Studies National Conference on Immigration Law, held in Washington, D.C. Each volume contains essays from leading government officials, lawyers, scholars, and immigration-policy practitioners focused on the issues and topics discussed at the convention.

Ueda, Reed. *Postwar Immigrant America: A Social History.* Boston: Bedford Books, St. Martin's Press, 1994.

Using an interdisciplinary focus and joining history and several social science perspectives, this volume probes the impact of arriving ethnic groups on the historic foundations of the United States, stressing how the new Asian and Hispanic immigrants have revitalized political and civic institutions inherited from the

Founders and reshaped the debate over how democracy could encompass ethnic groups with greater inclusiveness and egalitarianism. It applies demographic and quantitative analyses to the rise of worldwide immigration. It uses sociology and demography to understand the development of group life. Political science and law illuminate the relationship of immigration to the U.S. government and its ethnic policies.

U.S. Bureau of the Census. *The Foreign Born Population in the United States, March, 2000.* Current Population Reports. Washington, DC: U.S. Government Printing Office, 2001.

In its annual current population reports, the U.S. Census Bureau provides detailed and copious tabular data on a wide variety of social and economic characteristics of the foreign-born population, often in direct comparison to native-born populations, indicative of the degree of their incorporation into the U.S. workforce and their social integration (e.g., degree of formal education, acquisition of English, and so forth).

U.S. Department of Health and Human Services. *Temporary Assistance for Needy Families (TANF) Program: Third Annual Report to Congress.* Washington, DC: U.S. Government Printing Office, 2000.

The Welfare Reform Act of 1996 (IIRIRA) required annual reports on emerging data about welfare caseloads, family employment and earnings, state policy choices in assistance, and so on. This report provides a sharp statistical picture of the status of the program after four years of implementing welfare reform.

U.S. Department of Labor. *International Migration to the United States, 1999.* Washington, DC: U.S. Government Printing Office, 1999.

This report is one of the annual reports of the Department of Labor to study the flow of migration into the United States and the degree of its incorporation into the labor force.

U.S. Department of State. *Proposed Refugee Admissions for Fiscal Year 2001: Report to Congress.* Washington, DC: U.S. Government Printing Office, 2000.

The 1980 Refugee Act called for annual reports to Congress by the Department of State recommending the proposed number of refugee admissions and providing a rationale for the recommended levels. This fiscal year 2000 report provides the DOS recommendations for 2001.

———. *U.S. Refugee Admissions for Fiscal Year 2000.* Washington, DC: U.S. Government Printing Office, 1999.

This Department of State report provides detailed statistical data and analysis to Congress on the number of refugees admitted for the fiscal year.

Wolfe, Alan. *One Nation, After All.* New York: Penguin Putnam, 2002.

The book takes the reader on a "tour" through what middle-class Americans think about God, country, family, racism, welfare, immigration, homosexuality, the Right, the Left, and each other.

Yang, Philip O. *Post-1965 Immigration to the United States: Structural Determinants.* New York: Praeger Publishers, 1995.

Yang examines why countries differ in the size of their legal, permanent immigration population in the post-1965 period by investigating the structural determinants of cross-national variation in post-1965 immigration. He seeks the integration and development of international migration theories. He discusses the policy implications of how the U.S. should regulate and control immigration.

Yans-McLaughlin, Virginia, ed. *Immigration Reconsidered: History, Sociology, and Politics.* New York: Oxford University Press, 1990.

A collection of eleven original essays by scholars presenting at a conference in New York City in 1986, this volume covers various topics: immigration patterns, ethnicity and social structure, the study of new immigration, new approaches to the study of immigration, and the politics of immigration policy and its reform.

Zhou, Min, and Carl Bankston III. *Growing Up American: How Vietnamese Children Adapt to Life in the United States.* New York: Russell Sage Foundation, 1999.

This book examines the single largest group of refugee children—the Vietnamese refugees—as they experienced growing up in

America. Chapters examine such topics as the scattering by the war, resettlement, reconstruction of an ethnic community, social networks, language and adaptation, experiences in adaptation in U.S. schools, bicultural conflicts, gender role changes, and delinquency.

Zimmerman, Klaus F. *European Migration: What Do We Know?* New York: Oxford University Press, 2002.

This book offers a thorough assessment of the current situation of migration in a comprehensive range of European countries. It includes chapters on the United States, Canada, and New Zealand for comparative purposes. The "case study" for each country is written by a local expert, and the overall editor is one of Europe's leading scholars on the economics of immigration.

Zolberg, Aristide, Astri Suhrki, and Sergio Aguayo. *Escape from Violence: Conflict and the Refugee Crisis in the Developing World.* New York: Oxford University Press, 1989.

This cogent treatment of the causes of refugee flows emphasizes domestic and international causes of the flows and regional differences around the globe. The case studies are rich in detail; the analysis is systematic and comprehensive.

Zucker, Norman L., and Naomi Flink Zucker. *The Guarded Gate: The Reality of American Refugee Policy.* 1987.

This critical assessment of U.S. asylum policy stresses the political elements of the asylum debate. The work emphasizes U.S. government asylum policy rather than refugee policy broadly construed.

Journals

American Demographics
Seema Mayar, Editor
470 Park Avenue South
Eighth Floor
New York, NY 10016
Phone: (212) 545-3600
Fax: (917) 981-2927
Website: http://www.demographic.com

Published ten times per year, this peer-reviewed journal is an out-let for multidisciplinary articles dealing with all topics related to demography, occasional articles and reflective essays on migration and immigration, and an annual resource guide.

American Geographical Society
120 Wall Street, Suite 100
New York, NY 10005-3904
Phone: (212) 422-5456
Fax: (212) 422-5480
E-mail: AFS@amergeog.org
Website: http://www.geography.unr.edu

This quarterly journal of the American Geographical Society publishes research on all topics related to geography, and hence occasional ones dealing with migration and immigration and with the incorporation of immigrants. It also contains related book reviews.

American Journal of Sociology
Andrew Abbott, Editor
University of Chicago Press, Journal Division
1427 East Sixtieth Street
Chicago, Illinois 60637
Phone: (773) 753-3347
Fax: (773) 753-0811
E-mail: ajs@src.uchicago.edu
Website: http://www.journals.uchicago.edu/AJS

This scholarly, peer-reviewed quarterly journal of sociology has frequent articles concerning assimilation and integration, social trends and policies regarding migration and immigration, and book reviews on immigration-related topics.

Citizenship Studies
Engin F. Isin, York University, Canada
Taylor and Francis Group, Carfax Publishing
1185 Avenue of the Americas
New York, NY 10036
Phone: 44 (0) 2078422001
Fax: 44 (0) 2078422298
E-mail: isin@yorku.ca
Website: http://www.tandf.co.uk/journals

This quarterly journal publishes internationally recognized scholarly work on contemporary issues in citizenship, human rights, and democratic processes from an interdisciplinary perspective covering politics, sociology, history, and cultural studies.

Columbia Law Review
Margaret L. Taylor
435 West 116th Street
New York, NY 10027
Phone: (800) 828-7571

This law review is published eight times per year. It frequently has case reviews and analytical articles and original essays dealing with immigration law matters.

Demography
Barbara Entwisle, University of North Carolina, Chapel Hill
S. Philip Morgan, Duke University
Editors, *Demography*
Department of Sociology
The Ohio State University
Columbus, OH 43210
Phone: (614) 292-2858
E-mail: demography@osu.edu

This peer-reviewed journal of the Population Association of America publishes scholarly research of interest to demographers from a multidisciplinary perspective, with emphases on social sciences, geography, history, biology, statistics, business, epidemiology, and public health. It publishes specialized research papers and historical and comparative studies.

Ethnic and Racial Studies
John Solomos, South Bank University, UK
Taylor and Francis Group, Carfax Publishing
1185 Avenue of the Americas
New York, NY 10036
Phone: 44 (0) 2078422001
Fax: 44 (0) 2078422298
E-mail: isin@yorku.ca
Website: http://www.tandf.co.uk/journals

A bimonthly journal for the analysis of race, ethnicity, and nationalism in the present global environment, this interdisciplinary forum for research and theoretical analysis uses the disciplines of sociology, social policy, anthropology, political science, economics, geography, international relations, history, social psychology, and cultural studies.

Ethnohistory
Neil Whitehead, University of Wisconsin, Madison
905 West Main Street, 18-B
Durham, NC 27701
Phone: (713) 358-2600
Website: http://www.questia.com/index/jsp?CRID=ethnohistory

This quarterly publication of the *Journal of the American Society for Ethnohistory* contains articles on original research, commentaries, review essays, and book reviews.

Ethnology
Leonard Plotnicov, University of Pittsburgh, Department of Anthropology
3H29 Posvar Hall
Pittsburgh, PA 15260
Phone: (215) 624-8900
Fax: (215) 625-2940
E-mail: ethnology@pitt.edu
Website: http://www.questia.com/index/jsp?CRID=ethnohistory

This international journal of culture and social anthropology publishes original research articles by scientists of any country regarding cultural anthropology with substantive data. Topics of interest relate to ethnicity, social integration, and migration adaptation.

Foreign Affairs
James F. Hoge Jr., Editor
58 East Sixty-Eighth Street
New York, NY 10021
Phone: (800) 354-1420
Fax: (212) 434-9859
E-mail: foraff@palmcoastd.com or ForAff@email.cfr.org

This bimonthly magazine publishes articles and original essays on topics related to foreign policy by both scholars and practitioners. It also contains book reviews.

The Geographical Journal
Andrew Millington, Department of Geography,
University of Leicester
University Road, Leicester
LEI 7RH, UK
Phone: + 4 (0) 1865 244083
Fax: + 4 (0) 1865 381381
E-mail: acm4@le.ac.uk or jnlinfo@blackwellpublishers.co.uk
Website: http://www.blackwellpublishers.co.uk

The quarterly academic journal of the Royal Geographical Society publishes research reports and review articles of refereed articles related to all subjects concerning geography.

The Geographical Review
Paul Starrs, University of Nevada, Editor

Georgetown Immigration Law Journal
Georgetown University Law Center
Office of Journal Administration
600 New Jersey Avenue NW
Washington, DC 20001
Phone: (202) 662-9635 or (800) 828-7571
Website: http://www.law.georgetown.edu/journals/gilj

This quarterly law review is *the* most specifically related law journal dealing with U.S. immigration law, its current developments, and reform-related matters concerning all three branches of the U.S. government. It contains case reviews, articles, notes and commentaries, and workshop reports devoted to the topic.

Harvard Law Review
Harvard Law Review, Gannett House
1511 Massachusetts Avenue
Cambridge, MA 02138
Phone: (617) 495-3100
Website: http://www.law.harvard.edu/publications

The review is published eight times per year. It contains original articles, case reviews, essays, commentaries, and book reviews occasionally on topics related to immigration law and its reform.

Identities
Jonathan D. Hill, Southern Illinois University

Taylor and Francis Group, Carfax Publishing
1185 Avenue of the Americas
New York, NY 10036
Phone: 44 (0) 2078422001
Fax: 44 (0) 2078422298
E-mail: isin@yorku.ca
Website: http://www.tandf.co.uk/journals

This journal explores the relationship of racial, ethnic, and national identities and power hierarchies within national and global
arenas. It has an interdisciplinary focus, using social, political,
and cultural analyses of the processes of domination, struggle,
and resistance and of the class structures and gender relations in-
tegral to both maintaining and challenging subordination.

Immigrants and Minorities
Frank Cass, Gainsborough House
11 Gainsborough Road
London Ell 1RS
England
Phone: 44 (0) 2089202100
Fax: 44 (0) 2084478548
Website: http://www.frankcass.com/jnls/i&m.htm

This British quarterly focuses on immigrant minorities in Western
societies.

INS Reporter
Houston District Office, INS
126 Northpointe Drive
Houston, TX 77060
E-mail: ins.houston.district.director@houusdoj.gov
Website: http://www.immigration.gov/graphics/fieldoffices

This quarterly publication provides brief surveys of recent developments in U.S. immigration law.

INS Statistical Yearbook
Immigration and Naturalization Service
425 I Street NW
Washington, DC 20536
Phone: (800) 375-5283
Website: http://www.immigration.gov/graphics/aboutus/index

This annual publication gives statistical data in text, graphic, and tabular form. It also presents the latest "official" numbers on U.S. immigration.

International Migration
International Organization for Migration
Blackwell Publishing
108 Cowley Road
Oxford, UK
Phone: 44 (0) 1865791100
Fax: 44 (0) 1865791347
Website: http://www.blackwellpublishing.com/contacts/uk_us

This quarterly is an intergovernmental publication featuring documents, conference reports, and articles dealing with international migration topics.

International Migration Review
Center for Migration Studies
209 Flagg Place
Staten Island, NY 10304
Phone: (718) 351-8800
Fax: (718) 667-4598
E-mail: CMSLFT@aol.com
Website: http://www.cmsny.org

The leading quarterly journal in the field of migration, *International Migration Review* contains current research articles, book reviews, documents, and bibliographies.

International Organizations
The MIT Press
Five Cambridge Center
Cambridge, MA 02142-1493
Phone: (617) 253-5646
Fax: (617) 258-6779
Website: http://www.mitpress.mit.edu/IO

This journal is published quarterly by MIT Press for the World Peace Foundation. It carries articles on all aspects of world politics and international political economy.

International Review of the Red Cross
International Committee of the Red Cross
19 Avenue de la Paix
CH-1202 Geneva

Switzerland
Phone: 41 (22) 734 6001
Fax: 41 (22) 733 2057

This journal, published six times annually, contains articles on international humanitarian law and policy matters.

International Social Sciences Journal
John Crowley
5HS/SR8 UNESCO
1 Rue Miollis
75732 Paris Dedex 15
France
Phone: 33 (1) 45 68 38 28
Fax: 33 (1) 45 68 57 24
E-mail: j.crowley@unesco.org
Website: http://www.unesco.org/issj

This quarterly journal is published by Blackwell Publishers for UNESCO. It regularly contains articles concerning international migration and its impact on societies and social systems, as well as other topics related to UNESCO.

International Studies Quarterly
James M. McCormick, Iowa State University
108 Cowley Road
Oxford, OX4, JF
England
Phone: 4 (0) 1865 244083
Fax: 4 (0) 1865 381381
and
350 Main Street
Malden, MA 02148
E-mail: ceaisa@iastate.edu
Website: http://www.public.iastate.edu/~isq

Another scholarly quarterly journal published by Blackwell Publishers, as above.

International Studies Review
Linda Miller, Brown University
108 Cowley Road
Oxford, OX4, JF
England

Phone: 4 (0) 1865 244083
Fax: 4 (0) 1865 381381
and
350 Main Street
Malden, MA 02148

This quarterly journal is published by Blackwell for the International Studies Association. It contains original scholarly articles on research, review essays, book reviews, and an annual special issue on a theme.

Journal of American Studies
Richard Gray, University of Sussex, Cambridge University Press
40 West Twentieth Street
New York, NY 10011-4211
Phone: (212) 924-3900
Fax: (212) 691-3239
E-mail: information@cup.org
Website: http://www.cup.cam.ac.uk

Published three times per year, this multidisciplinary, scholarly, refereed journal is multinational, with an emphasis on articles on politics, economics, and geography and book reviews that will often relate to immigration matters.

Journal of Economic History
Jan De Vries, Stanford University
Social Science History Institute
Building 200, Room 3
Stanford, CA 94305-2024
Phone: (520) 621-2575
E-mail: sisaac@u.arizona.edu

This journal publishes original scholarship on the study of the economic aspects of the human past from a diversity of perspectives, most notably history and economics.

Journal of Economic Issues
Department of Economics
Bucknell University
Lewisburg, PA 89557-0207
Phone: (570) 577-3648
Fax: (570) 577-3451
E-mail: afee@bucknell.edu

This economics scholarly journal covers all aspects of economic issues, and hence has occasional original research on immigration and migration with a focus on economic impact, labor market issues, and so on. It includes book reviews of related matters as well.

Journal of Economic Perspectives
Alan Krueger, Princeton University
Hubert Humphrey Institute of Public Affairs
University of Minnesota
301 Nineteenth Avenue South
Minneapolis, MN 55455
Phone: (651) 696-6822
Fax: (651) 696-6825
E-mail: jep@macalester.edu

This journal of the American Economic Association publishes occasional symposium issues and regularly publishes original scholarly articles, features, economic analyses of a variety of public policy issues, including immigration, and book reviews of related books.

Journal of Ethnic and Migration Studies
Russell King, University of Sussex, UK
Taylor and Francis Group, Carfax Publishing
1185 Avenue of the Americas
New York, NY 10036
Phone: 44 (0) 2078422001
Fax: 44 (0) 2078422298
E-mail: isin@yorku.ca
Website: http://www.tandf.co.uk/journals

Edited from the Sussex Center for Migration Research at the University of Sussex, this journal publishes quality research on all forms of migration and its consequences, with articles on ethnicity, ethnic relations and ethnic conflict, race and racism, multiculturalism and pluralism, nationalism and transnationalism, citizenship and integration, identity and hybridity, globalization, and cosmopolitanism; it also contains policy debates and theoretical papers.

Journal of Intercultural Studies
Pete Lentini and Jan van Bommel, Monash University, Australia
Taylor and Francis Group, Carfax Publishing
1185 Avenue of the Americas

New York, NY 10036
Phone: 44 (0) 2078422001
Fax: 44 (0) 2078422298
E-mail: isin@yorku.ca
Website: http://www.tandf.co.uk/journals

This journal presents international research related to intercultural studies across national and disciplinary boundaries. One issue per year is thematic. It examines a common issue across a range of disciplinary perspectives. The journal presents peer-reviewed research, theoretical papers, and book reviews.

Journal of International Refugee Law
Oxford University Press
Walton Street
Oxford OX2 6DP
England
Phone: 44 (0) 1865 353907
Fax: 44 (0) 1865 353485
Website: http://www.3.oup.uk/jnls

This quarterly journal publishes articles on refugee law and policy matters, including legislation and documentation, and abstracts of recent publications in the field.

Migration
Berlin Institute for Social Research
Postfach 1125
1000 Berlin 30
Germany
E-mail: info@emz-berlin.de
Website: http://www.emz-berlin.de/migration/migration.htm

This European journal concerns international migration and ethnic relations.

Migration News
Philip Martin, University of California at Davis
Department of Agricultural Economics
One Shields Avenue
Davis, CA 95616
E-mail: migrant@primal.ucdavis.edu
Website: http://migration.ucdavis.edu

This monthly newsletter published by the University of California, Davis, concerns all manner of topics related to migration, especially as immigration affects U.S. society.

Migration World
Center for Migration Studies
209 Flagg Place
Staten Island, NY 10304
Phone: (718) 351-8800
Fax: (718) 667-4598
E-mail: cms@smsny.org
Website: http://www.cmsny.org

This journal publishes articles and information about migration and refugee problems worldwide in a readable and accessible way. It is a good source for school and college reports.

National Identities
Peter Catterall, Queen Mary University of London, UK
Taylor and Francis Group, Carfax Publishing
1185 Avenue of the Americas
New York, NY 10036
Phone: 44 (0) 2078422001
Fax: 44 (0) 2078422298
E-mail: isin@yorku.ca
Website: http://www.tandf.co.uk/journals

This journal, published three times annually, focuses on identity and ethnicity by examining how they are shaped and changed and on the transmission and persistence of national identities.

Patterns of Prejudice
David Cesaraini, University of Southampton, UK
Brian Klug, Saint Xavier University, Chicago (U.S. Consulting Editor)
Taylor and Francis Group, Carfax Publishing
1185 Avenue of the Americas
New York, NY 10036
Phone: 44 (0) 2078422001
Fax: 44 (0) 2078422298
E-mail: isin@yorku.ca
Website: http://www.tandf.co.uk/journals

This new journal provides a forum for exploring the historical roots and contemporary varieties of demonizations of "the other." It probes language and the construction of "race," nation, color, and ethnicity as well as the linkages between these categories. It also addresses issues and policy agenda such as asylum, immigration, hate crimes, Holocaust denial, and citizenship.

Policy Studies Journal
Uday Desai, Southern Illinois University, Carbondale
Mark C. Shellby II, Iowa State University
Policy Studies Organization (Stuart Nigal)
711 South Ashton Lane
Champaign, IL 61820
Phone: (217) 352-7700
Fax: (217) 352-3037
Website: http://www.moh.govt.nz/notebook

This journal of the Policy Studies Organization is produced at Iowa State University's College of Education. It is published quarterly and contains articles related to all issues of public policy, and it has occasional symposium issues and regular book reviews.

Policy Studies Review
Georgia State University
Department of Public Administration and Urban Studies
Policy Studies Organization (Stuart Nigal)
711 South Ashton Lane
Champaign, IL 61820
Phone: (217) 352-5094
Fax: (217) 352-3521
E-mail: info@ipsonet.org
Website: http://www.ipsonet.org/index

This journal is a product of the Policy Studies Organization.

Political Science Quarterly
Demetrios Caraley, Bernard College, Columbia University
475 Riverside Drive
Suite 1274
New York, NY 10115-1274
Tel: (978) 750-8400
Website: http://www.jstor.org

This quarterly scholarly journal is the journal of public and international affairs for the Academy of Political Science. It is nonpartisan, with scholarly, reviewed articles devoted to the study and analysis of government, politics, and international affairs. It contains original articles and essays, review essays, and book reviews.

Race, Ethnicity, and Education
David Gilborn, University of London, UK
Taylor and Francis Group, Carfax Publishing
1185 Avenue of the Americas
New York, NY 10036
Phone: 44 (0) 2078422001
Fax: 44 (0) 2078422298
E-mail: isin@yorku.ca
Website: http://www.tandf.co.uk/journals

This interdisciplinary, refereed journal publishes international scholarship, research, and debate on issues concerning the dynamics of race, racism, and ethnicity in educational policy, theory, and practice, focusing on the interconnections between race, ethnicity, and multiple forms of oppression, including class, gender, sexuality, and disability.

Refugee Reports
U.S. Committee for Refugees
1717 Massachusetts Avenue NW, Suite 701
Washington, DC 20036
Phone: (202) 347-3507
Fax: (202) 347-3418
E-mail: uscr@irsa-uscr.org
Website: http://www.refugees.org

This is a monthly report of information and documents concerning refugees and legislation, policies, and programs affecting them. A year-end statistical issue is published every December.

Refugee Survey Quarterly
Center for the Documentation on Refugees
UNHCR Case Postale 2500
1211-Geneva 2 Depot
Switzerland
Website: http://www.3.oup.co.uk/refqt

This quarterly journal lists abstracts of the many publications concerning refugees, including a selection of "country reports" and one on human rights–related legal documents.

Rural Migration News
University of California at Davis
One Shields Avenue
Davis, CA 95616
Phone: (530) 752-2320
Fax: (530) 752-5451
Website: http://www.migration.ucdavis.edu

This quarterly publication of the University of California, Davis, summarizes the most important immigration developments affecting cities and towns in California and rural areas throughout the United States.

Social Identities
Abebe Zegeye, University of South Africa
David T. Goldberg, University of California, Irvine
Taylor and Francis Group, Carfax Publishing
1185 Avenue of the Americas
New York, NY 10036
Phone: 44 (0) 2078422001
Fax: 44 (0) 2078422298
E-mail: isin@yorku.ca
Website: http://www.tandf.co.uk/journals

This interdisciplinary and international journal focuses on issues addressing social identities in the context of the transformation of the political economies and cultures of postmodern and postcolonial conditions.

Social Science Quarterly
Robert Lineberry, Department of Political Science
University of Houston
47 PGH
Houston, TX 77204-3011
Phone: (713) 743-3935
Fax: (713) 743-3927
E-mail: ssq@mail.uh.edu

Published for the Southwestern Social Science Association by Blackwell Publishing, this interdisciplinary quarterly presents articles of original research, review essays, book reviews, and occasional symposium issues. It frequently contains articles dealing with U.S. immigration and immigration policy and with issues related to the incorporation of immigrants and their children into U.S. society.

State of the World Population
UN Population Fund
United Nations
UN Plaza
New York, NY 10017
Phone: (212) 297-5050
E-mail: serrano@unfpa.org
Website: http://www.unfpa.org/swp/swpmain.htm

This annual publication covers world population growth and the problems resulting from it. It contains the latest in official statistics.

Videos

Angel Island: A Story of Chinese Immigration
Length: 12 minutes, color
Date: 2002
Cost: $69.95
Source: Films for the Humanities and Sciences
P.O. Box 2053
Princeton, NJ 08543-2053
Website: http://www.films.com

From 1910 to 1943, Chinese immigrants passed through Angel Island in San Francisco Bay, the Ellis Island of the West. Slated for destruction, the station was spared in 1970 when a park ranger discovered, beneath layers of paint, poems written by anxious detainees over their fear of deportation. This program looks at how two women are raising funds and awareness to have the old immigration station restored.

The Asianization of America
Length: 26 minutes, color
Date: 1993
Cost: $89.95
Source: Films for the Humanities and Sciences
P.O. Box 2053
Princeton, NJ 08543-2053
Website: http://www.films.com

This program examines the role of Asian Americans half a century after repeal of the Chinese Exclusion Act. It seeks to determine what accounts for Asian Americans' success in academia and the extent to which they can, should, or want to blend into the American melting pot.

Blue Collar and Buddha
Length: 57 minutes (color)
Date: 1990
Cost: $150
Source: Filmakers Library, Inc.
124 East Fortieth Street
No. 901
New York, NY 10016
Phone: (212) 808-4980
Fax: (212) 808-4983
E-mail: info@filmakers.com
Website: http://www.filmakers.com

This video explores the problems of Laotian refugees resettled in Rockford, Illinois, and their need to balance preserving their own culture and adapting to their new environment. Readjustment problems are complicated by the intolerance of their working-class neighbors.

Caught in the Crossfire: Arab-Americans in Wartime
Length: 54 minutes, color
Date: 2002
Cost: $298
Source: First Run/Icarus Films
32 Court Street
21st Floor
Brooklyn, NY 11201
Phone: (800) 876-1710
Website: http://www.frif.com

This film covers New York City's Arab population, who are caught in the cross-fire of President Bush's War on Terrorism, and the cold welcome they now experience. Raghida Dergham, CNN diplomatic correspondent for the leading independent Arab newspaper is featured, as is Khader El-Yateem, an Arab-Christian whose Arabic Lutheran Church serves as a haven for Brooklyn Arabs, Muslim and Christian alike, and Ahmed Nasser, a Yemen-born police officer stationed at Ground Zero after September 11, 2001, who relates how Arab American calls for help when they were harassed were ignored in his precinct. The film shows how Arab Americans are torn between their adopted country and their homelands as they wrestle with their place in wartime America.

Death on a Friendly Border
Length: 26 minutes, color
Date: 2002
Cost: $250
Source: Filmakers Library, Inc.
124 East Fortieth Street
No. 901
New York, NY 10016
Phone: (212) 808-4980
Fax: (212) 808-4983
E-mail: info@filmakers.com
Website: http://www.filmakers.com

The border between Tijuana, Mexico, and San Diego, California, is the most militarized border between "friendly" countries anywhere. Since 1994, when the United States began Operation Gatekeeper, an average of one person per day dies trying to cross. This film puts a face on that daily tragedy by following the story of a young woman who makes the perilous journey, with its hardships of heat, thirst, and abusive border guards.

The Double Life of Ernesto Gomez
Length: 54 minutes, color
Date: 2001
Cost: $295
Source: Filmakers Library, Inc.
124 East Fortieth Street
No. 901
New York, NY 10016
Phone: (212) 808-4980
Fax: (212) 808-4983
E-mail: info@filmakers.com
Website: http://www.filmakers.com

This film focuses on fifteen-year-old Ernesto Gomez, who has two identities, two families, and three nations: the United States, Mexico, and Puerto Rico. It follows his journey from Mexico to the United States to meet his Puerto Rican birth mother and to learn of his heritage. This award-winning film documents his struggle for identity.

Dying to Get In: Illegal Immigration to the E.U.
Length: 58 minutes, color
Date: 2002
Cost: $149.95
Source: Films for the Humanities and Sciences
P.O. Box 2053
Princeton, NJ 08543-2053
Website: http://www.films.com

This video surveys the high-tech methods used to secure the European Union's borders against refugees and asylum seekers. It interviews human smugglers, illegal immigrants, and European immigration bureaucrats who attempt to maintain "Fortress Europe" by keeping out as many immigrants as possible.

El Chogui: A Mexican Immigrant Story
Length: 57 minutes, color
Date: 2002
Cost: $295.00
Source: Filmakers Library, Inc.
124 East Fortieth Street
No. 901
New York, NY 10016
Phone: (212) 808-4980
Fax: (212) 808-4983
E-mail: info@filmakers.com
Website: http://www.filmakers.com

This film follows Louis Miguel, a young peasant from Oaxaca, Mexico, as he tries to lift his family out of poverty by boxing. He emigrates to the United States, as have countless of his compatriots. The film follows his transition over six years, from his tension-filled, illegal border crossing with his sisters, to his later crossings to bring his four brothers to California.

English Only in America
Length: 25 minutes, color
Date: 2002
Cost: $149.95
Source: Films for the Humanities and Sciences
P.O. Box 2053
Princeton, NJ 08543-2053
Website: http://www.films.com

When California passed its "English-only" law, it set off a storm of legal and social debate that continues to rage today. This film interviews persons in favor of and opposing the English-only policy from social, legal, and education perspectives.

Escape to the E.U.? Human Rights and
Immigration Policy in Conflict
Length: 58 minutes
Date: 2002
Cost: $149.95
Source: Films for the Humanities and Sciences
P.O. Box 2053
Princeton, NJ 08543-2053
Website: http://www.films.com

This video covers human rights policy, focusing on the European Union since 1960. It examines the processing of refugees and asylum seekers in Sweden and Great Britain and the UN and EU policies addressing human rights issues. News-making stories of a Bangladeshi detainee's suicide, a Kosovar-Albanian detainee's deportation to face near-certain death, and Cameroonian political activists are featured. The film looks at xenophobia as a political tool.

From a Different Shore: The Japanese-American Experience
Length: 50 minutes, color
Date: 2002
Cost: $129.95
Source: Films for the Humanities and Sciences
P.O. Box 2053
Princeton, NJ 08543-2053
Website: http://www.films.com

Japanese Americans are often considered a "model minority." By looking at three families whose members span three generations, this video explores the experiences of the first immigrants, the Isei; of their children, the Nisei, who endured confinement in camps during World War II; and of their grandchildren.

The Golden Cage: A Story of California's Farmworkers
Length: 29 minutes, color
Date: 1990
Cost: $295
Source: Filmakers Library, Inc.
124 East Fortieth Street

No. 901
New York, NY 10016
Phone: (212) 808-4980
Fax: (212) 808-4983
E-mail: info@filmakers.com
Website: http://www.filmakers.com

A modern *Grapes of Wrath,* this film offers a vivid and moving portrait of contemporary farmworkers using historical footage, interviews, newspaper clippings, and black-and-white stills. It traces the history of the United Farm Workers Union from the 1960s to 1990, showing the tactics used by many companies to avoid using union labor. It shows candid interviews with legal and illegal migrant workers, growers, doctors, and others.

Human Contraband: Selling the American Dream

Length: 22 minutes, color
Date: 2002
Cost: $89.95
Source: Films for the Humanities and Sciences
P.O. Box 2053
Princeton, NJ 08543-2053
Website: http://www.films.com

This ABC news program investigates the lucrative trade in smuggling desperate human beings from all over the world into Mexico, which is viewed as the back door to the United States. INS officials discuss multilateral efforts to combat illegal entry into the United States.

Illegal Americans

Length: 45 minutes, color
Date: 2002
Cost: $129.95
Source: Films for the Humanities and Sciences
P.O. Box 2053
Princeton, NJ 08543-2053
Website: http://www.films.com

This CBS news documentary looks at the hazardous enterprise of coming to the United States illegally, focusing on the plight of illegal aliens. It examines their living conditions in detention centers; the growing strains they place on U.S. cities, which provide assistance to those who manage to evade capture; the sweatshops that exploit them; and the efforts of some to beat the system via fake ID's and marriages of convenience.

The Immigrant Experience: 1900–1940
Length: 29 minutes, color
Date: 2002
Cost: $89.95
Source: Films for the Humanities and Sciences
P.O. Box 2053
Princeton, NJ 08543-2053
Website: http://www.films.com

This ABC documentary, anchored by Peter Jennings, dramatically relates the story of the transformation of the United States into a truly multicultural nation, from ethnic neighborhoods in New York to black migration to northern cities during the Great Depression. It discusses the terror tactics of the Ku Klux Klan and ugly incidents of racism, including the fears that prompted the internment of 120,000 Japanese and Japanese Americans in World War II.

Immigration: Who Has Access to the American Dream?
Length: 28 minutes, color
Date: 2002
Cost: $89.95
Source: Films for the Humanities and Sciences
P.O. Box 2053
Princeton, NJ 08543-2053
Website: http://www.films.com

This program reviews the ways new policy directives affect the survival of new immigrants to the United States. It covers a variety of questions, such as how many immigrants should be allowed in, who, if anyone, should receive preferential treatment, and how illegal immigrants should be handled. It examines these issues from various perspectives: from the perspectives of those seeking entry and the organizations who assist them, an immigration judge, an immigrant from Kenya, and a Korean immigrant owner of a New York City deli.

Immigration, Social Policy, and Employment
Length: 30 minutes, color
Date: 2001
Cost: $239

Source: Insight Media
2162 Broadway
New York, NY 10024–0621
Phone: (800) 233-9910
Fax: (800) 721-6316
Website: www.insight-media.com

This film presents students discussing the history of immigration. The discussion examines the successive waves of immigrants to the United States and the reasons people chose to migrate to the United States, and it explores the immigrants' reactions and contributions to U.S. culture and their impact on the increasing diversity of the current and future workforce.

In the Land of Plenty
Length: 62 minutes, color
Date: 1999
Cost: $295
Source: Filmakers Library, Inc.
124 East Fortieth Street
No. 901
New York, NY 10016
Phone: (212) 808-4980
Fax: (212) 808-4983
E-mail: info@filmakers.com
Website: http://www.filmakers.com

This video follows Mexican migrant farmworkers—most of whom do not speak English, are undocumented, and lack means to protect themselves from exploitation—through the strawberry fields of Watsonville, California. It follows the lives of the workers, showing their long hours at poor wages, exposure to toxic chemicals, and lack of health insurance and child care. It documents how they return far more to the economy than they take from it. Their meager wages are taxed, even though they receive no benefits, yet they are looked upon with hostility by the government as well as by private citizens.

The Latino Family
Length: 28 minutes, color
Date: 1993
Cost: $239.00
Source: Insight Media
2162 Broadway

New York, NY 10024–0621
Phone: (800) 233-9910
Fax: (800) 721-6316
Website: www.insight-media.com

This film follows the paths of three generations of one Mexican American family and, by looking at the roles of the elderly as they adjust to their families' changing needs, demonstrates how patterns of migration and cultural change have affected traditional Latino families.

Legacy of Shame: Migrant Labor, an American Institution
Length: 52 minutes, color
Date: 2002
Cost: $89.95
Source: Films for the Humanities and Sciences
P.O. Box 2053
Princeton, NJ 08543-2053
Website: http://www.films.com

This video, a CBS news documentary, is a follow-up to the award-wining 1960 film *Harvest of Shame.* It documents ongoing exploitation of migrant laborers in the United States by highlighting the efforts made to protect them. It investigates pesticide risks, uneven enforcement of employment and immigration regulations, and peonage conditions. It covers the efforts of rural legal services as advocates for this "silent minority."

Muslims in America: Islam in Exile
Length: 57 minutes, color
Date: 2002
Cost: $149.95
Source: Films for the Humanities and Sciences
P.O. Box 2053
Princeton, NJ 08543-2053
Website: http://www.films.com

This film examines the surprisingly fast growth of Islam in the heart of the U.S. Bible Belt. Muslims living in Appalachia face daily challenges, less over acceptance by their neighbors than over practicing their religion in a country whose overall culture is so often at odds with their beliefs and values. The film contains interviews with refugees and with experts in U.S. Islam. It touches briefly on the history of Islam and its rich contributions to the arts and sciences.

A Nation of Immigrants: The Chinese-American Experience
Length: 20 minutes, color
Date: 2002
Cost: $129.95
Source: Films for the Humanities and Sciences
P.O. Box 2053
Princeton, NJ 08543-2053
Website: http://www.films.com

This video explores the plight of Chinese immigrants, including their hard work for pitifully low wages, the racial discrimination against them, and their victimization in race riots.

Natives: Immigrant Bashing on the Border
Length: 25 minutes, black and white
Date: 1992
Cost: $295
Source: Filmakers Library, Inc.
124 East Fortieth Street
No. 901
New York, NY 10016
Phone: (212) 808-4980
Fax: (212) 808-4983
E-mail: info@filmakers.com
Website: http://www.filmakers.com

This video captures the unabashed xenophobia of many Californians living along the U.S.-Mexican border as they react to the influx of illegal aliens who they believe are draining the community's resources and who they also believe are often criminals. It critiques the nativists' position by contrasting their professed love of country with racist and antidemocratic attitudes. One interviewee advocates machine-gunning down a few illegal aliens at the border as a warning to others.

The New Generation: Vietnamese-Americans Today
Length: 35 minutes, color
Date: 2002
Cost: $129.95
Source: Films for the Humanities and Sciences
P.O. Box 2053
Princeton, NJ 08543-2053
Website: http://www.films.com

This video presents candid interviews with first- and second-generation Vietnamese Americans and documents the process of their assimilation into U.S. culture. College students, professionals, and clergy explore what it means to be of Vietnamese descent in the United States today. Topics include stress on family life due to cultural and generational differences, gang membership, and drug abuse, as well as anti-Vietnamese racial bias.

Obachan's Garden: A Japanese Immigrant's Memoir
Length: 95 minutes, color
Date: 2002
Cost: $159.95
Source: Films for the Humanities and Sciences
P.O. Box 2053
Princeton, NJ 08543-2053
Website: http://www.films.com

After the 1923 earthquake that shook Tokyo, twenty-five-year-old Asayo Murakami resettled in Canada. Using dramatization, newsreel footage, family photos, and interviews with the 103-year-old Asayo, the *obachan*, or grandmother, this film traces one woman's tumultuous life story from her early life in Japan, internment during World War II, and reunion with her long-lost daughter. Her remarkable life story exemplifies the Asian American experience during the twentieth century.

One-Way Ticket to Ghana: Forced Deportation from the E.U.
Length: 58 minutes, color
Date: 2002
Cost: $149.95
Source: Films for the Humanities and Sciences
P.O. Box 2053
Princeton, NJ 08543-2053
Website: http://www.films.com

This video tells the story of a Ugandan, Peter Ulewiri, whose application to migrate to the European Union was denied. He was forcibly deported to Ghana. The film examines the corrupt system in which EU police and immigration authorities pay Ghana to act as a transfer point for black deportees, for whom being sent to Ghana typically means years of imprisonment and an obscure death. The film explores evidence of European racial bias against black Africans.

Pieces of Dreams
Length: 15 minutes, color
Date: 1991
Source: UNHCR
Liaison Office to UN Headquarters
UN Plaza
New York, NY 10017
Phone: (212) 963-6200

This video was made by UNHCR as a training film for people doing fieldwork. It is a sort of case study of a Mozambican family who fled to safety in Zambia.

A Promise to Keep
Length: 9 minutes, color
Date: 1991
Source: UNHCR
Liaison Office to UN Headquarters
UN Plaza
New York, NY 10017
Phone: (212) 963-6200

A training film for people working with refugee children, this video examines the needs of refugee children and shows them to be like children the world over.

Refugees in Our Backyard
Length: 58 minutes, color
Date: 1990
Cost: $395
Source: First Run/Icarus Films
32 Court Street
21st Floor
Brooklyn, NY 11201
Phone: (800) 876-1710
Website: http://www.frif.com

This film concerns the migration of Central Americans to the United States, stressing the causes of migration and the means of entering the United States illegally. It considers laws regarding the problem and legal and humanitarian efforts to help migrants.

Serving with a Purpose
Length: 25 minutes, color

Date: 1990
Source: UHRWA
UN Building
DC2–0550
New York, NY 10017
Phone: (212) 963-2255

This video presents a vivid chronological account of the Palestinian experience from 1948 to 1990.

The Stolen Eye
Length: 50 minutes, color
Date: 2002
Cost: $195
Source: California Newsreel/Resolution
P.O. Box 2284
South Burlington, VT 05407
Phone: (877) 811-7495
Website: http://www.newsreel.org

This Jane Elliot film documents her diversity training exercise set in Australia, in which she brings together a group of Aborigines and white Australians for an unusually dramatic and candid encounter. The Aborigines eloquently reveal the story of the expropriation of their lands by European settlers and the deliberate attempts to destroy their culture via government-sponsored assimilation programs. The whites seem genuinely surprised and shocked by the pain their white compatriots have inflicted.

Stories from the Mines: How Immigrant Miners Changed America
Length: 57 minutes, color
Date: 2002
Cost: $149.95
Source: Films for the Humanities and Sciences
P.O. Box 2053
Princeton, NJ 08543-2053
Website: http://www.films.com

The U.S. rise to superpower status was fueled to a great degree by the social and industrial impact of coal mining in northeastern Pennsylvania. This meticulously researched program uses location footage, archival film, period photos, dramatizations, and academic commentary to examine U.S. labor. It vividly captures the agitation and the often violent suppression that characterized the times, and it emphasizes the precedents for social justice, including child-labor laws and the right to collective bargaining, against the stark backdrop of immigrant miners being exploited by industrialists.

The Strangers Next Door: Welcoming Muslims
Length: 28 minutes, color
Date: 2002
Cost: $89.95
Source: Films for the Humanities and Sciences
 P.O. Box 2053
 Princeton, NJ 08543-2053
 Website: http://www.films.com

This film focuses on the proposed building of a mosque in a wealthy Detroit suburb and illustrates the need for ecumenical dialogue. This CBS news program looks at interfaith efforts to welcome the Muslims, practitioners of one of the "three religions of the book," more readily into U.S. culture.

The Sun and the Light
Length: 26 minutes, color
Date: 1990
Source: Indiana University Audio Visual Center
 601 E. Kirkwood
 Bloomington, IN 47405
 Phone: (812) 855-8065
 E-mail: avcenter@iuk.edu

This video focuses on the UNHCR through observation of daily operations at refugee camps in Thailand and eastern Sudan.

Ties That Bind: Immigration Stories
Length: 58 minutes, color
Date: 2002
Cost: $129.95
Source: Films for the Humanities and Sciences
 P.O. Box 2053
 Princeton, NJ 08543-2053
 Website: http://www.films.com

This film examines the human drama behind the current immigration debate on both sides of the Texas-Mexico border while at the same time exploring the root causes of why Mexicans emigrate. It emphasizes the role of transnational corporations and their social and economic impacts on both Mexicans and U.S. residents. It explores the increasingly restrictive nature of immigration policies as well as the strong family values that immigrants bring with them and their positive impact on U.S. culture.

UNHCR: A Global View
Length: 16 minutes, color
Date: 1992
Source: UNHCR
Liaison Office to UN Headquarters
UN Plaza
New York, NY 10017
Phone: (212) 963-6200

This video looks at UNHCR operations around the world, at how UNHCR deals with the growing refugee crisis, and at recent successful repatriation programs.

When East Meets East
Length: 53 minutes, color
Date: 2002
Cost: $129.95
Source: Films for the Humanities and Sciences
P.O. Box 2053
Princeton, NJ 08543-2053
Website: http://www.films.com

This genre-breaking documentary explores the issues of ethnic and cultural identity through interviews with some of today's most prominent Asian film figures.

With Us or Against Us: Afghans in America
Length: 27 minutes, color
Date: 2002
Cost: $295.00
Source: Filmakers Library, Inc.
124 East Fortieth Street
No. 901
New York, NY 10016
Phone: (212) 808-4980
Fax: (212) 808-4983
E-mail: info@filmakers.com
Website: http://www.filmakers.com

This film explores the experiences of Afghan refugees who fled in the 1970s, many of whom settled in Fremont, California. After September 11, 2001, they found themselves in a cultural cross-fire as their adoptive homeland was at war with their native land. Ironically, in 1996, most of the Fremont Afghan community rejected the Taliban. The film introduces people who tell what it means to be Afghan in the United States today.

Women at Risk
Length: 56 minutes, color
Date: 1990
Cost: $295.00
Source: Filmakers Library, Inc.
124 East Fortieth Street
No. 901
New York, NY 10016
Phone: (212) 808-4980
Fax: (212) 808-4983
E-mail: info@filmakers.com
Website: http://www.filmakers.com

Produced collaboratively with UNHCR and the Canadian International Development Agency, this film examines the cases of three women living in refugee camps in different parts of the world and shows the hardships they must endure.

Yellow-Tale Blues
Length: 30 minutes, color
Date: 1990
Cost: $295
Source: Filmakers Library, Inc.
124 East Fortieth Street
No. 901
New York, NY 10016
Phone: (212) 808-4980
Fax: (212) 808-4983
E-mail: info@filmakers.com
Website: http://www.filmakers.com

This video is aimed at high school and college classes on multiculturalism. It looks at elements of prejudice against Asians in the United States through interviews with members of two Asian American families and through clips taken from Hollywood films.

Glossary

Adjustment to Immigrant Status   A procedure whereby a non-immigrant may apply for a change of status to that of a lawful permanent resident if an immigrant visa is available for his or her country. The alien is counted as an immigrant as of the date of adjustment.

Alien   A person who is neither a citizen nor a national of a given nation-state.

Amicus curiae   A "friend of the court" legal brief submitted by a state or an interest group that is not a party to a case but that has an interest in the outcome of the case in which it argues its position on the case.

Amnesty   The granting of legal relief or pardon; in IRCA, granting legal temporary resident status to a previously illegal (undocumented) alien.

Asian-Pacific Triangle   An area encompassing countries and colonies from Afghanistan to Japan and south to Indonesia and the Pacific Islands. Immigration from the area was severely limited to small quotas established in the McCarran-Walter Act (1953). The Asian-Pacific Triangle replaced the Asiatic Barred Zone.

Asiatic Barred Zone   A region designated by the Immigration Act of 1917, few of whose natives could enter the United States.

Asylee   A person in the United States who is unable or unwilling to return to his or her country of origin because of persecution or fear of persecution. The person is eligible to become a permanent resident after one year of continuous residence in the United States.

Asylum Temporary legal entrance granted to an individual who is an asylee.

Border card A card allowing a person living within a certain distance from the United States border to legally cross back and forth for employment purposes without a passport or visa.

Border Patrol The law enforcement arm of the Immigration and Naturalization Service.

Bracero Program A temporary farmworker program in operation from 1942 to 1964 that allowed migrant farmworkers to come to the United States for up to nine months annually to work in agriculture.

Certiorari A writ issued by the U.S. Supreme Court requiring the records of a lower court case to be sent up for its review upon appeal.

Cuban-Haitian entrant Status accorded Cubans who entered the United States illegally between April 15, 1980, and October 10, 1980, and Haitians who entered illegally before January 1, 1981. Those qualified who were in residence continuously for one year were allowed to adjust their status to that of legal immigrants by IRCA.

Debarkation Leaving a ship or airplane to enter the United States.

Deportation A legal process by which a nation sends an individual back to his or her country of origin after refusing him or her legal residence in the United States.

Diversity immigrants A special category of immigrants established by the 1990 IMMACT to allow a certain number of visas to be issued to immigrants from countries that previously had low admission numbers.

Due process of law The constitutional limitation on governmental behavior requiring the government to deal with an individual according to prescribed rules and procedures.

Emigrant An individual who voluntarily leaves his or her country of birth for permanent resettlement elsewhere.

Emigration   The act of leaving one's place of origin or birth for permanent resettlement.

Employer sanctions   A restrictive device of IRCA that imposes penalties (fines, imprisonment, or both) for knowingly hiring an illegal immigrant.

Equal protection of the law   The constitutional requirement that all persons be treated the same before the law.

Escapee   An individual fleeing persecution from a government (originally from a Communist or Communist-dominated one), usually for racial, religious, ethnic, social organization, or political reasons.

Eugenics   A pseudoscientific theory of racial genetics.

EWIs   An acronym for "entered without inspection," another term for undocumented or illegal aliens, those who came without proper documentation or a visa.

Excluded categories   A listing in immigration law of those persons specifically denied entrance to the United States for stated reasons for the purpose of permanent settlement.

Exclusion   The denial of legal entrance to a sovereign territory.

Exempt   An individual or class or category of individuals to whom a certain provision of the law does not apply.

Expulsion   The decision of a sovereign nation to legally compel an individual to leave its territory permanently.

Green card   A document issued by the INS that certifies an individual as a legal immigrant entitled to work in the United States.

Guest-worker program   A program enabling the legal importation of workers for temporary labor in specified occupations.

Identity papers   Legal documents recognized by a government as establishing a person's identity.

Illegal alien   An individual who is in a territory without documentation permitting permanent residence.

Immediate relatives   In recent immigration law, spouses, minor children, parents (of a citizen or resident alien over twenty-one years of age), and brothers or sisters of a U.S. citizen or permanent resident alien.

Immigrant An alien admitted to any country as a lawful permanent resident.

Investor immigrant An individual permitted to immigrate based upon a promise to invest $1 million in an urban area or $500,000 in a rural area to create at least ten new jobs.

Legalized alien An alien lawfully admitted for temporary or permanent residence under the Immigration and Nationality Act of 1965 or under the Immigration Reform and Control Act of 1986.

Literacy test A device imposed upon immigrants by the 1917 Immigration Act to restrict immigration to persons able to read and write.

Mortgaging A legal device to "borrow" against future fiscal year immigration quotas to allow the entrance of immigrants, for refugee or humanitarian purposes, after their national-origin fiscal year quota had been filled.

Naturalization The legal act of making an individual a citizen who was not born a citizen.

Net EWIs Estimates of the total number from each country who entered without inspection and established residency in the United States, a large majority of whom are from Mexico. Net EWIs are computed by adjusting the count of undernumerated aliens and subtracting the estimated legal resident population and subtracting the estimated number of visa overstays.

Nongovernmental organizations (NGOs) In immigration matters, organizations, usually for advocacy or immigrant assistance, that are not government agencies.

Nonimmigrant An alien seeking temporary entry into the United States for a specific purpose other than permanent settlement, for example, a foreign government official, tourist, student, temporary worker, or cultural exchange visitor.

Nonpreference A category of immigrant visas apart from family and employment-based preferences that was available primarily between 1966 and 1978 but that was eliminated by the Immigration Act of 1990.

Nonquota immigrant A person allowed entrance for a specific reason who was not charged against a nation's annual quota.

Pacific Triangle   An area in southeast Asia from which immigration was specifically excluded during most of the quota era that was ended by a provision of the McCarran-Walter Act (1952).

Parolee   An alien, appearing to be inadmissible to the inspecting officer, allowed to enter the United States for urgent humanitarian reasons or because that alien's entry is determined to be a significant public benefit.

Passport   A legal identification document issued by a sovereign nation-state attesting to the nationality of an individual for international travel purposes.

Permanent resident   A noncitizen who is allowed to live permanently in the United States, who can travel in and out of the country without a visa, and who can work without restriction. Permanent residents are also permitted to accumulate time toward becoming citizens.

Preference system   A device used in immigration law to establish rules and procedures to determine the order in which annual limits of immigration visas were to be issued.

Preferences   Specific categories of individuals to be awarded visas for permanent immigration.

Protocol   An international agreement governing the understanding and procedures that member states who are parties to a treaty agree upon for a given purpose, as in the UN protocols regarding the status and treatment of refugees.

Pull factor   A characteristic of a country that attracts immigrants for permanent resettlement.

Push factor   A reason that compels an individual to emigrate from his or her nation of origin and seek permanent resettlement elsewhere.

Quota immigrant   An individual seeking entrance to the United States or coming under the system that fixed an annual number of visas to be awarded to persons from a particular nation or territory.

Refugee-parolee   A qualified applicant for conditional entry between 1970 and 1980 whose application for admission could not be approved because of inadequate numbers of seventh-preference visas. The applicant was paroled into the United States under the parole authority granted to the attorney general.

Relocation camps   A number of places established by executive order for holding Japanese aliens or Japanese American citizens during World War II on their way to the ten permanent internment camps.

Special agricultural workers   Aliens who performed labor in perishable agricultural crop commodities for a specified period of time and who were admitted for temporary and then permanent residence under the Immigration Reform and Control Act of 1986.

Transit alien   An alien in immediate and continuous transit through the United States, with or without a visa. Transit aliens are principally aliens and their families serving at the UN headquarters and foreign government officials and their family members.

Unauthorized alien   An individual who is in a territory without documentation; an illegal immigrant.

Undocumented alien   An individual in a sovereign territory without legal authorization to be there; an illegal alien.

Visa   A legal document issued by a consular or similar State Department official allowing a person to travel to the United States for either permanent or temporary reasons such as immigrant, student, tourist, government representative, business person, or cultural exchange student.

Withdrawal   An alien's voluntary removal of an application for admission in lieu of an exclusion hearing before an immigration judge.

Xenophobia   An unfounded fear of the foreigner.

Index

About the Author

Michael C. LeMay is professor of political science and assistant dean of the College of Social and Behavioral Sciences at California State University San Bernardino.